JULIE BATTILANA *and*
TIZIANA CASCIARO

Mae Power to You!

Tiziana & Julie

POWER,
*for*ALL

Simon & Schuster

New York London Toronto Sydney New Delhi

POWER, *for* ALL

How It Really Works and Why It's Everyone's Business

Julie Battilana
and Tiziana Casciaro

Simon & Schuster
1230 Avenue of the Americas
New York, NY 10020

First Simon & Schuster hardcover edition August 2021

SIMON & SCHUSTER and colophon are registered
trademarks of Simon & Schuster, Inc.

For information about special discounts for bulk purchases,
please contact Simon & Schuster Special Sales at 1-866-506-1949
or business@simonandschuster.com.

The Simon & Schuster Speakers Bureau can bring authors to
your live event. For more information or to book an event,
contact the Simon & Schuster Speakers Bureau at 1-866-248-3049
or visit our website at www.simonspeakers.com.

Manufactured in the United States of America

10 9 8 7 6 5 4 3 2 1

Library of Congress Cataloging-in-Publication Data
has been applied for.

ISBN 978-1-9821-4163-9
ISBN 978-1-9821-4165-3 (ebook)

To Jean-Pierre, Marica,
and Emilie for paving the way,

To Romain for charting it forward
and always being by my side,

And to Lou and Noé, and the vibrant
young people of their generation, for continuing
our collective march toward social justice.

JB

To my mother, Maria Teresa Tarsitano, who has
powered me with love, virtue, and knowledge, and
a "sgridatina" once in a while.

TC

Contents

Introduction
Power Is Misunderstood

Returning to his flock after a bone-rattling storm, a shepherd sees ·a startling sight. In what had been undisturbed pastureland the day before lies a crevasse revealing an underground cavern. Stepping through the opening, the curious shepherd finds himself in a crypt containing an imposing bronze sculpture of a horse. Inside the statue is a cadaver wearing nothing but a gold ring. The shepherd pockets the ring and leaves. Soon afterward, he discovers that this is no ordinary ring; it's a magic ring that renders its wearer invisible. Realizing his newfound ability, the shepherd quickly plots his next moves: He makes his way to the palace, seduces the queen, murders the king, and takes control of the kingdom.

The shepherd's tale, the Ring of Gyges, appears in Plato's *Republic*,[1] dating back to the fourth century BCE. The Greek philosopher's story has captivated human imaginations across the ages. Another tale about a ring that grants invisibility, along with other more sinister powers, has managed no small feat: keeping readers engaged for more than 1,500 pages. This is none other than twentieth-century English writer J.R.R. Tolkien's *The Hobbit* and *The Lord of the*

Rings, in which the One Ring corrupts its bearer with the promise of absolute dominance.

For millennia, people have told stories like the Ring of Gyges and *The Lord of the Rings*. In a folk tale from the Middle East, Aladdin, sent by an evil sorcerer to retrieve an oil lamp from an enchanted cave, discovers a genie who can grant him wishes. A Vietnamese legend recounts how King Lê Lợi liberated his people from Ming occupation in the fifteenth century, after a decade-long war, with the aid of the mythical sword Thuận Thiên (Heaven's Will). In Richard Wagner's *Der Ring des Nibelungen* cycle, Alberich possesses a magic helmet that gives the wearer the ability to change form or become invisible. More recently, millions of readers have delighted in following Harry Potter's saga, which culminates in his search for the Deathly Hallows, a trio of enchanted objects that, together, allow their bearer to become Master of Death.

Tales of a protagonist setting out on a quest to find a magic object that will give him (or lately her) the ability to control their own destiny and triumph over evildoers exist in every culture. What these timeless stories share is also what makes them so enthralling: They are all fundamentally stories about power. The heroes and villains fight and kill to gain possession of the magic artifacts that can enable them to control not only their own fortunes, but also the behavior of others. This, after all, is what power ultimately is: *the ability to influence another's behavior*, be it through persuasion or coercion.

ENDLESSLY FASCINATING, OFTEN MISUNDERSTOOD

These epic stories endure because power fascinates us. It keeps us turning the pages of books, glued to the news, and binge-watching movies and TV series. Power is one of the world's most talked about, and perhaps most written about subjects because it is an inherent part of our lives. From our personal relationships and disputes at work, to the highest levels of international diplomacy and big business, power is everywhere.

After studying and teaching this subject for two decades, we have come to realize that, despite its ubiquity—or perhaps because of it—power is still vastly misunderstood. Every fall, as students file into our classrooms at Harvard University and the University of Toronto, they seek answers to the same set of questions: How can I gain power and keep it? Why don't I feel more powerful even though I've been promoted? How can I convince people to change? Why is it so hard to stand up to abusive bosses? How can I ensure that I won't abuse power myself when I have it?

They are also concerned with what is happening around them in the world, and they wonder whether they have the potential to make a difference. In these past few years especially, we have been asked repeatedly, in various ways, why do I feel like the world is blowing up in our faces and I can't do anything to stop it?

Our classrooms aren't the only places where people come to us with such pressing questions. Our research and advising have taken us around the world, where we've heard similar concerns from people of all ages and backgrounds: teenagers to nonagenarians, some highly educated and others who never had the opportunity to learn to read. All these encounters both inside and outside the classroom have given us a unique window into how people grapple with power in places as different as a public hospital in the inner city of Rio de Janeiro, the well-appointed office of a former French president in Paris, and a bustling open-space incubator for social enterprises in New York.

Despite their great diversity, the people we've met and worked with think about power in similar ways. For the most part, they care about improving their own lives and often those of others. They want to have more control over their environment and make a difference, whether in their immediate families, their jobs, their communities, or society. Yet they find the path a rocky one. For every success they experience, they have stories of struggle or downright defeat. Intuitively they know that power is the key to the impact they aspire to effect. But acknowledging that power is at play and understanding how it works are very different. And this brings us to the second thing people tend to have in common: Most of us have deep-seated misconceptions about power. Three fallacies, in particular, prevent many people from properly grasping it and, ultimately, being able to exercise it.

THREE PERNICIOUS FALLACIES

The first fallacy is the belief that power is a thing you possess, and that some fortunate individuals have special traits that enable them to acquire it. If you have those traits, the reasoning goes, or you can find a way to obtain them, you will always be powerful. Those special characteristics are not too different from the magic artifacts that figure in epic stories and myths; not surprisingly, people are curious to discover what these "ideal traits" are. But think about the relationships in your own life. You probably feel more in control in some of them than you do in others; and yet, most of the time you bring with you the same underlying traits and capabilities. Although personal attributes can be sources of power in certain situations, you will come to appreciate why searching for special traits that would make someone powerful always and everywhere is largely a waste of time.

The second fallacy is that power is positional, reserved for kings and queens, presidents and generals, Board members and CEOs, the rich and the famous. It's common to mistake authority or rank for power, so common that we see it every year on the first day of class. When we ask students to list five people whom they view as powerful, 90 percent of the time they name people at the apex of some hierarchy. Yet you would be surprised by the number of top executives and CEOs who come to us because they struggle to get things done in their organizations. They realize that being at the top is no guarantee that their teams will do what they want them to do. Comedies, from the ancient Greek plays of Aristophanes to the British Monty Python sketches, have made audiences laugh by ridiculing figures of authority, from emperors to chiefs, ministers, and puffed-up bosses. Our analysis will reveal why being at the top may well give people authority, but it doesn't necessarily give them power.

The last and perhaps most widespread misconception is that power is dirty, and that acquiring and wielding it entails manipulation, coercion, and cruelty. Literature and film abound with ghastly examples: Shakespeare's Lady Macbeth and Iago, Voldemort in the Harry Potter series, and Frank and Claire Underwood in *House of Cards*. We can't look away, but we can't abide the thought of being like these characters, either. Power fascinates and repulses us at the same time. It seems like fire: bewitching, but capable of consuming us if we get too close. We fear it could make us lose our minds, or our principles. The shepherd in the Ring of Gyges transforms into a manipulative murderer, while Tolkien's One Ring turns its wearer gradually evil. In reality, there is nothing intrinsically dirty about power. Although the potential to be corrupted by it always exists, its energy is essential if we wish to achieve positive ends as well. When a third grader convinces her classmates to participate in a fundraising campaign to benefit a not-for-profit organization that cares for kids with disabilities, she is exercising power constructively. So is the manager who persuades the corporate office to give his team the resources they need to do better work in better conditions.

These three fallacies plague us individually and collectively. Individually, our confusion is the source of major frustration, because it significantly limits our ability to have control over our own lives, to influence others, and to get things done. We end up feeling at the mercy of the "politics" of our workplaces, jostled by puzzling dynamics bigger than ourselves.

Collectively, our misunderstanding of power is catastrophic, because it makes us less likely to identify, prevent, or stop abuses of power that threaten our freedoms and well-being. We risk—often without realizing it—letting our common destiny be decided by a small group of people who may have only their own interests at heart. History gives us innumerable examples of tyrants who disregarded others' lives and liberty. Yet dictatorships continue around the globe, depriving people of basic human rights. And even within democracies, hard-won freedoms are fragile, because the risk of power becoming concentrated in the hands of a few who will fight fiercely to defend their privileges is always present.

Entrenched as these three fallacies are, and severe as their consequences can be, we know from our research and teaching experience that the real dynamics of power can be taught. Be it to resist evil or to do good, understanding how power works and what it takes to acquire and exercise it is imperative. Providing this knowledge is what set us on the journey to write this book: We want to give you the keys to unlock these dynamics so that you will be better able to wholeheartedly pursue your objectives in your relationships, workplaces, communities, and society.

THE KEYS TO UNDERSTANDING POWER

At the end of our course, we ask our students to look back at a time they were blindsided by power and analyze the situation using what they've learned. We've heard about the shock of being unexpectedly fired, the gloom of running for office and losing by a handful of votes, and the confusion of failing to implement a change everyone in the community seemingly supported. These situations were painful puzzles, or as one student who unexpectedly lost his job explained: "It felt like I was starring in a movie without understanding the plot." As we debunk the three fallacies throughout the course, we witness our students slowly discovering the plot. Then, looking back, they realize how they misread situations, how they directed their energy at the wrong manager or politician, and what the forces were that made them feel so stuck. In short, they finally see power for what it is. We want to help you do the same.

Grasping the dynamics of power is the key not only to pursuing our personal objectives, but also to participating effectively in shaping our collective future. Individual and collective power are joined at the hip. The power we are able to exercise in our personal lives, whether at work or at home, is interdependent with the political systems that govern us, the economic systems that enable and constrain us, and the ecological and biological systems of the natural world with their whims and iron laws. It's foolish to think that we can pursue our individual objectives irrespective of how the distribution of power in society affects our own power.

In uncovering the workings of power in our lives, we will see that the psychological manifestations and consequences of feeling powerful and powerless are real and important, but no accurate analysis of power can be limited to what is in your mind and how you feel. It must also account for others: who they are, the relationships you have with them, the relationships they have with each other, and the broader context within which these relationships are embedded.

To this end, we will examine the dynamics of power in organizations and in society as well as in interpersonal relationships. In doing so, we will draw on insights from our own research, which examines power at all three levels, as well as from that of others across disciplines including sociology, social and evolutionary psychology, management, political science, economics, law, history, and philosophy. Building on this rich body of knowledge, we will show you—layer by layer—the many facets of power and its manifestations through time and in our lives today.

As two women and scholars with international backgrounds— Julie is a native of France and now a French and American citizen; and Tiziana grew up in Italy, lived in the United States for years, and then chose Canada as her home—we are acutely aware that how power is manifested and perceived varies greatly not only across time, but also across culture, gender, race, and class. To understand these variations and their implications beyond our own experiences, we conducted more than one hundred interviews with individuals on five continents with intriguing and diverse paths to and through power. Among them were a Brazilian doctor turned social entrepreneur, a Polish Holocaust survivor, an African American voting rights organizer, a Bangladeshi policeman, a Canadian investment banker, a world-famous Italian fashion designer, and a Nigerian social activist. You will hear their voices throughout this book. Their stories will help you uncover the workings of power and what it takes to use it effectively to have an impact.

GETTING STARTED ON OUR JOURNEY

More than five hundred years ago, Niccolò Machiavelli wrote *The Prince*, a landmark treatise read to this day by people in positions of power and those who aspire to emulate them.[2] These are the people Machiavelli wrote for, and herein lies a key distinction between this book and texts like *The Prince*: We are not writing exclusively for and about powerful people. This book is meant for everyone, including those groups that have been historically, and still are today, excluded from power. That they have been so long denied power does not mean they cannot have it. Power can be for all.

As we will show you, recognizable elements reliably explain who has power and who doesn't in any given situation. When you can identify these elements, it is like having a pair of infrared glasses that help you see in the dark. You will be able to discern the power relationships around you, at home, at work, and in the political, economic, and cultural context where your life unfolds. Together, these elements constitute the fundamentals of power, and when power is broken down to its fundamentals, analyzing who holds it and why depends on answering two key questions. Just two. And we will show you what it takes to answer them.

We will explain why, although power can change hands, its distribution in society is sticky, making it easy for some of us to gain, keep, and consolidate structural advantages, while clearly disadvantaging others. But as we will show you, these oppressive hierarchies can be disrupted when people take action by joining forces to fight them. New digital technologies have the potential to both facilitate and hinder this kind of collective action. Monitored carefully and used wisely, technology can give the power-disadvantaged access to resources that would otherwise be beyond their reach. Left unchecked, it can lead to ever greater concentrations of power. Technology, like power, is intrinsically neither good nor bad; its nature depends on how and for what purpose it is used. Here, as in other spheres, you will appreciate that power can ultimately be for all only if we keep it in check with mechanisms that prevent excessive concentration and hold its keepers accountable, lest they infringe on our rights and freedoms.

We have come a long way in giving more and more of us room to live our lives well, pursue our aspirations, and help others do the same. For millennia, the vast majority had to bear the whims and disregard of authoritarian rulers whose own interests and desires guided their decisions. Today, many of us live in democracies where we can express our views with our vote and decide for ourselves how we want to live. These advances happened thanks to the tireless work of people—some celebrated, most nameless—who articulated new ideas and advocated for a fairer world, even when others deemed them too radical. Nevertheless, the tides of history have left vast divides in their wake, with democracies still imperfect in giving equal voice to all, and social and economic inequalities still pervasive around the world.

If we are to survive and thrive as a species, living in harmony with each other and with our environment, we must continue the work of previous generations who fought for power to be more fairly distributed. Engaging in this work is both a moral imperative and in our own self-interest, as it is the only way to avoid excessive power concentration and ensure our individual and collective freedoms. Thankfully, we are not starting from scratch. Far from it. As we will show you throughout this book, tested ideas and solutions have the potential to make power accessible to all.

Chapter 1

The Fundamentals
of Power

W hen we met Lia Grimanis in Toronto in 2008, she had a motorcycle helmet under her arm and was wearing a hot-pink leather jacket that matched her hot-pink BMW F650GS. The high-performing technology sales executive was an arresting figure, to say the least. But what we were there to talk about wasn't high tech. Lia was passionate about creating an organization that would help homeless women regain control of their lives and futures. Why so passionate? Lia herself had risen from poverty and homelessness to security and stability. Now she wanted to help other women make a similarly transformative journey.

To understand how Lia accomplished this remarkable feat, we must first examine the dynamics of power—what it consists of and how it works. Power as we've defined it is the ability to influence others' behavior, be it through persuasion or coercion.* But what determines this ability? The answer is surprisingly simple: What enables

---

* For a review of definitions of power in the social sciences, see the Appendix.

one person to influence another is control over access to resources the other person values. Such control is the key to understanding the power dynamics in any situation, whether it's one in which you have power over someone else, or one in which they have power over you.

WHAT IS POWER MADE OF?

To have power over someone, you must first have something, or some things, the other person values. Anything a person needs or wants qualifies as a valued resource. The resource can be material, like money or clean water, acres of fertile farmland, a house, or a fast car. Or it can be psychological, like feelings of esteem, belonging, and achievement. And, as we will see, material and psychological resources are not mutually exclusive.

Whatever you have to offer—your expertise, stamina, money, track record, gravitas, networks—will give you power over someone else *only* if they want it. Think about a parent who promises their child a cookie to clean up a messy room. Controlling access to the cookie jar won't be much use if the child doesn't like cookies. In addition, the resource you have to offer must be something the other person can't easily get from others. Are you one of just a few who can provide that valuable resource? Or are there many? Do you, in essence, control the other party's access to resources they value, or are they widely available? If the child loves cookies, but can always get them from an indulgent neighbor, the parent's offer isn't likely to get much traction.

Knowing what the other party values and whether they have alternatives to access what they value tells you how much power you have. But that is not enough to fully understand the balance of power between you. You must also account for whether the other party has something you value and the extent to which they can control your access to it. The effects of having power over someone vary dramatically depending on whether they, in turn, have power over you.

Power is always relative. Does the other party in a given situation have power over you while you also have power over them? If so, you are mutually dependent. Then you must figure out if the current relationship is balanced, meaning your power over each other is similarly low or high; or, if it is imbalanced, meaning you are more dependent on the other party than they are on you (or vice versa). Power does not have to be a zero-sum game. The balance of power can shift over time, and as you will see, one party's gain does not have to be the other party's loss. But no matter who you are, where you live, or what kind of work you do, the fundamental elements of power, shown in the figure below, are the same. To be powerful, you need to offer valued resources over which you have unique control (or that are, at the least, hard to get from someone else). Then the strength of your grip on power will depend on your needs, and how much control the other party has over things you value. To illustrate these fundamentals, let's return to Lia's story.

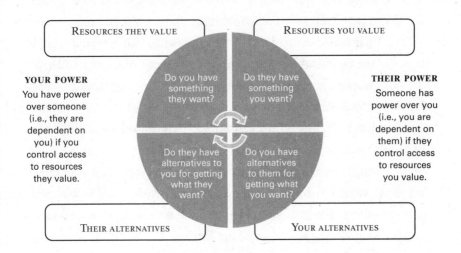

**THE FUNDAMENTALS OF POWER
IN A SOCIAL RELATIONSHIP**

FROM POWERLESSNESS TO EMPOWERING OTHERS

At sixteen, Lia was homeless, having run away from a home that had become violent after the death of her grandmother, the family matriarch. Navigating the dangers of homelessness was especially hard for Lia because she is autistic, and her autism (diagnosed only later in life) manifests as an inability to read facial expressions and interpret social cues. "It's like a blind spot," she explained. "You don't see the train coming until you get hit by it." After periods of couch surfing and a traumatic episode of sexual abuse, she landed, broken, in a women's shelter. Only nineteen, she didn't think she'd live to be twenty-one. "For a time," she said, "the only question in my mind was: *Do I live? Or do I die?*"[1] It seemed to her that the women who left the shelter just kept coming back. She saw no sign that homelessness was anything but a dead end, no role models that gave her reason to hope her life would be anything other than a constant struggle.

Lia found new motivation to live in becoming that role model. She swore to herself that she would leave the shelter and return with a story that would inspire other women who, like her, had fallen through the cracks. After ten years of financial precarity and odd jobs—including running a rickshaw through the streets of Toronto, day in and day out, rain or shine, for four years—Lia had a chance encounter with "a guy who'd made $900,000 selling software."[2] She decided that was the way to go and applied to every software sales job she could find, never mind that all of them required a BA and preferred an MBA. Through all the rejections, for once her autism was an asset, she recalled. "If you can't read the way people are thinking, then it doesn't occur to you to be embarrassed or to doubt yourself. I had no idea that these people were quietly and politely telling me to go jump in a lake, so I just kept calling. Eventually, I must have worn someone down, because someone took a chance on me."[3]

From that point on, Lia worked insane hours, driven by the vow she'd made when she left the shelter. A few years in, she was making her company so much money that they didn't hesitate about hiring an executive coach for her and investing five hundred dollars an hour in her career development. The coaching was a revelation; and as Lia reflected on how valuable it would have been when she was moving off the streets, the idea for what became Up With Women was born: She would found a charity to make the intensive, personalized developmental coaching she had received available to homeless women. To do that, however, she would need to convince certified coaches[4] to provide their services pro bono for a year, and that, Lia quickly realized, meant offering them something they valued.

Lia's first small cohort of coaches were attracted by the same things that draw Up With Women's volunteers and donors today: both Lia herself—her passion and determination, as well as her stunning story of trauma, survival, and success—and the transformative impact of the charity's mission, with coaching at its core. Other charities might provide coaching as an add-on to other services, but at Up With Women, the coaches are *the* most valued contributors; and Lia was promising them that their work would help transform someone's life.

In the beginning, however, everyone struggled. The coaches, accustomed to working with executives, had neither the tools nor the experience to connect with women who had been so marginalized and traumatized. Nor had Lia yet figured out how to identify candidates who would be ready to accept coaching and benefit from it. As a result, the clients weren't finding the coaching helpful; and the coaches, for all their genuine desire to help, weren't seeing the transformative impact Lia had promised them. So, "the early years were really tough for recruiting [coaches]," she told us. "Painfully tough."[5]

Money was also a challenge. Having left her corporate job in 2012 to focus entirely on Up With Women, Lia was quickly running out of the personal savings she'd been using to keep Up With Women going. And without enough coaches, clients, and results, she couldn't attract new funders. "I was staring down the last five thousand dollars in my bank account, and I was telling our shelter partners that they might need to make room for me! I seriously thought I would become homeless again. I went bankrupt to save Up With Women." But Lia's years running a rickshaw, pulling as many as eight people at a time, had made her "insanely strong," and she came up with a solution to fortify Up With Women financially in a way no one else would have thought of: She earned two Guinness World Records for "Heaviest vehicle pulled 100 ft (female)" and "Heaviest vehicle pulled in high heels (female)." The ensuing publicity attracted the attention of the media, potential donors, and corporate partners, and the donations started coming in. And with her feat, Lia sent a powerful signal to struggling women: "You are stronger than you think."[6]

Lia still had to find a way to give her coaches what they needed and wanted to keep them "hooked." And although she had been coached herself, she knew very little about the process, or what made a coaching relationship successful from the coach's perspective. Fortunately, however, there were three coaches who were committed to the vision and eager to help her learn and recruit others. They articulated what an effective program would look like, and then took responsibility for creating it with her. For prospective coaches, it included providing them with the specialized skills that this most challenging client base required, such as proficiency in trauma-informed coaching, which most volunteers had little or no background in. For prospective clients, it included devising screening criteria for identifying women ready to take the next step. One such criterion was to focus on women who had recently come out of homelessness and were actively trying to regain their footing. Guided by this new approach, Lia started visiting shelters to get recommendations from staff who could best identify potential candidates.

Before long, Up With Women was flourishing, as were the coaches and their clients. With the help of the coaches, the women were learning to uncover their motivations and strengths and find their own agency. The coaches were not only mastering new skills but also becoming active partners in a learning community unlike any they had ever experienced. As one of them told us, "This clientele really stretches a coach's muscles and bandwidth, brainwidth, heartwidth." As Lia talked with other coaches, she realized that they, too, valued the opportunity to stretch professionally in a community of like-minded colleagues whom they could relate to and learn from. So, she made that learning more accessible by establishing regular coach meetings and mentor-coach roles to give all the volunteers an increasing sense of mastery and belonging. She also engaged evaluation experts to develop measures of impact that would allow the coaches to see the tangible results of their work—a level of rigor not typically found in the corporate world, where rarely does anyone systematically assess the ROI from executive coaching.[7] What ultimately mattered most to the coaches, though, couldn't be quantified. As one of them put it, "It is one thing to see a VP get a promotion in the corporate sector; it is another to see a woman who hit rock bottom blossom. How do you measure *that*!?"

Lia—who was completely dependent on the certified coaches to achieve her mission—had finally sorted out what the coaches valued most: inspirational purpose, transformative impact, deep learning, and a community of like-minded colleagues. Over time, she had made Up With Women irreplaceable for the coaches to access those valued resources all at once. It's no wonder that you couldn't find a more loyal group of volunteers if you tried. By understanding what the coaches needed and wanted, and then figuring out how she could give them access to those resources, Lia introduced a level of mutual dependence into the relationship. You could argue that the power was still imbalanced in the coaches' favor—after all, Lia couldn't deliver the program she had envisioned without them. But now she, too, had some power. Yet, she did not use it to coerce the coaches; she used it to enable them to help the women they coached. Lia had developed the kind of power relationship that pioneering social scientist Mary Parker Follett referred to as "power-with," "a jointly developed power" used to facilitate "the enrichment and advancement of every human soul."[8]

We purposefully didn't give you the example of a Caesar or a Napoleon to start on our journey to understand power because we want to help you see it differently. So we took you to a place where people seldom turn to look for it: a shelter for homeless women. Was Lia powerful? Absolutely! She managed to regain control over her own life against all odds, and then she was able to harness enough power to convince certified coaches to join Up With Women to help other women rebuild their lives and careers. But Lia not only gained power for herself, despite not having been born into an already powerful position, she also used her power to empower others. Her trajectory perfectly illustrates the lesson that Toni Morrison, the Nobel laureate author, gave her students, "If you have some power, then your job is to empower somebody else."[9]

REBALANCING POWER

Lia's story shows both the interplay of the fundamental elements of power and how these elements can be rebalanced over time. Just as there are four elements that define the distribution of power across two parties in any relationship—the resources each party values, and whether they each have alternatives to access those valued resources—there are four strategies for shifting the balance of power: *attraction*, *consolidation*, *expansion*, and *withdrawal*, as shown in the figure to the right.[10] These strategies are used today, as they have been since antiquity, and they are relevant for all kinds of relationships—those you have with family, friends, and colleagues, and those that emerge between organizations, industries, and nation-states. To illustrate, we will use the diamond industry as our lens, looking at each of them in turn, starting with the attraction strategy advertising agency N.W. Ayer developed to persuade generations of prospective brides and bridegrooms that the sparkly gems are much more important to them than they might have thought.

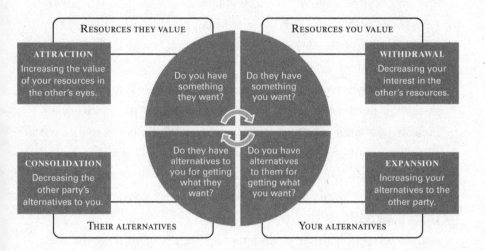

FOUR WAYS TO SHIFT
THE BALANCE OF POWER

In 1938, the Great Depression was beginning, fitfully, to lift, but war was on the horizon as the world watched Hitler march into Austria. Many families still struggled to make ends meet, and diamonds were not much on people's minds. Only 10 percent of engagement rings contained diamonds.[11] Harry Oppenheimer, the South African president of De Beers Consolidated Mines Ltd., the world's largest diamond company, was worried, and so were his bankers. They were pressing Oppenheimer to find a way to increase demand, drive the price up, and make De Beers more profitable.

Hoping that advertising could help, Oppenheimer traveled to New York to meet with the Ayer executives.[12] The agency more than met the challenge: The core elements of the campaign they developed—associating diamonds with eternal love, success, and marriage—still resonate today. Ayer achieved this by deploying advertisements with movie idols and socialites to promote the gems and amplify the campaign's iconic tagline, "A diamond is forever." Less than three years later, diamond sales in the United States were up 55 percent.[13] By 1990, 80 percent of engagement rings had diamonds.[14]

Salespeople and marketers may be particularly adept at using attraction as a strategy, but they are not alone. Attraction—or increasing the value of a resource in the eyes of others—is one of the moves most often used to rebalance power. Think about Lia: The promise of transformative impact along with new professional skills and networks is what attracted coaches to Up With Women and kept them hooked.

An attraction strategy can hinge on both perception and reality. The impact of Lia's coaches on the lives of their clients is real: These women get out of poverty, give their children a stable home, and start careers—undoubtedly tangible changes. But the value of a diamond owes a lot to perception, and psychologists have taught us how easy it can be to shift people's perception of a resource's value by using simple levers of persuasion.[15] This is true even when the value of a resource is easy to assess objectively. Diamonds are a case in point: cut, color, clarity, and carats determine their quality. And yet, a study of 1.5 million eBay transactions found that diamond rings of exactly the same quality received lower bids when the seller described them as being for sale for a "tainting" reason, like a cheating fiancé, versus a benign one, like an heirloom from a happily married aunt.[16] Whether real or perceived, increasing the value someone sees in a resource you have to offer can be an essential strategy for rebalancing power in your favor.

But even an attractive resource gives you little power if it is available from many. In such cases, you can increase the other party's dependence by reducing the number of alternatives they have. Doing so requires consolidating with other providers of the same resource. Cartels are one example of a consolidation strategy designed to decrease the number of providers of a valued resource. That's how OPEC has increased the power of petroleum-exporting countries since its founding in the 1960s. One of the most extreme and well-known incarnations of this approach is the power of monopolies. The etymology of the word "monopoly" is *monos* and *pōlein*, which in Greek mean "single" and "sell." In other words, "you've only got me." When a company acquires providers of the same resource to eliminate its competition, it is also using consolidation to increase its market power. This is why antitrust laws are important: They prevent companies from concentrating too much power in their hands. But whether voluntary or coercive, consolidation rebalances power in favor of the providers of a resource, who come together to reduce the alternatives available to the other party.

This was the case with De Beers, which used a consolidation strategy for decades to win control over the world's supply of rough diamonds. To increase its power over suppliers, De Beers created a Central Selling Organization that developed exclusive contracts with diamond sellers. At the same time, De Beers also increased its power over its customers by setting up an exclusive club for the world's top diamond buyers. By the 1980s, De Beers controlled 80 percent of the world's supply of rough diamonds.[17] If you wanted to trade in diamonds, you had almost no alternative but De Beers.

Different as they may seem from monopolies and quasi-monopolies like De Beers, unions also leverage consolidation. How much power does a single worker really have in his relationship with his company? As long as the company needs his work to produce its products or services and he is protected by labor laws, he certainly has some. Yet his power is limited, as the company could likely find a replacement either internally or through external recruiting. This creates a real power asymmetry, which is even greater when there are a lot of available recruits able to accomplish the work and looking for jobs. Such asymmetries can make it hard for workers to protect their rights, which is why they created unions. As the etymology of the word "union" (*unus*, the Latin term for "one") reminds us, by unionizing, workers can be represented as one group and, in so doing, prevent their employers from simply turning elsewhere should there be disagreements about acceptable working conditions.

While attraction and consolidation are both about increasing the other party's dependence, expansion and withdrawal are the other two ways to rebalance power by decreasing one party's dependence on the other party. Thus, withdrawal can be thought of as the countermove to attraction, and expansion as the countermove to consolidation.

Withdrawal entails walking away from the resource the other party has to offer, becoming less interested in it. This is the challenge that De Beers and other diamond sellers started to face at the turn of the twenty-first century, as some consumers turned their backs on diamonds. The number of marriages has been shrinking, with evolving gender norms challenging traditional marriage rituals. In the past decades, competition for luxury goods, from travel to handbags and electronics, has also been exploding.[18] Blood diamonds—gems mined in war zones and sold to finance military insurgencies—have further tarnished diamonds' once-pristine reputation as the symbol of eternal love. These social trends have lessened De Beers's and, more generally, the diamond industry's power, with some analysts calculating a drop in sales growth by as much as 60 percent between 2000 and 2019.[19]

But De Beers had been losing power in the industry even before these trends began to play out, so much so that by 2019, its share of the global rough diamond market had fallen to roughly 30 percent.[20] De Beers's change of fortune resulted partly from strategic moves by its suppliers and competitors: The collapse of the Soviet Union in 1991 weakened De Beers's partnership with Russian diamond producers, while new mines opened in Canada, and start-ups began to use new technology to grow synthetic diamonds in their labs. Suppliers could now connect directly with buyers to negotiate prices, and buyers had more options for suppliers, further weakening De Beers's power. Meanwhile, the company was caught up in antitrust litigation that enabled its suppliers and customers to further increase their alternatives. This kind of expansion strategy can radically change the balance of power not only in economic exchanges, but also in everyday life. Think about the child who loves cookies and has a friendly neighbor. Nothing like an outside option to take power away from your parents!

In sum, to increase another's dependence on you, you can try to increase how much they value a resource you have access to, or you can try to increase your control over this resource by becoming one of its only providers. Conversely, to decrease your dependence on the other party, you can try to diminish the value you place on the resource to which they have access, or try to decrease their control over it by finding alternative providers of that resource.[21] Far from being fixed, power relationships evolve over time as the parties engage in these moves and countermoves. So, as the rise and fall of De Beers exemplifies, while a diamond may be forever, power is not. This is true for organizations as much as it is for every one of us. Even those who are so powerful that we view them as power personified do not own power.

POWER IS NOT A *THING* WE POSSESS

For many of his contemporaries, Senator Lyndon Baines Johnson was the most powerful person in Washington in the 1950s. And he went on to become arguably the most powerful man in the country when he became the 36th president of the United States following the assassination of President John F. Kennedy. Two years later, after being elected president in his own right, he seemed to be at the apex of his political career. His presidency was notable for the passage of the Civil and Voting Rights Acts and the anti-poverty programs of the Great Society, but it was also marred by his escalation of the Vietnam War. As more and more troops were sent overseas, youth across the nation rose to demonstrate against the war's continuation. LBJ's unpopularity was such that he eventually announced he would not run for re-election. He focused instead on negotiating peace in Vietnam, only to see it elude him and be achieved by his successors.

Johnson's rise to power is often attributed in part to his unique persona: At almost six feet four inches tall, he towered over most of his fellow senators and often used his height to intimidate them. Physical intimidation was, however, only one component of what later became known as "the Johnson treatment," described by one reporter at the time as "an incredible, potent mixture of persuasion, badgering, flattery, threats, reminders of past favors and future advantages."[22] But although he was just as tall at the end of his presidency, and he still had access to his signature "Johnson treatment," neither helped him retain his hold on power. What, then, made him so powerful in the first place, and why was it not enough for him to sustain power during his presidency?

No one has spent more time dissecting Johnson's use of power than Robert Caro, whose monumental biography of the man follows every step of his rise and fall. Remarkably, when Caro was asked in an interview about what traits made Johnson powerful, he referred neither to his personality nor to the specifics of the Johnson treatment.

Instead, he pointed to his "genius in creating political power."[23] In Caro's account, Johnson's unique capacity to gain and exercise power during his years in the Senate rested on this: He understood, better than most, what his colleagues valued, and he deployed this knowledge to maximum effect by controlling their access to it. When he joined the Senate in 1949, Johnson made a point of carefully observing fellow senators, as Caro notes: "He watched which senators went over to other senators to chat with them—and which senators sat at their desks and let other senators come to them. He watched two senators talk, and watched if they talked as equals. He watched groups of senators talk, and watched which one the others listened to. And he watched with eyes that missed nothing."[24] Johnson was at his most effective when he was one-on-one. He had an uncanny ability to read people, and made a habit of keeping people talking, always working to discover what his interlocutor *really* wanted. Then, he would find a way to control their access to it. For some, it was important committee assignments and seats; for others, it was enabling the bills they supported to proceed to a vote; and for others, it was going on junkets and eating in fancy restaurants. Providing his colleagues with what they needed and wanted enabled him to become one of the most powerful senators in more than a hundred years.

Once he became president, however, his fellow senators, mostly middle-age and older White men like him, were no longer the only people he had to deal with. Now he had to engage with the American citizenry in all their great diversity, and with foreign leaders, among them Ho Chi Minh, the North Vietnamese president. American involvement in the struggle between North and South Vietnam sharply escalated during Johnson's tenure. While the geopolitics of the Vietnam War are much too intricate to cover here, one factor that contributed to this escalation was Johnson's belief that he could broker a deal with Ho Chi Minh the same way that he had done so many times in the halls of the U.S. Capitol. But none of the resources Johnson could make available, such as generous developmental aid, were of interest to Ho Chi Minh, whose unrelenting purpose was creating a unified Vietnam under a Communist-led government. Johnson's frame of reference was too detached from the cultural, historical, and ideological roots of Ho Chi Minh's uncompromising pursuit. The Johnson treatment that served LBJ so well in the Senate was of no avail in the context of the Vietnam War. This time around, he could not intimidate or cajole his way to victory.

Johnson's extraordinary trajectory is a stark reminder that no one ever owns power, even those who seem the most powerful among us. Personal skills or attributes that help us gain power in one environment can actually harm our chances of gaining and keeping it in another.[25]

Why, then, do so many people believe power is a personal possession? Because we tend to personalize it. *L'Homme Providentiel,* or "the great man" who determines the course of events and the fate of masses, is a prominent figure in chronicles and legends throughout history.[26] In the 1970s, psychologist Lee Ross coined the term "fundamental attribution error," which refers to our bias to explain another person's behavior by their personal qualities rather than any situational factors.[27] The media, biographies, movies, and more perpetuate the idea that one person can naturally possess power and achieve greatness alone.

This misconception is dangerous. For the powerful, it leads to an illusory sense of permanence, invulnerability, even hubris. And pride — the proverb goes — comes before the fall.[28] For the powerless, the idea that the powerful have attributes simply beyond their reach breeds passivity, the belief that they cannot do anything, that they are trapped in their own powerlessness.

Once you understand the fundamentals of power, it becomes easy to debunk this fallacy: No one can ever possess power, because one's power over another party depends on what the other party needs and wants, and whether one can control their access to it. The other party's power, in turn, depends on the extent to which they control access to resources the other values. As such, power exists only in the context of a relationship. No one is ever powerful or powerless in general. Power is a force through which the parties in a relationship can influence one another's behaviors. In and of itself, this force is neither good nor bad. It is up to each of us to harness it so as to have the kind of impact we aspire to have.

Chapter 2

Power Can Be Dirty, But It Doesn't Have to Be

"Conceal your intentions."

"Get others to do the work for you, but always take the credit."

"Use selective honesty and generosity to disarm your victim."

"Pose as a friend, work as a spy."[1]

These are among the recommendations in *The 48 Laws of Power*, Robert Greene's bestselling book, first published in 1998. No wonder people believe that power is dirty. Or perhaps you remember that the ends justify the means and that "it is much safer to be feared than loved" from Niccolò Machiavelli's sixteenth-century political treatise, *The Prince*.

What we forget is that, according to Machiavelli, the prince also "ought to . . . proceed in a temperate manner with prudence and humanity, so that too much confidence may not make him incautious and too much distrust render him intolerable."[2] But if there is humanity, too, in Machiavelli's prince, why is it that the prince's cruelty is what fascinates us? We humans have a well-documented negativity bias, which causes us to pay greater attention to negative events, objects, and traits than we do to positive ones, and we respond to them more strongly.[3]

But portraying power exclusively as exploitative and manipulative misses its essence: Power is neither inherently moral nor inherently immoral. History shows us that power can be used for virtuous purposes as well as dishonorable ones. Whether it becomes dirty in our hands depends on how we gain and keep it and the purpose for which we use it. As such, each of us confronts three ethical decisions with respect to power: whether to acquire it, how to do so, and what to use it for.

Acquiring power means acquiring the capacity to take action and effect change. "Power is the very essence, the dynamo of life," in the words of American community organizer and political activist Saul Alinsky.[4] Power, as the British philosopher Bertrand Russell put it, is "the fundamental concept in social science . . . in the same sense in which energy is the fundamental concept in physics."[5] And even though this energy can be channeled toward self-serving and, at times, evil ends, it can also be channeled toward principled aims that transcend self-interest. In fact, having power is indispensable to pursuing such ends, because, as Lia's story taught us, you need to be able to influence others to achieve any kind of positive change. By seeing power for what it is—a force residing in the control of valued resources that is inherently neither amoral nor moral—we open ourselves up to wielding it responsibly. This requires overcoming the intoxicating effect it can have on our psyches, on the one hand, and learning how we can use it without abusing it, on the other hand.

POWER INTOXICATES

Miriam Rykles was born in Vilnius, in what was then Poland and is now Lithuania. A teenager at the time of World War II, Miriam[6] was the only member of her immediate family to survive the Holocaust.

After two years in Nazi concentration camps, she knew the horrors of abusive power intimately. She had seen firsthand how people with total and unchecked power can use it to destroy lives and all that makes us human. Immunized against any form of power abuse by her experiences, she would never succumb to its exhilaration—or so she thought.

By her thirties, Miriam had resettled in Boston, where she worked as an administrative assistant in the physics department at Harvard University. At the invitation of her cousin Elwood, she visited him in London. Before the war, Elwood had waited tables and studied socialism with serious interest; after it, he made millions as a lawyer with celebrity clients from Hollywood and around the globe. His world, separated not just by an ocean but also by enormous wealth, couldn't be more different from Miriam's.

On a sunny Thursday morning, Noel, her cousin's chauffeur, picked her up in Elwood's limousine for a day of museum-going. Their first stop was the Tate Gallery. "Noel pulled up to the entrance," Miriam recalled, "and opened the door. I got out and saw people craning to see who was coming out of the car. I walked through the crowd feeling, *Oh, they think I'm somebody!* but the feeling didn't penetrate somehow. I went from museum to museum and had a ball." The only moment that gave Miriam pause was when she stopped for a late lunch and Noel demurred when she invited him to join her.

By the time evening approached, the weather had become chilly. "We were driving through Trafalgar Square," she told us, "and people were walking along quickly, shivering, trying to shelter from the drizzle. I looked out the window and felt warm and comfortable and very indifferent [to those we were driving by]: *They are them, and I am me*, I thought. *I am in the car, and they are out in the cold.* In that instant, I felt superior."

Miriam's experience of feeling caught up in the comfort of power and becoming insensitive to others is not uncommon. Reflecting upon what a fleeting experience of power and privilege had done to her, Miriam explained, "It occurred to me that when you're born into privilege, or experience it for a while, you feel the way I did that day all the time. You don't even know that you feel that way! I was there for just one day. One day, and that's how I felt? Me, so sure in my convictions, my sense of justice, so aware that good and evil coexist in all of us, and that it is imperative to keep the evil side of humanity in check to protect civil society. I got scared, because if something like that can happen to me in just a day, anything can happen, to me and to other people."

Power, Self-Focus, and Hubris

As history attests, and psychologists have documented, Miriam is right: The experience of power can engender less empathy and respect for others, and more self-serving impulsivity and feelings of exceptionalism.[7]

In the lab, social psychologists have shown the impact of reflecting even briefly on one's power relative to others. In one study, experimenters asked participants to reflect on either those with the most wealth and prestige in the U.S. or on those with the least, and then to mark on a ten-rung ladder where they themselves fell. Thinking about the country's most powerful people led participants to feel relatively powerless, and to rank themselves lower. In contrast, participants who thought about the least powerful in society felt comparatively powerful and ranked themselves higher. Participants then were given a well-known test, *Reading the Mind in the Eyes*,[8] which measures people's level of empathy by asking them to discern others' emotional states based on photos cut to show just the top of their face, around their eyes. The people who had been led to feel of high rank were significantly less accurate than those who had been led to feel of low rank.[9] The experience of power made them less attentive and more insensitive to others' emotions.

Beyond increasing what psychologists call a person's "self-focus," the experience of power also tends to make people more self-confident. Feeling high in social status leads to an increased sense of well-being;[10] and some research even suggests that those holding power tend to have greater tolerance for pain[11] and lower heart rates in the face of stress.[12] Such feelings can encourage risk-taking,[13] which can be good in some situations, but dangerous when a person is blinded by hubris.

References to the dangers of hubris, excessive pride, and self-confidence abound in the myths and tragedies of the ancient Greeks, who considered it a character flaw serious enough to elicit the wrath of the gods.[14] Remember Icarus, whose father made him wings of feather and wax to help him escape from the island of Crete? Warned by Daedalus not to fly too low, lest the feathers become wet and useless, nor too high, lest the sun melt the wax, Icarus, overcome by his newfound likeness to the gods and "rejoiced by the lift of his great sweeping wings,"[15] ignored his father's admonitions, flew too close to the sun, and tumbled into the sea to his death.

What individual with power has not been tempted to fly too close to the sun? The experience of power can give us the impression that nothing and no one can resist us. Experiments in social psychology show that the powerful are more disinhibited and believe that they have greater control over the effects of their actions than they actually do.[16] In an emblematic study, some participants were asked to write about a time when they felt powerful, while others wrote about a time when they felt powerless. Participants were then given a die, offered a monetary reward for predicting the outcome of a roll, and asked if they would like to throw the die themselves or have the experimenter do it. Every single participant who wrote about a time they had felt powerful chose to roll the die themselves, while only 58 percent of those who had written about feeling powerless rolled for themselves. Simply recalling an experience of power can lead us to greatly overestimate our abilities—even to the extent of controlling the random outcome of a roll of the die![17] If this is what thinking about power for a few minutes can do to us, can you imagine the psychological implications of occupying top positions of power for years?

David Gergen,[18] who served as a key governmental advisor over the course of three decades, under four U.S. presidents (Nixon, Ford, Reagan, and Clinton), appreciates better than most the need to remind those in power that they too are mortal. While in Washington, he observed the emergence of hubris again and again, especially for presidents in their second term, when they were more prone to believe that they were the "master of the universe," David told us. President François Hollande,[19] who served as the president of France for one term, between 2012 and 2017, was aware of this danger when he was elected. Reflecting back on his years as president, he told us that one of the biggest challenges he faced was not only trying to avoid the trap of hubris himself, which he admitted was difficult, but also having to deal with the situation when the people he nominated fell into it.

Presidents, politicians, and their appointees aren't the only ones whose behavior can be changed by hubris. Miriam's experience is a reminder that anyone who has some power risks falling victim to its dangers. And the more power you have, the higher the risk of abusing it. "Power tends to corrupt, and absolute power corrupts absolutely," Lord Acton wrote in 1887, in a letter to Mandell Creighton (who would later become a bishop of the Church of England), as part of a conversation about how historians should evaluate the past. Acton argued that, contrary to Creighton's opinion, not only should moral standards apply to everyone, but they should be particularly stringent for figures of authority.[20] "I cannot accept your canon that we are to judge Pope and King unlike other men, with a favourable presumption that they did no wrong. If there is any presumption it is the other way against holders of power, increasing as the power increases," Acton pressed.

Unchecked absolute power is quite likely to corrupt absolutely.

And, interestingly, while those who do not have power are aware of this trap and are then more prone to think of power as dirty, those who do have power seldom do, because the experience of power makes us less likely to feel morally impure. Let's see why.

POWER CAN MAKE US FEEL VIRTUOUS, TOO

Do you have pen and paper handy? Or perhaps your phone? When you have something to write with, consider the list of words below, and fill in the missing letters as quickly as you can to compose words in the English language.

W _ _ H
F _ O _
S H _ _ E R
B _ _ K
S _ _ P
P A _ _ R

Now look at the words you wrote and count how many of them are related to cleansing. Perhaps you wrote shower? Or soap? Do you have one such word in your list? Two? Three? The number matters because the word-task you just completed reveals unconscious feelings of moral impurity.

That's right. Research in moral psychology has demonstrated that people who behave in morally questionable ways embody their shame, such that they wish to cleanse themselves physically to rid themselves of the moral dirtiness of their actions.[21] This instinct to wash away our sins is not news to people with keen insight into human nature. William Shakespeare, for one, had Lady Macbeth cry: "Out damned spot! Out, I say!" when she was overtaken with guilt for the murder she had led her husband to commit. Although she had no actual blood on her hands, she felt the stains acutely.[22]

You don't have to connive at murder to feel morally impure and fill the blanks with words like wash, shower, and soap, instead of neutral ones like wish, shaker, and step. The focus of this chapter on the perceived dirtiness of power might have been enough to conjure cleansing-related words in your mind as you wrote because it doesn't take much to make us feel morally queasy. Take networking, a perfectly legitimate professional activity many of us engage in, at least on occasion.

Across multiple lab and field studies, we have seen hundreds of working professionals come up with many more cleansing-related words when asked to think about a time that they went networking to advance their career and job performance than when they recalled socializing to make new friends. The moral value of altruistic behavior explains why. When we network socially, for friendship, we can easily feel altruistic, because the purpose is a mutually supportive relationship.[23] In contrast, when we network for professional reasons, we typically do so to get valued resources such as information, job opportunities, or profitable new clients from others. The selfish intent behind our networking makes us feel morally questionable — unconscious as those feelings often are.

And yet, there are exceptions: In all our studies, the people least likely to feel dirty when they network professionally, even when they do so with the explicit purpose of accessing resources from others, are those who feel powerful. Being powerful means, by definition, having control over resources others value. People who feel powerful, therefore, are more likely to network with a clear conscience, since they know they can benefit other people by giving them access to resources they control. When it's a two-way street — at least in their mind — it takes the shadow of exploitation away from their networking. This doesn't mean that powerful people always reciprocate benefits; nor that they are generous with their resources as they acquire resources from others. We all act selfishly at least some of the time. But the powerful can more easily justify their networking to themselves as altruistic and virtuous, because they have something of value, potentially, to contribute.

Power thus liberates us to pursue access to valued resources without incurring moral qualms about feeling selfish. We saw this effect clearly when we studied professionals in a large North American law firm. We found that lawyers who networked to advance their team and share their collective expertise with clients felt cleaner than lawyers who networked to advance their own careers and personal success.[24] Because these collectively oriented lawyers didn't feel dirty about their professional networking, they networked more often and got more clients, thereby confirming its effectiveness. Here's the catch, though. The lawyers who networked the most were the firm's powerful senior members, while the most reluctant—those who felt queasier about cultivating relationships to access clients and connections—were the junior lawyers, who had the least power and needed networking most but didn't feel they had something of value to offer.[25] You can see how easily this phenomenon can perpetuate existing power hierarchies, since those who are most powerful are also the most unabashed in leveraging their power to gain yet more power, while the least powerful feel most uneasy about getting out there and seeking the resources they need.

POWER AND MORALITY: A CATCH-22?

Wanting to have an impact in the world without having power is like wanting to produce electricity without a source of energy. It's simply impossible. Yet as we have seen, holding power makes us more self-absorbed and arrogant—even when we think we are using our power for the purpose of benefitting others. Does this mean that it's impossible to acquire and wield power without losing one's moral compass? This is the catch-22 that Dr. Vera Cordeiro[26] had to navigate as she worked to help the impoverished mothers and children in her care at Rio de Janeiro's bustling Lagoa public hospital.

As months turned into years, and her young patients cycled in and out of the hospital, Vera's anger mounted. Illnesses that would be easily treated in private hospitals serving Brazilians with stable jobs, healthy sanitary conditions, and regular meals were death sentences for too many of her patients. In 1991, she founded a nonprofit organization, Associação Saúde Criança (now the Instituto DARA), to break this cycle via an innovative and, at the time unique, multipronged approach: In addition to providing the medicine children needed, the organization also supported the rehabilitation of their homes, the vocational training of their parents, and the health of all their household members.[27]

Funding these activities wasn't easy. Initially, Vera raffled off personal items from her home and relied heavily on the volunteer support of family and friends. But that could take her only so far. As the number of full-time employees grew, Vera realized she could no longer avoid seeking support from the rich and the powerful. In her mind, power was the sleek cars that crept through Rio's shantytowns, and the politicians who took lavish vacations abroad—in short, greedy and corrupt. She wasn't one of these powerful people, and she didn't want to have anything to do with them. But if Vera wanted to sustain and grow the impact her NGO was having, she could not shy away from power. From that point on, she and her team worked hard to attract the attention of private donors, public authorities, and the general public. They sharply increased their engagement with the media and their networking, not only in Brazil but also internationally in social entrepreneurship circles. An avalanche of accolades for Vera soon followed, and her NGO became one of the most highly regarded in Brazil. By 2016, it had directly helped seventy thousand people.[28]

Along the way, Vera noticed that she had become more comfortable with power. She wasn't so concerned about interacting with powerful people, and she realized that she herself had built a strong power base. She was well connected nationally and internationally, a frequent speaker at prestigious conferences like the World Economic Forum at Davos, where she could meet potential new funders.

At the same time, she was starting to get some new and unexpected feedback from her staff and family: Colleagues told her that she was always interrupting them and didn't let them speak their mind enough in meetings; her adult daughter questioned her about why she seemed to care so much about attending award ceremonies and public events. Their comments made her pause. Had she become one of those people who wanted more and more power to advance her own fame and interests?

Having once been wary of power is no guarantee that you will be immune to abusing it. That Vera—a social entrepreneur who dedicated her life to trying to address the root causes of poverty and who initially shunned power—could be changed by the experience of power is another reminder that we are all susceptible to its intoxicating effects. The challenge is finding a balanced relationship that avoids the strictures of dirtiness and the perils of hubris and insensitivity to others. This balancing act hinges on both personal development and structural design—the way things work in the context where we wield power. Insights from the social sciences, neuroscience, and philosophy can guide us in tackling both dimensions.

A DEVELOPMENTAL PATH TO POWER: CULTIVATING EMPATHY AND HUMILITY

Developing a balanced relationship with power seldom happens overnight, not least because our emotions, not just our thoughts, are at play. Freeing oneself from the "power is dirty" narrative and understanding power's potential as a source of energy to effect change is the first step, as we've seen. The next is recognizing that one has valuable resources to offer others—power that *could* be used to advance their well-being. This developmental process can help us to deploy our power as a force for good; and research finds that people who focus on the altruistic, collective benefits of building their power base feel worthier and are more likely to achieve better performance.[29] But it is not devoid of pitfalls: The risk is that we convince ourselves that our motivations and behaviors are purely moral, that they transcend our own self-interest, when in fact they do not.[30] As Vera discovered, engaging with power for a good purpose still makes us vulnerable to becoming self-focused and hubristic. We can, however, overcome these challenges to accruing power by cultivating both empathy (the antidote to self-focus) and humility (the antidote to hubris).

The Cultivation of Empathy

Diana, princess of Wales, broke many norms in her brief life as a British royal, perhaps none more so than how she mothered her sons, William and Harry. With public displays of affection for her children and her insistence on taking them with her on official trips, she was a warmer mother than the typically reserved British royal family had experienced. Nor did her break with convention stop at her own interaction with the princes: She was also determined to develop their empathy and took the unprecedented step of taking them with her to visit people in deeply challenging situations, such as AIDS patients. Asked why, she responded, "I want them to have an understanding of people's emotions, people's insecurities, people's distress, and people's hopes and dreams."[31]

Princess Diana's approach assumes that empathy can be developed by regularly exposing children to life experiences different from their own, giving them a chance to understand others emotionally and feel what they feel. Both neuroscience and psychology back up Princess Diana's method, which, when sustained over time, can develop empathy in adults, too.

Neuroscience has demonstrated that our brains are dynamic systems, constantly changing and adapting in response to the environmental stimuli to which we are exposed.[32] Pioneering psychological research on empathy development is consistent with these findings on the plasticity of the brain. It shows that empathy is not a fixed trait that one is either born with or not; it is a skill, a capability that we all can build up and strengthen.[33] Interventions to enhance empathy can be amazingly simple. In the lab, it's enough to ask people to read a story of someone's illness and imagine how the disease affected that person's life, for the reader to feel more empathy not only for the individual featured in the story, but also for all those afflicted by the same condition.[34] And if instead of just reading about someone we get to live their experience more vividly through immersive virtual reality technology, the engrossing simulated environment can greatly enhance our empathy for them.[35]

Scientific interventions are hardly the only way to develop empathy. The more embedded you are in someone else's reality, the deeper the empathy: The manager who works entry-level jobs before continuing to climb up the corporate ladder will appreciate the contributions of front-line personnel and blue-collar workers more than colleagues who leave their offices only for power lunches with clients and investors. The university student from an affluent family who takes a summer job at a fast-food restaurant will know what it means to be at the bottom of a corporate hierarchy, and how tough it is for people to live on a minimum-wage job. The banking executive who volunteers at an inner-city school or a local homeless shelter will think differently about the social role of a financial institution.

What these interventions and experiences tell us is that increasing someone's empathic accuracy requires asking them to put themselves in someone else's shoes. Incredibly, even psychopaths—whose defining traits are impaired empathy and uninhibited egotism[36]—respond to such nudges.[37] Neuropsychologists have shown that asking psychopaths to focus on others' pain, and to do their best to imagine how they felt, elicits mirrored suffering in their brains similar to that exhibited by non-psychopaths. Empathy nudges work. But sustaining their effects over time and beyond the immediate context in which they are applied is a lot more challenging.

Deep and lasting development of empathy requires more than temporarily seeing the world through someone else's eyes. It entails sustainably shifting from a focus on the self to an awareness and appreciation of interdependence. Psychologists think of this shift in terms of self-definition: People can view themselves as separate from and independent of others, or they can see themselves as connected to and interdependent with others.[38] Like perspective-taking, this interdependent view of the self can be stimulated with simple interventions, like asking someone to read a story written with independent pronouns (I, mine) but substitute interdependent pronouns (we, ours) instead.[39] The self is malleable, and, unsurprisingly, an interdependent view inspires greater empathy, more cooperation, and a collective orientation.

The development of the self is ultimately about expanding what an individual is aware of and feels connected to and responsible for. We start self-focused and—if our development isn't otherwise stunted—we evolve toward seeing ourselves as interdependent with something larger: family, community, country, and ultimately humanity and the planet.[40] In chapter 8, we will appreciate how a society can cultivate this awareness of interdependence in its citizens, and through the empathy it produces, curb the nefarious effects of power when they emerge, and achieve collective prosperity.

Social psychology isn't alone in believing that empathy rests on the awareness and appreciation of our interdependence. In Buddhist thought, all things are dependent on all other things, and interdependence is at the root of empathy and altruism.[41] The Buddhist path of liberation from self-focus hinges, in part, on the practice of meditation, which helps cultivate the wisdom to see how the things we crave—wealth, fame, power itself—keep us compulsively focused on ourselves.[42] Buddhism holds that training our minds to nonjudgmentally direct our attention to the present moment can help us let go of these destructive cravings, recognize our interdependence, and see the pursuit of the well-being of others as the pathway toward our own.[43]

Seeking a way to break out of the tendency to get caught up in self-centeredness, Vera Cordeiro turned to meditation to help her come to grips with her self-focus. Developing a regular practice, she told us, "helped me have more empathy for my staff and families that our NGO serves, reminding me of the primacy of our social mission." In connecting empathy with her organization's mission, Vera took a fundamental step along the developmental path to power: the recognition that all people are part of the same human family, and all things are interconnected. This recognition is central in the philosophy of Martin Luther King Jr., who famously remarked, "all life is interrelated. We are all caught in an inescapable network of mutuality, tied in a single garment of destiny. Whatever affects one directly, affects all indirectly."[44] Recognize this interdependence, and empathy will spring naturally from it and, with it, a cleaner relationship with power.

Sometimes, as we struggle to see through the fog of our self-focus, events much larger than ourselves remind us and rekindle our empathy. The COVID-19 pandemic helped some to see that the unilateral exercise of individual power is futile and counterproductive.[45] And many more of us have awakened to the truth of scientists' dire warnings about the boomerang effects of invading and destroying ecosystems[46] and "the need for a more holistic 'one health' approach [that] views human, animal, and environmental health as interconnected."[47]

Life-altering experiences such as the pandemic also make us more aware of our impermanence, which has long been one of the defenses humans put up against the other great danger of power: hubris.

The Cultivation of Humility

When it comes to celebrating military victories and putting personal power on display, Rome has been the reference point for monarchs and autocrats for the last two millennia.[48] Yet, in an interesting juxtaposition, some historians tell us that behind every victorious general riding in a chariot through the streets of Rome stood a slave whispering, "*Hominem te memento*" ("Remember you are [but] a man"), in his ear.[49] Cultivating this awareness that we are mortal and that success is fleeting is key to protecting ourselves from the dangers of hubris. Nothing dampens illusions of invincibility and infallibility more than remembering the impermanence of our own lives and all life.

What can we do to remember we are mortal and keep our hubris in check, not only at our zenith but also day-to-day? Mashroof Hossain,[50] a special representative of district police in Bangladesh, found his reminder in a life-changing exchange with a refugee during the Rohingya crisis. In 1982, the Rohingya, a Muslim minority group in Myanmar, were excluded from the list of 135 officially recognized national ethnic groups eligible for "citizenship by birth"[51] and became officially stateless. In 2017, civilian massacres, executions, infanticides, gang rapes, and village burnings caused hundreds of thousands of Rohingya to flee to refugee camps on the Myanmar-Bangladesh border, where living conditions are bleak and perilous.[52] Among those called to help manage the situation at the border was Mashroof, who had joined the police force seven years prior.

Of the many people Mashroof encountered in the camp, an unassuming old man was one of the most memorable. Mashroof enjoyed listening to his stories, and they became friends. One day, he was surprised to learn from other people that the old man had been a general in the army. "And in Myanmar," Mashroof explained, "if you're a military officer, you're like the king." Yet in the blink of an eye, this man fell from the height of power to profound powerlessness. "Today, Mashroof, you may feel like you are on the top of the world," the old man warned him, "but tomorrow you could lose everything."

The man's words stayed with Mashroof. Since that encounter, whenever he feels hubris lurking, he checks himself by remembering the general. "Feeling strong and powerful can be like a drug. When it happens to me . . . I remind myself of this general who is now a refugee with just one bag, like so many others who lost everything. And I know that this can happen to any one of us, so we should never take anything for granted."

Mashroof was right to believe that cultivating humility is necessary for avoiding the trap of hubris. Empirical research shows that when we display humility, we enable others to help us stay grounded, because we give them permission to speak up with ideas, questions, concerns, or mistakes without fear that they will be punished or humiliated. Organizational scholar Amy Edmondson has identified a number of practices that nurture such a climate of psychological safety.[53] To encourage interpersonal risk, for example, leaders can first frame the work by reminding their team of the complexity, uncertainty, and ambiguity in their environment, so that it is plain to see that no single individual can have all the answers. They can then invite engagement by making it a habit of asking questions to surface different perspectives, all the while acknowledging the limits of their own current knowledge. By admitting their own fallibility, they encourage others to follow suit. And when they do, the leaders must respond appreciatively: thanking those who speak up and destigmatizing errors by flagging them as opportunities for learning. The psychological safety these practices engender not only helps a leader keep hubris in check but also enhances the team's innovation and effectiveness.[54] When leaders express humility, the quality of team members' contributions increases, together with their job satisfaction and retention, and their engagement and learning orientation.[55]

Humility—the acknowledgment of one's limitations and the accurate perception of one's abilities and accomplishments—increases our openness to learning and boosts our altruism, generosity, and helpfulness.[56] Together, humility and empathy are thus what allows us to use power to achieve a higher purpose.

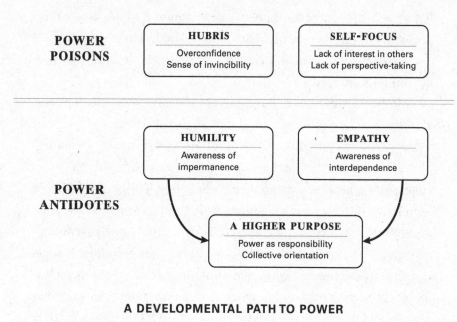

POWER POISONS		
	HUBRIS	**SELF-FOCUS**
	Overconfidence Sense of invincibility	Lack of interest in others Lack of perspective-taking

POWER ANTIDOTES		
	HUMILITY	**EMPATHY**
	Awareness of impermanence	Awareness of interdependence
	A HIGHER PURPOSE Power as responsibility Collective orientation	

A DEVELOPMENTAL PATH TO POWER

PUTTING POWER IN GOOD HANDS

Beyond guiding our own development, understanding how to engage constructively with power should also guide whom we give power to, whenever that choice is available to us. A psychopath might fleetingly respond to empathy nudges, as we've discussed; but do we really want to put a psychopath in power and hope that he, or she, will morph into a paragon of wisdom? Of course not. And yet history is filled with instances in which awesome power fell into the hands of exactly the wrong people.[57] These include individuals, chosen democratically, who became autocrats, and others who elbowed their way into positions of great influence and proceeded to make the worst possible use of it. The question is: Why does power end up in the wrong hands so often? Why do we allow power to go to people who proceed to take us down a spiral of abuse and loss?

One reason is self-selection, in that people who want power the most are often the ones who seek and get it. People vary in their desire to occupy positions of influence; and one study has shown that those who do the best job in these roles are neither the people most eager to get them nor those who adamantly eschew them. They are, instead, the individuals who are somewhat reluctant to be at the helm.[58] The reluctantly powerful, as it were, are most likely to use power well, but also less likely to acquire it, because they don't seek it.

Selection is another reason power often ends up in the hands of people ill-suited to use it well. We allow such people to occupy positions of power they have attained illegitimately, and sometimes we actively choose them in free and fair elections. Why? Because many of us, across cultures, are disposed to prefer people who project an air of strength and a sense of supreme control, people who give us a feeling of security and stability.[59] By the time we realize whom we have given power to, their hold on it, and their control of the narrative around themselves and their actions, may be too tight to overcome.

What must we do instead? We should apply the same insights from psychology and philosophy that can guide our own approach to power when we choose the people who will exercise it on our behalf: individuals who have demonstrated empathy and humility; a proven tendency toward altruistic pursuits and not only selfish ones; and competence, of course, without which even the best intentions fall flat. These are the criteria we should judge every political candidate against, and the standards by which every business leader should be measured. Our job should be to look for cues that a potential power holder isn't so unwise and needy as to crave power for power's sake. The evidence suggests that much too often we fail to use these anchors and let other, flashier signs of strength, confidence, wealth, and status lure us into giving the wrong people power. The lessons of science and the humanities allow us to do better.

In sum, embracing power while avoiding its pitfalls rests on two foundations: an awareness of interdependence, which allows us to counteract self-focus with empathy; and an awareness of impermanence, which fights hubris with humility. Empathy and humility, in turn, make it easier to let go of selfish goals and to pursue altruistic ones—the key to a virtuous use of power. This is, of course, easier said than done. If it were easy, we would all use power wisely, shrug off its intoxicating dangers, and counter our individualistic desires. This is why we cannot rely exclusively on developing ourselves into more empathic and humble individuals. We also need structural limits to help keep our worst responses to power in check.

MORE THAN PERSONAL DEVELOPMENT: THE NEED FOR STRUCTURAL SAFEGUARDS

Vera found personal practices like meditation immensely helpful in cultivating empathy and humility, yet she also recognized that they weren't enough. If she were to manage the intoxicating effects of power and avoid riding roughshod over her team members' ideas and opinions, she would need some external checks and balances as well. To that end, she structured her organization's weekly executive team meetings so that everyone had the same amount of time to report on their activities and to share ideas and concerns. She also committed publicly not to interrupt her colleagues and to listen carefully before sharing her reactions; and she asked others to do the same.

These external efforts helped facilitate teamwork by creating processes that ensured inclusivity and a shared sense of responsibility. Vera was right to do so: Research on team performance has demonstrated that, together with colleagues' average empathy (measured as their ability to read others' emotions from their faces), the extent to which team members take turns speaking is among the strongest predictors of team performance.[60] Establishing protocols, such as those Vera put in place, to prevent a few (over)confident people from hoarding airtime and silencing dissenting opinions is critical. So are formal processes and organizational norms that keep everyone—especially leaders, who have more power—accountable for their actions. Such practices lead the powerful to focus on others and to act in a less self-serving manner.[61] They also keep the newly empowered team members accountable: the psychological safety to speak up and be heard enhances team learning and effectiveness when everybody feels accountable for using their share of power to accomplish collective goals.[62]

The idea that underlies all these practices is that power sharing and accountability accomplishes two objectives: It doesn't let power go to the leader's head; and it improves the effectiveness of the group. Vera had applied this key principle of good governance. In doing so, she stayed faithful to the higher purpose of her team *and* improved its performance. But she knew that she had to remain vigilant, as power sharing and accountability need to be constantly reinforced to curb hubris and self-focus. And as we will see in chapter 8, these limits on power matter as much for a small team in an NGO as they do for a giant corporation or the political system of an entire country.

So, power doesn't have to be dirty. If we cultivate both empathy and humility and put in place structural safeguards that ensure power sharing and accountability, we can avoid the pitfalls of power. Such knowledge frees us to seek the power we need to pursue objectives of our own choosing, instead of resigning ourselves to letting others—"the powerful people"—decide for us. Equipped with the developmental and structural tools to help us engage with power and use it responsibly, the next step is figuring out how to get it. This brings us back to the fundamentals of power, to the idea that power is always situated in a specific relationship. To be powerful in that relationship, you must have some control over resources the other party values. And vice versa, others will have power over you if they have control over things you value. Take these fundamentals seriously, and you will realize that diagnosing where the power lies in any situation comes down to answering two questions:

What do the people involved value?
Who controls access to what they value?

The answers to these questions vary across contexts and over time, of course. But this variability contains patterns that we can make sense of to reliably diagnose any power relationship, whatever the context, and give ourselves a chance to harness power, instead of being swept away by its force. Let's start with the first question: What do people value?

Chapter 3

What Do People Value?

How can we possibly know what another person values when human needs and desires are so diverse, multifaceted, and mutable over time? Philosophers, poets, and writers from Lucretius and Dante to Shakespeare and Yourcenar have devoted some of humankind's finest thinking to answering this question, as have psychologists, biologists, neuroscientists, and social scientists of every stripe. The arts and sciences have given us scores of models of human nature and motivation, each emphasizing different drivers of people's behavior. What follows is not an exhaustive account of this vast literature; that would be a feat far beyond the scope of this book, were it even possible. Rather, it is our distillation of the points of convergence we have found among these many bodies of work. Other scholars could—and undoubtedly would—make different, equally valid choices.[1] Recognizing this, we offer our analysis not as some new "last word" on human motivation, but as a useful guide for those who seek to uncover the needs and desires that activate power relationships.

HUMANITY'S TWO BASIC NEEDS:
SAFETY AND SELF-ESTEEM

Observed from afar, humanity is but a speck of dust in an endless universe, our position as inconsequential as it is fleeting. At the deepest level, what we humans long for are two defenses against this existential dilemma: first, protection from the whims of dangerous forces much greater than our own that could annihilate us in a moment; second, reassurance of our value as individuals in a universe that is indifferent to us. Ultimately, then, we aim to satisfy two basic human motives: safety from harm and confirmation that we are worthy of esteem. The need for safety and the need for self-esteem are so fundamental that they reliably shape power relationships across time and space.

Consider the dire perspective of psychologist Mihaly Csikszentmihalyi, chillingly summing up the vulnerability of the human condition:

> It seems that every time a pressing danger is avoided, a new and more sophisticated threat appears on the horizon. No sooner do we invent a new substance than its by-products start poisoning the environment. Throughout history, weapons that were designed to provide security have turned around and threatened to destroy their makers. As some diseases are curbed, new ones become virulent; and if, for a while, mortality is reduced, then overpopulation starts to haunt us . . . The earth may be our only home, but it is a home full of booby traps waiting to go off any moment.[2]

In the face of such looming danger, is it any wonder that we value safety from harm first and foremost? Our survival instinct is primal, which is why controlling access to resources that are critical to our physical and physiological safety—water, food, shelter and protection from illness and violence—is an effective strategy for wielding power. We shrink from what threatens our safety and embrace what promises to protect us from harm.

If this sounds nefarious, it's because it can be. Threatening someone's physical safety is as blunt an instrument of power as it is effective. It is a way that autocratic regimes squash dissent and control the people they rule,[3] mafia bosses keep families and businesses under their thumb,[4] and violent spouses hold their families hostage.[5] Threatening someone's livelihood is likewise a way to exercise power, albeit without the need to resort to physical violence. Holding someone's job hostage is a potent threat, given the physical and mental stress of unemployment.[6] Firing employees who refuse to work in dangerous conditions,[7] or ousting public officials who won't stand silent in the face of a political leader's unethical behavior[8] sends an unmistakable message about where the balance of power lies in the relationship.

Before our need for safety leads you to conclude that we live in a Hobbesian world of each against all,[9] however, remember that the promise of protection from harm is also a highly effective source of power. This promise is why human beings agree to form governments, create public institutions, and enact laws to safeguard our rights and protect our societies from falling back into a state of nature. Such protection is essential, because it is only when we do not depend on the goodwill of others for our security that we can all "look others in the eye without reason for fear" and act as free people, as philosopher Philip Pettit has pointed out.[10] But, the line between safety from harm and threats to safety can be easy to cross. Faced with a new and unpredictable danger, people tend to be less attentive to safeguarding their freedom, as the acceptance of increased government surveillance of private citizens after September 11 illustrates.[11] And, when they give power up willingly, they leave themselves open to its abuse.

While our basic need for safety stems from the precariousness of the human condition, our need for self-esteem responds to our relative insignificance. Across the millennia, over 100 billion people have come and gone,[12] leaving little or no trace, almost invariably forgotten. Questions about the meaning and value of existence are therefore at the root of humankind's robustly documented need for self-esteem, or the desire to maintain a positive view of ourselves, both privately and publicly.[13] The profound existential problem to make sense of our time on earth triggers the need to understand the worth of our life and its value for others.[14] Viewing oneself as a valuable person is, by some accounts, the superordinate goal toward which most other goals in life are oriented.[15]

Maintaining high self-esteem is critical to our well-being and our capacity to set and pursue goals, savor positive experiences, and cope with challenging ones.[16] Yet our pursuit of self-esteem can be *both* dysfunctional and functional.[17] When we seek it because we are feeling insecure and vulnerable about our self-worth, we engage in strategies that are motivated by the need to protect or aggrandize ourselves. The esteem this behavior produces is fragile—unstable and relative, contingent on external validation from events and accomplishments. In contrast, when our behavior is grounded in a realistic acceptance of who we are, without defensiveness, the resulting self-esteem is secure—congruent and stable, an authentic expression of a person's core self.[18]

Much as we might aspire to genuine self-esteem, achieving it is a lifelong quest. So, those who wish to influence us can do so by appealing to our self-esteem; and we can use the same appeal in turn, when we seek to influence others.

HOW DO WE SATISFY THESE TWO BASIC NEEDS?

Knowing that we are all driven by the pursuit of safety and self-esteem is the starting point in deciphering any power relationship; how each person satisfies these needs varies. Research in social psychology tells us that self-esteem depends on our subjective assessment of ourselves, including how we view our personal competence, the social rank we occupy, the degree of influence we have, and how worthy of love and morally upright we believe we are.[19] Likewise, safety depends on securing basic physiological necessities, such as food and shelter, but also psychological resources, such as relationships with people who care for us and protect us from harm, or competences that allow us to cope with the danger and uncertainty around us.

How we each prioritize these resources at different times and in different situations varies. And we're also influenced by those around us, with what we value shaped by our social context and the cultural beliefs of our community. Despite all these differences, we share commonalities in our quest for safety and self-esteem. Let's see what they are and how they affect power dynamics, starting with the resource that—many say—makes the world go 'round: money.

Material Resources

"The present trend of fossil fuel consumption will cause dramatic environmental effects before the year 2050." While this quote could come from almost any newspaper published over the past few years, it actually dates back to 1979. Who made such a pioneering prediction? None other than Exxon, one of the world's biggest oil producers.[20] Three years later, another Exxon internal report on the greenhouse gas effect provided predictions on global warming that, to this day, remain frighteningly accurate.[21]

As the scientific understanding of human-caused global warming grew, the fossil fuel industry started a full-fledged operation to hide what they had discovered. A leaked memo dated 1998 set out the industry's strategy: Working with the same public relations group big tobacco used to hide the health effects of smoking from the public, the fossil fuel industry launched a deep-pocketed, full-throttle effort to sow doubt around climate science.[22] Think tanks and advocacy organizations, funded by families who had made their fortune in oil, launched ads, published reports, and trained skeptical "scientists" to become ambassadors of climate change denialism. Between 2003 and 2010, some ninety-one conservative organizations received half a billion dollars in funding to undermine Americans' faith in climate science,[23] while, in parallel, oil companies were designing rigs from the Arctic to the North Sea to account for rising sea levels and coastal erosion.[24]

Perfectly aware of the long-term consequences of their greed, the barons of the oil and gas industry stayed the course. In the relentless pursuit of money, they are but one part of an economic system that places profit and consumption above everything else[25]—a system in which we are all complicit to some extent.[26] We want the latest appliances, electronic devices, and fashions for as low a price as possible, while the companies that provide these goods and services want to make as much money as possible. In this neoliberal capitalist system espousing Milton Friedman's thesis that "the social responsibility of business is to increase its profit,"[27] financial short-termism has been so legitimized that it has become the norm in many modern societies.

The logic of neoliberalism may have pushed the value we ascribe to money to an extreme, but wealth and material possessions have been highly prized and greatly desired throughout time.[28] Read any of Jane Austen's novels and you will find yourself evaluating a character's marital prospects based on how much income and property they would bring to the marriage. Nor was this approach to social relations exclusive to late eighteenth-century British landed gentry. People have always been willing to go to great lengths to put their hands on a pot of gold, a treasure chest, or a lucrative contract, even if it means engaging in immoral or illicit behavior.

We crave money because it feeds both our basic needs: safety and self-esteem. You can't eat or wear money, but you can exchange it for food and shelter and feel—and be—safer as a result. And you can use it to boost your self-worth, especially in individualistic societies, because wealth is the gateway to privilege that feeds people's social status—a precious source of self-esteem for many.[29] Money *does* indeed make the world go around. Control people's access to money, and you will have power over them.

And yet, money isn't always required to influence people's behavior. Think of the clever way Napoleon wielded power over his military after the French Revolution, when the abolition of hereditary nobility deprived him of titles (and prosperous landed estates that came along with them) to reward his bravest officers. That's when Napoleon created a universal order of merit, the Legion of Honor, as a symbolic reward to soldiers and civilians alike.[30] It worked. To this day, honorific ornamentation can replace material rewards so effectively that it remains relevant as a motivational tool across industries well beyond the military. Or consider the artisans in Channapatna, a city in southern India known for its traditional wooden toys. Like everyone, they need to earn a living. Yet, sociologist Aruna Ranganathan,[31] who studied their economic behavior, found that they chose to charge connoisseurs, who would be willing to pay more for their fine work, *lower* prices than they would accept from less-discerning buyers.

In the face of the outsize value most of us place on money and material possessions, what are we to make of Napoleon's officers and Channapatna's artisans? The key to these puzzles is that other resources, more psychological than material, can supersede money as an object of desire, even in economic exchanges. Status, which can be achieved through material possessions, but also through other, less tangible means, is one of these resources.

Status

We seldom come to a sense of our worth entirely on our own.[32] The respect, prestige, and esteem others accord us—our status, our value in the eyes of others—also matters. Status indicates where we are positioned in relation to those around us, and we value the distinctions of rank fiercely. But status is a social construct, and in any era and culture, people have demonstrated an almost limitless ability to invent new ways to signal it.

Think about the ancient Chinese custom of foot-binding. Although the origin of the practice is still contested, a prominent theory suggests that it started and ended with different conceptions of status.[33] Aristocratic families embraced it, possibly as early as the tenth century, to demonstrate that their highborn daughters had no need to work the fields or go to market as peasant girls did. Confining girls to the home also ensured their chastity and purity—another source of esteem for families, and a boon for their daughters' marital prospects. The practice persisted until geo-politics and international commerce at the end of the nineteenth century exposed the practice to the rest of the world, reshaping its significance. To newcomers, the custom was barbaric, and those who practiced it culturally backward. The ancient practice of foot-binding was banned and eventually abandoned.[34]

The esteem others confer on us satisfies our need for self-esteem. For the aristocratic families of imperial China, women's "lotus feet" signified their family's place in the social hierarchy. For many of today's consumers, luxury goods are the ultimate marker of social status: Recall how diamonds weren't popular a century ago but later became an expensive symbol of everlasting love.[35] The resources that satisfy people's need for self-esteem change across place and time depending on cultural, economic, and institutional forces. What doesn't change is that we can influence others when we are the gateway to their social status, and vice-versa.

Affiliation

Status is not the only resource that can replace money as a means to influence people's behavior. Social connection—in the form of relationships, reciprocated commitment, and care—is another deeply valued resource. We long for friendship, trust, and acceptance; to both give and receive love or affection; to belong to a group.[36]

The Harvard Study of Adult Development, begun in 1938, is one of the longest-running research programs in all of psychology. Its goal was to understand why some people aged more successfully than others. The initial participants were two groups of men: 268 sophomores from Harvard University, and 456 boys from the toughest neighborhoods of Boston. In time, it grew to include more than two thousand boys and, eventually, their spouses.[37] At first, the researchers were concerned with changes in participants' physical attributes and intellectual ability, but over time, their focus shifted. George Vaillant, the psychiatrist who led the research from 1972 to 2004, observed, "When the study began, nobody cared about empathy or attachment. But the key to healthy aging is relationships, relationships, relationships."[38] The healthiest octogenarians, the researchers found, were people most satisfied in their relationships at age fifty. For longevity, loneliness matters as much as smoking or alcoholism.[39]

How do affiliation and belonging relate to power? Objectively, surrounding ourselves with people who care for us makes us safer. Subjectively, their presence and affection enhance our sense of self-worth. Research in evolutionary psychology highlights how people internalize experiences of social acceptance and rejection in ways that can profoundly shape their assessment of their own worth.[40] Kids understand early on the power of threatening to withdraw their friendship from another child, even if they don't understand that the power derives from depriving a vulnerable peer of a key source of self-worth and a potential defense against mean-spirited bullies.

Ultimately, the people we love matter more to us than anything else. Anyone who has come close to death will tell you that their loved ones were all they thought about in those final moments.[41] The pain of being denied a last farewell to hospitalized family members was what made COVID-19 so heartbreaking for so many people. We can accept death, but not death without those we love.[42] Love is easily leveraged as a source of power: Threaten someone I love, and I will yield to you to ensure the safety of my loved one. At the same time, I will do all that's in my power to stop you.

Affiliation can also be leveraged to divide us. Our desire to belong can lead us to define our self-worth on the basis of our group's superiority to others.[43] The people who give us opportunities to feel good about ourselves by discriminating against others, seen as "lesser," gain power over us by exploiting our affiliations to feed our craving for self-esteem. Hostility toward immigrants, ethnic cleansings, and history's long list of racial and genocidal regimes illustrate how toxic the exploitation of this lever of influence can be.

Thankfully, hate isn't the only form of identification that influences us. Remember the artisans of Channapatna who identify so closely with their work that they value customers who they know will care for it beyond the point of sale, even if it means making less money. The value of labor changes when it's a labor of love, which is why they want to share their work with those who understand it and will love it as much as they do.

Achievement

The intensity of the Channapatna artisans' emotional investment in their work may be unusual, but they are far from alone in the value they place on mastering their craft. The drive to achieve and feel competent propels us to solve problems and overcome challenges by learning, analyzing, observing, and acting. We value feeling competent and accomplished because it helps make us feel safe and worthy. The more we master a craft or body of knowledge, the more control we are able to exercise in our daily lives, and the less threatened we feel by what we do not understand. And the more we stand out for our superior skill and insight, the more special and worthy we feel.

What constitutes achievement varies from person to person and across cultures. Young people in East Asia, for example, have ranked highest in international comparisons of math, reading, and science scores,[44] which is partially attributable to cultural differences in what constitutes achievement. Conversely, Anglo-American culture often defines youthful achievement in terms of the "student athlete," who epitomizes the Roman ideal of *mens sana in corpore sano* (a healthy mind in a healthy body).[45] But while definitions differ, achievement itself is universally valued.

In organizations, the value people place on achievement offers discerning managers a constructive way to influence employees' behavior. Research shows that the feeling of progress—born out of increasing competence and achievement—is an important source of motivation for people at work. The manager who can create an environment in which people experience progress will have a major influence on their behavior.[46]

Since achievement is demonstrated in myriad ways, those who define competence or "success" in a given arena have considerable leverage over those active in it. Parents' attention to grades and the assessment methods teachers use can influence students' behavior for good or ill. The selection committees that recognize heights of achievement—from Nobel Prizes to three-star Michelin restaurant reviews to college acceptance letters—wield enormous power because they control whose achievements in the lab, the kitchen, or at school are most worthy of commendation. If we did not attribute value to achievement and competence, prizes and grades would not exert such sway over our behavior. Yet, these external sources of validation for our achievements are not always what people are after. Some chefs stop pursuing more Michelin stars. Some artists refuse to collect awards. In doing so, they withdraw from the power relationship with those who grant these prizes and regain control over another resource that they value: their autonomy.

Autonomy

People who feel that they are in control of the choices they make, and that their actions are the result of their own volition, have autonomy. We value autonomy deeply. Indeed, the primary driver of our desire for power is not the desire for influence over the lives of others, but rather freedom from the influence of others over us.[47] Autonomy makes us feel safer, by protecting us from the unwanted consequences of choices made by others; and it enhances our self-esteem, because the actions we engage in by choice feel authentic—a genuine reflection of who we are—and therefore morally worthy.[48]

Employees who are able to act autonomously and perceive their managers as supportive of their autonomy express more satisfaction than those who have little or no control over their work lives. In turn, their satisfaction is reflected not only in better performance evaluations, but also in healthier psyches.[49] Conversely, the lack of autonomy takes a toll on employees' physical and mental health. Respecting the autonomy of others—acknowledging our desire to decide for ourselves—is what allows managers to motivate their employees, teachers to engage their students, and parents to have children who talk to them.

The fear of losing autonomy, or the realization that it has been lost already, is easily leveraged. In his book, *Heroic Failure: Brexit and the Politics of Pain*, journalist Fintan O'Toole credits this fear as a major contributor to the UK's exit from the European Union.[50] Politicians like Nigel Farage and Boris Johnson understood how much many in England resented the collapse of the British Empire, the increase in immigrants, and their real or perceived loss of autonomy to the European Union.[51] "Make Britain great again," they said. "Don't let those EU bureaucrats outlaw your favorite prawn cocktail-flavored potato chips!" Leveraging people's desire to control their own destiny can be a powerful way to influence others' behavior and thereby exercise power.

A deficit in autonomy can lead people to seek control over others to make up for the lack of control they have over their own lives.[52] In its most extreme form, this need for control can devolve into a craving for dominance—the capacity to intimidate, coerce, and instill fear and submissiveness.[53] Territorial behavior is one example.[54] When deeply valued resources, starting with food and water and extending to shelter, material property, and social position, are scarce or threatened, territorial behavior can satisfy our deep need for safety, just as it did for our hunter-gatherer ancestors.

In more mundane aspects of our lives, the appeal of dominance can explain why many enjoy spectator sports, particularly those with the potential for violence. One theory for why violence in sports is entertaining holds that "spectators live vicariously through athletes, so that when a player slams [another], it's as if the spectator accomplished the play."[55] And, conveniently, spectators get to feel dominant from the safety of their seats. Fans demand aggression and violence in spectator sports, which teams and leagues are happy to provide. There's money to be made from exploiting the human desire to dominate.

At its worst, the need for dominance comes in the form of torture, terrorism, and other direct assaults on human life. What are these if not twisted variations of the need to feel in control—if ever so briefly—by controlling whether other people suffer or flourish, live or die. People who commit such acts are seeking a warped and perverted sense of self-worth. New Zealand Prime Minister Jacinda Ardern made this clear in the way she dealt with the perpetrator of the Christchurch Mosque terrorist attack on March 15, 2019:

> He sought many things from his act of terror, but one
> was notoriety. And that is why you will never hear me
> mention his name. He is a terrorist, he is a criminal, he

is an extremist—but he will, when I speak, be nameless. And to others, I implore you, speak the names of
those who were lost rather than the name of the man
who took them. He may have sought notoriety, but we
in New Zealand will give him nothing, not even his
name.[56]

By denying the terrorist a name known around the world, Prime
Minister Ardern thwarted what likely motivated his act of hatred:
the desperate need for self-esteem.[57] She also took away his control
of the narrative by focusing it not on his horror, but on others' de-
cency and worth.

Morality

Can someone influence us by giving us a way to feel morally upright?
As Ardern demonstrated, it's possible, because virtue—goodness
and adherence to high standards of right and wrong—figures significantly in our pursuit of safety and self-esteem. Moral philosophy, sociology, biology, and evolutionary psychology provide at least three,
not mutually exclusive, explanations for why we place so much value
on morality.

The first explanation is that morality is born out of necessity and
interdependence: We depend on one another to find refuge from
danger and suffering, and our individual well-being is intertwined
with the well-being of others.[58] We value virtuous conduct because
adhering to moral norms and conventions keeps us safe from the
dangers of both the natural world and of a social world in which the
only law is the "war of all against all."[59] According to this view, virtuous conduct has instrumental value.

The second explanation is evolutionary: An innate moral sense
emerged and took hold in human nature because of its role in natural selection. The moral element of cooperative, prosocial behavior,

for example, likely evolved in the context of shared infant care: If you help me protect and raise my children and I reciprocate, we both stand a better chance of keeping them alive and passing on our genes.[60] Like the instrumental explanation for the value of morality, the evolutionary view is "greatly complicated by the ultimately self-serving quality of most forms of altruism," as biologist Edward O. Wilson puts it.[61] But ultimately selfish though it may be, morality has evolved to be at the core of our view of ourselves and our worth. We apply moral sentiments, such as sympathy and inclusivity, beyond our kin; and when our conduct diverges from what we consider moral, we feel the need to justify the deviation to ourselves, as well as to others.[62]

The third explanation sees morality as the highest expression of our humanity. To be moral is to be fully human. In Greek philosophy, for example, Epicurus—narrowly remembered for proclaiming that the highest goal of human life is the enhancement of pleasure and the reduction of pain—believed that it is impossible to live pleasurably "without living prudently and honorably and justly, and also without living courageously and temperately and magnanimously, and without making friends, and without being philanthropic."[63] In Aristotelean virtue ethics, living in accordance to virtue is necessary for human flourishing.[64] In the modern philosophy of Immanuel Kant, being moral is a categorical imperative (that is, a rule of conduct that is unconditional for all of us), because, unlike all other beings, humans can use reason to articulate moral principles that have universal and intrinsic value.[65] Despite their differences, these bodies of thought are congruent in one respect: People develop moral standards, and value adhering to them as an ideal of human fulfilment. Moreover, these moral principles appear in remarkably similar ways across epochs and traditions. In the philosophy of Confucius and Mencius, for example, *rén* (benevolence, compassion, and humanity), *yì* (honesty and righteousness), *lǐ* (propriety and good manners), *xin* (faithfulness and integrity), and *zhi* (knowledge and wisdom) are considered the five constant virtues.[66]

Whether being moral has instrumental, evolutionary, or intrinsic value, the individuals, organizations, institutions, and communities that enable us to develop and assert our moral sense can influence us, because we all strive to act in accordance with our moral principles and, when we fail to do so, we risk feeling uneasy, misaligned, or downright ashamed.[67] We are drawn to groups that reflect what we value because we wish to associate ourselves with those values and consequently see ourselves as virtuous. In the realm of consumer behavior, brands, organizations, and leaders can gain or lose power because they align or fail to align with contemporary moral values.

Appealing to moral principles to mobilize people for change is also a universal source of power. If you think back to social change icons like Mahatma Gandhi, Nelson Mandela, and Mother Teresa or, more recently, Malala Yousafzai, their ideals are what enabled them to influence others. This is also how, in 2019, sixteen-year-old Greta Thunberg's Fridays for Future mobilized an estimated 4 million people in 163 countries to march, protest, and join strikes for climate action.[68] But while moral appeals are powerful, they are not always virtuous. Painting "other" individuals or groups or nations as "immoral" is a tried-and-true strategy for mobilizing people. As Edward O. Wilson cleverly put it, "Human beings are consistent in their codes of honor, but endlessly fickle with reference to whom the codes apply."[69]

Although the desire to be moral is universal, how highly each of us values and cultivates our moral self varies greatly.[70] For some, the inordinate love of money or the desire to dominate crushes any aspiration to be virtuous. There is not much moral about the behavior of those who profited from fossil fuels for decades while knowing that their impact would pose an existential threat to humankind. For others, by contrast, morality is valued above all else. Think about all those resisting fascist occupation during World War II, the student protesters in Beijing's Tiananmen Square, and all who have died throughout the ages to uphold justice and freedom from tyranny. Unsurprisingly, people who see morality as important to their identity are less likely to use power for self-interested reasons.[71]

As is the case with status, affiliation, and achievement, the criteria we use to define morality are subject to social construction and interpretation. The nineteenth-century philosopher Friedrich Nietzsche saw morality not as a timeless, objective truth, but rather as the product of cultural and historical circumstances.[72] For example, we still embrace Aristotle's cardinal virtues—prudence, temperance, courage, and justice—but we cannot condone his justification of slavery and rejection of human equality. Foot-binding was for centuries a marker of status for aristocratic Chinese families, but it eventually became seen as a barbaric and immoral practice. And while fur was a marker of social class and high style until the 1980s, in the 1990s its symbolic value began to plummet in the U.S. thanks to the public activism of People for the Ethical Treatment of Animals (PETA),[73] which tapped into people's moral compass to transform it from a symbol of elegance to a symbol of cruelty.

DISCOVERING WHAT, EXACTLY, OTHER PEOPLE WANT

We have seen that people fulfill the basic human needs for safety and self-esteem in many ways: material possessions, status, achievement, affiliation, autonomy, and morality are all valued resources (as shown in the figure on page 58). But we have also seen that these resources are not equally compelling to every person, at every moment in time, or in every context. So, while these commonalities give us essential insights into what people value and why, knowing what, exactly, someone else wants often requires careful observation of their situation. Only then can you know whether your power hinges on giving them a badge of honor, a pot of gold, a measure of autonomy, a sense of virtue, or something else altogether.

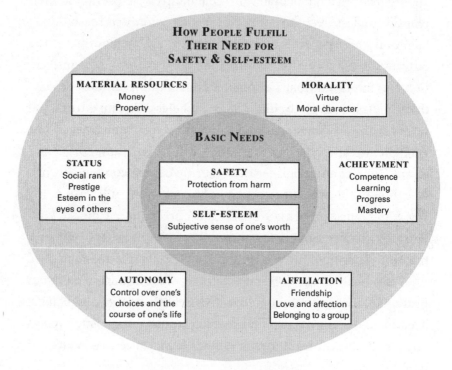

**A FRAMEWORK TO UNDERSTAND
WHAT PEOPLE VALUE**

To illustrate, let us tell you a story about Ning.[74] A native of China, he accepted a position as a strategy advisor at a large Australian enterprise after receiving his MBA. His assignment—to improve the lackluster performance of the organization's call centers—was a challenge, because despite his seemingly lofty title, he had no formal authority over the call-center manager or agents, nor did he have much knowledge about what motivated their behavior and how to change it. One thing he did know, though: Morale at call centers is always a major issue.

"Nobody ever calls in to say, 'Hey, your service is working won-ders, I love it!' Callers are almost always angry," he told us.[75] "These agents hear people yell at them 24/7. You're constantly fearful of yet another tense, unpleasant call; and you feel pretty crappy about yourself when you can't solve the caller's problem and make them happy—which is often. It's no surprise that absenteeism and turn-over are very high."

Ning felt for the call-center agents. It was already clear to him that they were sorely lacking safety and self-esteem. Hard to feel safe when another screaming customer is always around the corner, and managers from headquarters regularly come in announcing job cuts. Hard to have high self-esteem when you're paid very little for doing alienating work in a cubicle. Employees were miserable, and when Ning came to us for advice on how best to succeed in his new job, he was determined to figure out something to make their lives better.

Ning knew that his ability to make a positive difference de-pended on being able to understand what the call-center employees needed and delivering the resources they valued most. But some of those valued resources, like higher pay, weren't an option because he had no control over them. What else, then, might these people want that he could give them?

To learn what the agents valued, he began visiting one of the centers, mindful that the people he met were suspicious of anyone from headquarters. "The moment I walked in," Ning said, "every-body stopped talking; pin-drop silence." He responded by adjusting his approach. He started spending every Wednesday there, working on his laptop at an empty cubicle on the main floor instead of asking agents about their work.

From his perch on the main floor, he noticed immediately that visual barriers around the sides and front of the cubicles made the agents feel alone while fending off callers. When Ning asked whether those barriers could be removed, HR at first refused, citing the confidential customer information on the agents' screens. They relented, however, when he quickly pointed out that privacy screens on the agent's monitors would address that concern, and high-quality headsets would protect agents from the sounds of calls around them. "All of a sudden, people were able to see each other, make eye contact, feel that their colleagues are right there." It was a simple way to feed their need for safety and affiliation.

Noticing that the more formally he dressed, the more nervous people became, Ning also took to wearing jeans and a T-shirt like everyone else. As the agents became more relaxed around him, they started to feel bad that he always sat by himself and nobody talked to him. Soon enough, they invited him to join their lunches. "The first time it was very weird," Ning recalled. "People didn't want to say anything, so I started talking to them about my life, the problems I was having. Once they realized that I had problems similar to theirs, they started opening up."

These conversations immediately made it clear that the agents found no purpose in their work—the job was nothing to them but a paycheck. But they were passionate about their second jobs and the volunteer activities they were involved in: a theater troupe, a dairy farm, a family bakery, an animal rescue. Ning thought about what he was hearing and came up with an ingenious idea: Why not replace the news shown on the cafeteria TV with photos and videos of the agents' activities outside the call center? At first, he had to beg for submissions. But once he put together the first slideshow, the photos and videos poured in. Agents who couldn't find their sense of worth in the call center found it by sharing their achievements, loved ones, and friends with their colleagues.

As the agents became more forthcoming about the problems they encountered at work, Ning took notes, keeping track of every single issue they mentioned, big and small. The callback information in a script they were required to follow was one of the irritants. While the script promised a call within two business days, Australia's holiday schedule, which varies across its states and territories, often shrank the timeframe to one day, making it harder for the agents to solve the customer's issue. Ning heard about the issue at lunch one Wednesday, and he had the authority to change the script; but revising the text had to be done at headquarters. Ning went back to his hotel room, called the corporate office where he had built a great network, and by lunchtime the next day, he was able to tell the agents, "The script has changed. You can go online right now and check. It's done." He also told them what, exactly, he had been doing to start solving the other issues they had brought up, and when he expected to resolve them.

The agents were impressed: "Holy shit. You're efficient!" Without missing a beat, Ning replied, "That's what I'm here for. Now, tell me, how can I help you more?" The floodgates opened because the agents no longer feared the emissary from headquarters who boosted their self-esteem by getting them the resources they needed to do their job well. In just six months, their self-reported engagement, empowerment, autonomy, and satisfaction all went up by 27 percent. Management was equally thrilled, because the call-center's productivity doubled! Ning's approach was so successful that the company asked him to do his magic at every one of the country's call centers.

EARNING PEOPLE'S TRUST TO UNCOVER THEIR NEEDS

Ning navigated his challenging circumstances beautifully. At first, he had the title but not the power to influence call-center employees. But by figuring out what they valued that he did have access to, and finding clever ways to deliver those resources, he gained the power he needed to create the change he aspired to.

What made Ning's accomplishments even more impressive is that he had to overcome massive skepticism and downright suspicion. As his trial by fire demonstrates, even when you know to ask people what they need, they don't always tell you. Ning knew that he needed to gain the agents' trust if he really wanted to understand their needs. He also realized that they were sizing him up. Across cultures and contexts, people judge other individuals and groups on two criteria: competence and warmth.[76]

Competence encompasses our perception of a person's efficiency, skills, and ability. Warmth refers to our perception of a person's sincerity, honesty, and benevolence. Warmth is trust in someone's intentions; competence is trust in someone's ability to act on their intentions. We pay a lot of attention to the warmth and competence of the people we interact with because they offer safety. If I can trust you to look out for me (and not stab me in the back), I feel safe. And if you can deliver the goods and not leave me in the lurch, I feel safer yet.

Warmth and competence also feed our self-esteem. People who have good intentions toward us make us feel respected and cared for; and if they respect and care for us, we feel worthy of their benevolence. Surrounding ourselves with competent people makes us more competent, too, which also increases our self-worth. It's no wonder that these two attributes account for the lion's share of our interpersonal perceptions.

Ning understood that, to help the agents, he needed them to trust him, both for his intentions and his ability to act on them. He also intuited that he had to establish his good intentions first, because he knew he was perceived as an outsider (as a Chinese national in Australia) and as someone to fear (since he came from corporate headquarters). While people value both competence and warmth in their colleagues, warmth rises to the top when people are forced to make tradeoffs.[77] Given a choice between a competent jerk (a colleague who is skilled but not very nice) and a lovable fool (one with below-average expertise but warm and good-hearted), most people choose the lovable fool.[78] We avoid working with jerks no matter how competent they are, and we value every bit of competence we can get out of lovable fools.

Ideally, of course, we'd like to have both warmth and competence. But at the margins, giving people more reassurance as to your good intentions and moral character makes you a more attractive work partner than competence does (provided a minimal level of both, as is typically the case in organizations that select people based on ability and interpersonal skills). You might think that in highly competitive and profit-driven industries (such as consulting, investment banking, and private equity), or in technically demanding professions (such as surgery, software development, and the military), competence would override warmth. But we find the same dynamic across industries.

This is what Ning got so right. To overcome the suspicion of the call-center personnel, he used what social psychologists tell us are the most potent sources of interpersonal liking: familiarity (by plopping himself on the call-center floor right next to the other agents), and similarity (by showing that he and the agents had a lot more in common than met the eye).[79] And he did so genuinely with a real desire to improve their working conditions. Once his benevolence was established and the call-center agents felt that they could confide in Ning, he was relentless in demonstrating his ability to act on his intentions, his competence. He attacked their issues head-on, fast, leveraging his contacts at headquarters and delivering for the agents, over and over. He became the lovable star everybody wanted to work with.

What we have constructed through this chapter is a roadmap to understanding which resources matter most to others at a given moment in time. The first step is to uncover what someone values in their context: Money or status? Friendship and supportive relationships or a feeling of competence and progress? A sense of autonomy or a desire to feel virtuous? You can count on most, if not all, of these to be relevant to some degree in most situations. The second step is to identify who controls access to these valued resources. Ning was brilliant at uncovering what the call-center employees wanted, but he was equally clever about figuring out how to get access to those resources and deliver them to the call-center agents. How can we discern who controls access to the requisite valued resources, and why, in any given setting? What follows are the tools required to map the distribution of power in any context by identifying who, in that environment, holds the keys to accessing what people value.

Chapter 4

Who Controls Access to What We Value?

Donatella Versace never wanted the power that befell her on July 15, 1997. On that day, her brother Gianni—the creative genius behind the Versace empire—was murdered in Miami Beach, Florida, by a serial killer obsessed with the fashion icon. Overnight, Donatella found herself at the creative helm of the company her brother had dreamed up and turned into a global force in the fashion industry.

Ten years her brother's junior, Donatella was Gianni's first muse. When she was ten years old, Gianni would dress her for school in black leather miniskirts. When she turned eleven, he encouraged her to bleach her hair, outraging their mother but inspiring Donatella, who, by her teens, was a platinum blonde. As an adult, Donatella was Gianni's trusted creative advisor and scout, the only family member to work with him on the creative side of the Versace business. While Gianni designed, her keen eye and global outlook brought innovations to the company that heightened Versace's prominence in the fashion world. Her vision of the supermodel as a cultural icon transformed anonymous mannequins into public figures, women with distinctive identities and influence. "Carla Bruni, Claudia Schiffer, Naomi

Campbell, Cindy Crawford, Linda Evangelista. I'm the one who found them and brought them all into Versace," Donatella told us.[1] By 1993, she was so close to the business that few people realized Gianni had been ill with cancer, and that Donatella had quietly filled her brother's shoes to bring his collections to market while he recovered.

Despite these accomplishments, when Gianni was killed and Donatella officially replaced him as Versace's creative leader, few people inside or outside the company thought she could design iconic fashion the way her brother had. "Nobody believed in me—not even my team, the people who had worked with me all along. To them, I was just the little sister of a great genius. It didn't help that I was a woman in a company dominated by men in 1990s Italy. The weight of immense responsibility and total skepticism was crushing." Nevertheless, she said, "at the time, selling didn't cross my mind. Not for a second. I could never have given away my brother's creation, his sweat, his blood, his passion. I had to keep it in the family, for the family, for him."

Donatella paid a steep personal price for her commitment. "I was barely surviving," she remembered. "I had tunnel vision to get to the next collection. I couldn't see any farther. I knew I couldn't do it alone, and I kept asking everybody for input, not trusting myself. I needed to find my self-confidence, but it seemed that nobody around me had confidence in me," she recalled. "I had a seat on the Board of Directors, but in the eyes of the other Board members, I was there only because I was the founder's sister, so I didn't count."

At a loss for allies to sustain her through the turmoil of grieving her brother's death in the public eye and succeeding him, Donatella needed to be powerful and feel powerful, but power eluded her.

POWER AND AUTHORITY ARE NOT ONE AND THE SAME

As unique as Donatella's situation was, her experience of powerlessness at the top isn't unusual. Hierarchical positions seem, at first, like a useful proxy for power; and organization charts are indeed a good first step in identifying powerful individuals. In the military, orders flow down the chain of command. In politics, only presidents and prime ministers can issue executive orders. In business, managers can hire and fire subordinates. In these examples, title describes a person's authority, that is, their formal right to give orders and commands, and to make decisions.

Plenty of evidence exists, however, that authority does not always equal power. In a study we conducted in the United Kingdom's National Health Service, we saw how misleading it can be to rely solely on formal rank as a source of power. For one year, we followed sixty-eight clinical managers, all of whom had just launched a change initiative in their workplace. Some of these change agents were middle managers, while others were quite senior. But we found that a manager's rank and formal authority didn't improve the odds that their changes would be adopted. That's not to say hierarchy isn't important—in most organizations it is, as it was in the NHS—but it's not everything. How much power comes from authority varies considerably.[2]

For one, cultures ascribe varying importance to authority. For example, a comparative study of Citibank offices in China, Germany, Spain, and the United States showed that employees in the Hong Kong office were far more observant of workplace hierarchy than those in the other locations, even though they all had the same organization chart.[3] Psychologist Michele Gelfand, who has conducted research on cultural norms in thirty countries spanning five continents, found that such deference is common in places with Confucian philosophical traditions, which view adherence to clearly delineated roles, responsibilities, and authority relationships as essential to preserving social order.

Drawing on her analyses of people's behavior in organizations, states, social classes, and communities as well as in countries, Gelfand classifies cultures on a tight-to-loose continuum. Tight cultures, which have stricter social norms and higher social order—Singapore is a case in point—tend to be more rule-abiding and responsive to authority. Loose cultures, in contrast, are less hierarchical: In Israel, for example, the use of diminutive nicknames is common, and extends even to people with very high status.[4] (This is how Prime Minister Netanyahu turned into Bibi.)

Wherever your culture falls on the tight-to-loose continuum, limits to the power of authority affect everyone, including the heads of state in democratic countries, who are bound by checks and balances within the government and in society. "In reality, my power as the president of the republic was shared," François Hollande, France's president from 2012 to 2017, told us. "It resided in the prime minister, the ministers, the bureaucrats, local representatives, [and] civil society. People think that the president of the republic has the power to enact reforms unilaterally. It's a false preconception! The truth is: Power is the ability to effect change, and change is often slow in our democracy, because power is decentralized. Power is compromise."[5]

The sooner you stop conflating formal authority, or rank, with power, the greater the odds that you will identify who the power holders in a given environment really are, and whether you are one of them. As we've seen, the realization that being at the top isn't the same as being powerful wasn't lost on Donatella Versace. But if being the boss wasn't enough to make her powerful, what was? Or, to put the question more broadly: How and why does power deviate from what the formal hierarchy dictates?

To answer this question, you need to be able to identify both the resources the organization in question values, and the people who control them. In addition, you need to understand how individuals whose roles do not put them in a position to control those resources can become influential nonetheless. Navigating the path to exercising power and achieving our goals can be challenging for everyone, even those who are famous and privileged like Donatella. Travel this path with us, and we will take you back to Donatella and how she found her power at the journey's end.

THE DIFFERENCE BETWEEN RANK AND ROLE

In the 1950s, researchers at a French plant conducted a study that became foundational to understanding how people accrue power in organizations.[6] Workers in this plant reported to foremen who themselves reported to top management. Every step in the production process was thoroughly planned and strictly controlled. In such an environment, you would expect power to be strictly hierarchical and to reside with top management and foremen, who had the authority to set goals for the workers, monitor progress, and fire and hire employees. But they were not the most powerful people in the plant. In fact, the workers—mostly women making cigarettes on the factory floor—didn't seem to pay them much attention. Instead, it was the maintenance personnel who seemed to have the most power over other workers: Why?

Days of observation and interviews gave the researchers the answer: The plant's machines were prone to breaking down. When that happened, production was interrupted, jeopardizing not only the targets set by top management, but also the line workers' pay, which was based on the number of cigarettes produced each day. The maintenance workers were the only people with the expertise to fix the machinery. Knowing that they had sole control over this highly valued resource, the maintenance workers kept a tight grip on their expertise. Instead of teaching production employees how to perform basic repairs, or asking management to hire additional maintenance staff, they deliberately hoarded their critical knowledge and made sure they kept neither records nor repair manuals.

Depending on their role, employees may thus have more power than their formal rank would suggest because they control a resource critical to the organization's survival. This is why client-facing, profit-making roles in business organizations typically wield more power than back-office, cost-center roles like HR or accounting, removed as they are from having a direct impact on revenues and profits. Even in non-business contexts, those who deliver resources central to the organization's mission and survival have power regardless of where they are in the formal hierarchy.

So, while authority can be a source of power, it is no guarantee of power. The idea that power is only for those at the top is therefore a fallacy, one of the misconceptions that we must debunk. Authority lets bosses issue directives, but it doesn't necessarily mean people will follow them. And those who have no formal authority can still influence others' behavior if they control access to a critical resource. Sometimes this power is simply a function of role, as it was for the French maintenance workers. But the disconnect between authority and power can—and often does—emerge through another channel: one's network of relationships.

LIFTING THE VEIL FROM THE ORG CHART

To understand the power of networks, let's start with a story about Manuel, a manager hired to reorganize the audit department inside the aircraft engine manufacturing division of a large defense contractor. Internal auditing was critical to this company, which had to comply with federal government standards and deliver flawless work to maintain its access to contracts from the U.S. Department of Defense.[7] When Manuel joined the unit, they were taking 28 percent longer to process audits than their peers. His experience allowed him to see that the delays stemmed from a lack of coordination between the auditors and the administrative staff (the figure to the right shows the audit department's org chart). So, Manuel made a few basic changes that he had already used successfully in another unit: He assigned each auditor to a specific administrative assistant, being careful to pair more experienced assistants with auditors who performed the most complex audits. He also instituted a scheduling system that allowed the admins to see when they were likely to receive an audit, giving them more visibility into their workload and protecting them from receiving too many audits at the same time. He ran the changes by the group before implementing them, and people seemed just fine with his proposed course of action.

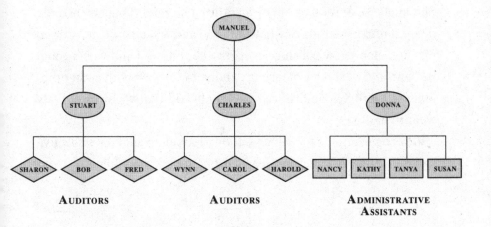

FORMAL POWER IN THE AUDITING DEPARTMENT

A few weeks later, however, the backlog was longer than before. Manuel was dumbfounded. The changes he had put in place were sensible and uncontroversial. Why hadn't they worked? At this point, desperate for an answer, he approached Professor David Krackhardt, an organizational scholar, for help. Using a simple questionnaire, Krackhardt asked each team member to describe who they went to with questions at work. The picture that emerged is shown on page 72, where the number of arrowheads going to one person corresponds to the number of people who reported seeking that person out for advice and information. The higher the number of arrows, the more prominent that individual was in the audit unit's advice network.

From a glance, Manuel knew that he was far from being the department's most connected person.[8] It made sense; after all, he was new. The only people who said they sought him out for advice were the managers who reported directly to him—demonstrating that the formal chart does indeed drive a portion of the informal advice networks that emerge in every organization.[9] On the other hand, Nancy was nearly everyone's point of reference, including Manuel himself. She might be at the bottom of the formal hierarchy, but she had the deepest understanding of what mattered and what didn't in the organization. She knew which rules had to be followed and which could be bent, and she had an "uncanny ability to forecast both audit problems and problem audits," as Manuel put it.[10] That's why everybody went to her.

Recognizing his foolishness in overlooking Nancy's perspective and influence, Manuel approached her to ask her opinion about

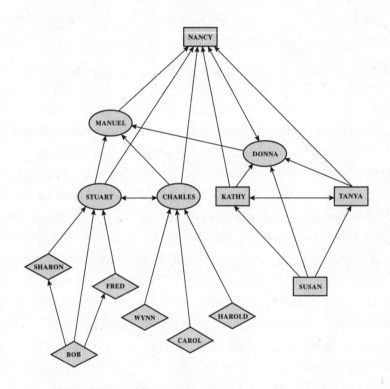

INFORMAL POWER IN THE AUDITING DEPARTMENT

pairing assistants with auditors. At first, she was reluctant to share her views. He was her superior. But with some prodding, she said that it was not a good idea, without elaborating. Manuel surmised that having been accustomed to allocating audits amongst themselves, the admins were unhappy about their loss of autonomy. Over the next two months, he and Nancy worked out a compromise that gave the admins a greater say in how they worked with the auditors. A month later, the team's performance was exceeding company targets, and Manuel had learned a key lesson: Driving change requires identifying and enlisting those who are well connected in the network of the organization.[11]

Remember Ning in the call center? His effectiveness came from the trust he inspired in people up and down the hierarchy: trust in his intentions to help and trust in his ability to deliver on his intentions. These "lovable stars" are the most likely to be sought out by their colleagues and to become highly connected in the advice network. All these connections, in turn, give them power by increasing their access to information, contacts, opportunities, and other resources that people value.[12] An administrative assistant who is well connected may be much better at effecting change than a manager, no matter how smart or talented, who is peripheral in the organization's network. Many CEOs and executives who come to us because their change efforts are failing learn this lesson the hard way. You can imagine their reactions when we advise them to delegate certain leadership duties to middle managers who are well connected within the organization. They cannot or, perhaps, do not want to understand that the middle manager may have more power in this context than they do. Over time, however, our advice pays off and the results speak for themselves: The executives witness the importance of network connections as a source of power.[13]

Their mistake is equating authority with power. Authority lets you command compliance, but you can never command commitment. Anyone who wants to enact change, no matter how high in the hierarchy they may be, must identify the right people to work with. Even the best change is unlikely to be adopted when placed in the hands of someone who isn't well connected to implement it.

MAPPING POWER: WHO HOLDS IT AND WHY

When faced with an environment you wish to influence—particularly if you have a new role, new goals, or an organizational change to advance—understanding who is best positioned to help you is critical. You will need help because effecting change, even a modest one, is hard. Change triggers primitive signals warning our safety may be at risk. In effect, we are hardwired to favor constancy and resist change. This instinct, which psychologists call the status quo bias, is so strong that people resist even trivial changes they themselves control[14]—like switching toothpaste brands. And when that sense of control is missing, as it so often is when dealing with others, our defensive alarm systems ring even louder. This is one reason we find that people well connected in their organizations' networks are more effective change-makers.[15] Others trust them, and trust is a conduit of influence, especially when people feel threatened.

Overcoming resistance to change requires lifting the veil from the formal structure, accounting for people's connections to one another, and building a detailed power map to answer the following questions: Who are the powerful players in your immediate circle, your organization or institution, your industry or profession? What resources do those players value, and what valued resources does each possess? How much control over access to those resources do they have? What are the alliances or coalitions among those players? And what is the nature of your relationship with each of them?

Research shows that the ability to map networks is itself a source of power. A study of a small entrepreneurial firm in the 1990s revealed that people who had an accurate understanding of who went to whom for advice tended to have more power, independent of their formal rank and network connections.[16] This means that, even when you are not at the top and you don't have a great network, viewing the map of power clearly—who is close to whom, who influences whom, who is indispensable but underappreciated, who will resist or support you—matters. These insights are themselves a source of power.[17] Power mapping may sound sneaky to some, but it is essential to having any kind of positive impact.

People often struggle to draw accurate power maps, however. They make mistakes of omission (for example, failing to see how central someone is, as Manuel did) and errors of commission (like seeing someone as more sought out for advice than they are). These errors are not surprising. We all have limited powers of observation, confined as we are to the social circles we inhabit and unaware of networks farther away from us.[18] Ironically, as people get more powerful, they become less likely to harness the power that comes from accurately viewing the network beneath them. The reason? The self-focus power induces: It's not that people at the top are more stupid than everybody else, but they do tend to be inattentive to people of lower rank and can't be bothered to map their subordinates' networks. Studies in the controlled conditions of a laboratory show that people who feel powerful are less adept at recognizing the social relationships around them than people who feel powerless.[19] The same pattern emerges in field studies conducted in organizations: The higher up in the hierarchy someone is—and hence the more powerful they feel—the less accurate they are about the networks linking employees in their organization.[20]

The best power mappers we know are master observers of their social environment. Instead of mentally checking out during the long meetings we all must sometimes endure, they gain invaluable insights by carefully noting other attendees' behavior, verbal and nonverbal, and analyzing their interactions: who defers to whom;

what alliances seem to emerge; which conflicts lurk beneath the surface; who is gaining influence and who's losing it. Remember Lyndon Johnson's watchful eye? You can also enlist help. When an executive we know began presiding over meetings where she was expected to do much of the talking, she recruited one of her employees, who was an excellent observer, as her power mapper. While the executive was in action, her observer was taking notes on people's body language and behavior—who was listening while his boss spoke and who was passing notes, for instance.

Another key question to answer through these observations is: What does the organization reward? Know what gets someone a raise, a promotion, or a plum assignment, and you'll know what the organization values (whether they admit it or not). In the quest for answers, never assume you know what someone else is thinking: Ning's experience at the call center makes it clear that people's needs and wants are rarely transparent. And your own position in the network will determine how good your vantage point is: If you are well connected, your power map is likely more accurate because you get information from many sources—who are often well connected themselves—bringing you closer to a widely shared view of who has power and why in your context. Conversely, if you're at the periphery of the network, your view of it is likely idiosyncratic and therefore potentially misleading.

How do you know if you're prominent in the network? In our research, we found that you can answer this question with surprising accuracy by asking yourself another question: Do people come to me for advice? If they do, you are likely in a position to both influence them and learn from them. If it's not you, then who is influential? Whom do people go to for advice? Observation, as described above, will help you make that assessment. Start with people you're closer to and ask questions like: "Who do people listen to around here?" "Who has been successful? Who has struggled? Why?" "How has this place changed since you've joined?" And then ask them: "Who else is a good person to learn from?" This snowball technique broadens your sources of insight and your power map. Then you can deepen it, by mapping not just who is powerful, but also who is likely to be your ally, your opponent, or someone you can sway.

MAPPING ENDORSERS, RESISTERS, AND FENCE-SITTERS

When you have a change initiative to advance, identifying the powerful people in your environment isn't enough. Your power map also has to track how those people feel about what you want to accomplish. That's why Manuel had to know not only that Nancy was the person most people sought for advice, but also what she thought about his changes. Influential people like Nancy—who can persuade others to embrace a change and are crucial to its success—typically come in three varieties: endorsers, who are positive; resisters, who are negative; and fence-sitters, who see both benefits and drawbacks to the change and are therefore ambivalent about it. Which of these people should you cultivate to help you reach your goals? With whom should you strive to establish a close relationship of mutual trust and liking?

"Keep your friends close and your enemies closer," Michael Corleone advises in *The Godfather II*.[21] Is he correct? We were determined to find out, because the time and energy required to build a coalition of support for an initiative is limited, and people need to allocate it carefully. So, we looked at the change agents in our NHS study and linked their eventual success and failure to the kinds of influential people they were close to, or became close to, as they attempted to implement their initiative.[22]

Here's what we found: Keeping endorsers close is not a priority. Don't get us wrong, you must identify your champions and keep them strongly engaged—for example, by letting them co-own the change. But how close you are with them doesn't affect how much they embrace your goals. Like you, they want the change to be adopted.

In contrast, keeping resisters close is treacherous. You must talk to them to understand why they resist—they may have a good point that will send you back to the drawing board—but be careful about the effect they can have on you. Spend a lot of time with them in hopes of converting them, and they may end up influencing you. When a change is relatively modest, like Manuel's, a resister might reluctantly support it because you're a friend and they want to help you do something you believe in or reciprocate your past kindness to them. But warm feelings are insufficient when you push for more radical changes that will disrupt the resister's access to valued resources. In that case, their opposition will be stronger than their affection; and seeing the people you're closest to push back on your idea can deflate your own enthusiasm for it and, with that, its chance of success. This is the mistake we see change-makers make most often: They focus on the influential resisters they are close to, convinced that they can convert them, and that they, in turn, will convince everyone else to get on board. But close relationships are two-way streets, and this is not how it works: The resisters convince the change-makers to give up on their project instead!

The only people you want to keep close, no matter what, are the fence-sitters—whom Michael Corleone didn't even mention. Closeness makes all the difference here, because we rarely want to disappoint people we like. In other words, we feel a sense of social obligation,[23] which is likely to sway us if we are teetering and all we need is a little push. This is why the fence-sitters always warrant a change agent's focused attention and consideration. The takeaway is not to manipulate people's affection for you. Remember that closeness is built on liking and mutual trust, and trust is as precious as it is fragile. The takeaway is to invest the time and energy to explain to people who are ambivalent about your project, but personally close to you, why you genuinely believe that change is needed.

POWER MAPPING BEYOND ORGANIZATIONAL BOUNDARIES

If your ambition extends to influencing larger, more diverse groups outside your department or organization, you can expect to encounter greater, even fierce resistance.[24] In this situation, being well connected within your team, like Nancy was, isn't enough. You also need to become a bridge across multiple groups and gain what network scholars call "betweenness."[25]

As the name suggests, betweenness has to do with being the "in-between," the bridge between two people or two groups who are not directly connected. Betweenness is thus a source of power, because those two people or groups must go through you to exchange information. As the bridge, they depend on you, because you control their access to a valued resource, the information flow between them. Betweenness also gives you access to bits of information that no one in those disconnected groups is likely to be aware of. Since you can control when and how to share this information, you will be in a better position than most to draw a more accurate power map, build

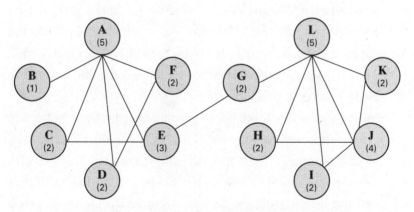

A and L have the most connections (high prominence or popularity), but E and G are information brokers between networks (high betweenness)

TWO WAYS TO HAVE POWER THROUGH YOUR NETWORKS

valuable relationships, and forge alliances. To illustrate, let's look at how Carol Browner used betweenness when she was the director of the U.S. Environmental Protection Agency (EPA).

Two years into Bill Clinton's presidency, the Republicans won a majority in the House of Representatives for the first time in four decades. To say they were elated is an understatement. Newt Gingrich's *Contract with America*, a rallying cry for most of the new Republican representatives, called for less government intervention and sweeping reforms to cut regulations and slice agency budgets.

At the EPA, Carol Browner oversaw seventeen thousand employees and managed a budget of $7 billion.[26] The agency's backbone was regulation and enforcement, so Republican attacks were hitting the EPA hard. Warned by colleagues in the West Wing that she would have to compromise, Carol retorted: "You know what, that's bullshit. People may have voted for Newt Gingrich, but they did not vote for dirty air and dirty water."[27] Instead of retreating, as some might have expected of a young woman new to the role of EPA administrator, she counterattacked.

Trying to win by forging close relationships with resisters, in this case prominent Republicans, was out of the question. "There were no enemies we could keep close . . . These people hated me because I stood up to them," she told us. "Once one of them literally threw the Constitution at me; he took it out of his pocket and threw it at me." Carol still did what every change-maker should do: She listened to the resisters to understand their views.

But she also understood that to galvanize support for the agency, she had to reach beyond the confines of Washington, DC, and take control of the narrative. She and her team scheduled meetings with every newspaper editorial board that would talk to them: "Here's what we did on air pollution in your community. Here's what we did on toxic waste. Here's what we did to help your kids' asthma and keep the water coming out of your tap clean. This is why you want an environmental cop on the beat." In no time, she had the editorial page editor of the *New York Times* on speed dial. But, as she admitted to us, she was also terrified. She was taking on one of the most influential Republicans in the House, leading up to a presidential re-election, and doing so in the eye of the storm. The media, of course, loved it.

Carol then sought alliances with leaders and organizations with different sources of power and access to influential people across domains, like the American Academy of Pediatrics, the American Lung Association, and public health and classic environmental organizations. They, in turn, started publishing opinion pieces in local newspapers, which complemented Carol's relationships with the national press, putting pressure on members of Congress who represented those districts' local needs. She also cultivated connections with broadcast media, giving her another channel to shape public opinion. In short, Carol built a diverse network across sectors and became the connector between organizations that would normally have had no way to coordinate action. One partnership, interview, and opinion piece at a time, the EPA became stronger and more able to fend off regulatory rollbacks.

Carol Browner couldn't have achieved this success had she focused solely on building lots of connections within the EPA network. That was not the only place where the resources she needed resided. To access those, she had to map a much broader network and be the bridge at the center of a diverse set of relationships, each contributing unique resources to her effort.

WITHOUT A POWER MAP, THE TERRAIN IS TREACHEROUS

A power map allows you to identify what is valued in your environment and who controls access to the resources that are most desired and rewarded there. As with any trek in a challenging environment, an accurate map will help you reach your destination safe and sound.

Without it, the terrain quickly becomes treacherous. In this respect, the troubled path of Aakash[28] in the world of investment banking provides a cautionary tale.

A native of India, Aakash began his career in the Asian offices of a leading American investment bank, then moved to Canada to earn an MBA. Upon graduation, he landed a coveted position in the mergers and acquisitions (M&A) group of a top Toronto bank. Despite his impressive track record, Aakash's experience in his new job was brutal. M&A is a tough environment: The work is hard, the hours long, and the pressure high. New hires are utterly powerless before these demands, and jocular camaraderie is an important coping mechanism. But that support wasn't forthcoming for Aakash. As "the only first-generation immigrant with brown skin" in his group, overtures from the others weren't offered, nor were his efforts to reach out particularly well received. Not belonging was new to Aakash, who had enjoyed his share of privilege as a well-off Indian man working in South East Asia, but he was undaunted. "I figured that the only way someone like me can get a bit of power in this context is to work your ass off and perform at a level that is so outstanding someone senior grows to love you."

Aakash earned that respect, but it exacted a higher toll than he ever imagined. His first review—by a manager who, it was clear to Aakash, "didn't like people like me"—was searing. Aakash responded by doubling down, seeking work with the most demanding boss he could find, an executive so fearsome and exacting that even Aakash's most talented and ambitious colleagues steered clear of him. In one respect, Aakash's strategy paid off. He survived a grueling eight-month assignment, delivered outstanding work, kept a job designed to weed out most new hires within a year, and earned respect and mentorship from the harshest judge of talent in his group. "I had delivered what the bank valued most: outstanding M&A products. And I gained something valuable in return: keeping my job. But I had lost what I valued most: my life with my wife, my friends, the books I love to read, all the simple pleasures that make life worth living. That's why I decided to leave and join a different bank."

The move was riskier than Aakash realized. Italians say that *"Chi lascia la via vecchia per la nuova, sa quel che lascia, ma non quel che trova,"* or, "Those leaving one path for another know only what they leave behind, not what they will find." Before you move to a new work environment, it's vital to do some reconnaissance to ensure you're moving into favorable territory, where you will have control over what's valued there. In his rush to leave an unhealthy workplace, Aakash didn't realize he'd find himself with even less control over his fate.

In his previous position, Aakash's job was to develop products without needing to interact much with the client. In his new position, what was valued was acquiring new clients, which rests on building relationships and getting powerful people to entrust you with profitable business. Looking like the client, speaking their language, and being connected to the "right" people is what matters in such a job, not working longer hours for the toughest boss. Any outsider would struggle building a network in the cliquey world of finance. But it wasn't until he started on the new job, Aakash told us, that he fully appreciated how exceptionally hard it would be for an Indian guy who "looks differently, talks differently, and thinks differently" to get clients in Toronto's mostly White world of investment banking. His strength—developing the best financial models and products—was no longer the most valued resource. Aware of this dynamic, one of Aakash's few brown colleagues quit, noting: "They will never trust us. And that's a problem if you want to grow in this business."

Aakash was stumped. He could admit defeat and conclude that someone without access to Canada's elite business circles and powerful networks—in other words, someone like him—should get out of that type of business environment and find one where he could succeed. But what if you refuse to give up on a job, a profession, or an endeavor only because you don't "fit" the dominant profile in that context? And what if you want to change the rules of the game that prevent someone like Aakash from succeeding, despite his talent and work ethic? Giving up is as humiliating as it is enraging to many of us. What are the alternatives, then? Remarkably, part of the answer to Aakash's quandary is related to Donatella Versace's.

DIFFERENT NETWORKS FOR DIFFERENT PEOPLE

Our power-mapping journey so far reveals key factors that determine who controls access to valued resources in any situation. First, formal authority is no guarantee of power, as Donatella Versace can tell you from experience. Second, regardless of rank, your formal role can give you power if it gives you control over resources essential to the success of the organization, as the tobacco plant maintenance workers demonstrated. Third, if you have neither high rank nor a formal role critical to the organization's success—say, you're an administrative assistant like Nancy—you can become influential if you are a hub in the informal network, the person everybody flocks to for advice. Fourth, having many connections is not the only way a network gives you power: You can also control access to valued resources by being the in-between, the information broker between networks. Fifth, regardless of your position in the formal chart or the informal network, you can gain power just by knowing who values what, and who controls access to those valued resources; building such a power map is critical and eminently feasible for anyone who pays attention and asks good questions. Sixth, you must map not only who has influence, but also who among those influential people is more likely to endorse you, resist you, or sit on the fence waiting for you to win them over. Seventh, the search for allies can take you far beyond the confines of your group or organization, as Carol Browner brilliantly demonstrated. And finally, danger lurks for those who venture into a terrain they haven't carefully power mapped, as Aakash will attest.

With a better understanding of how to ascertain who has power in any environment, and how networks can be bases of power, we're ready to return to Donatella Versace's predicament in the aftermath of her brother Gianni's untimely death. As you might have guessed, we're about to show you that Donatella's network was essential to her eventual success. But ask yourself, what kind of relationships would you have advised her to seek out? The challenge she faced was that people in her company and the industry saw her as lacking control over the resource that was most critical to the company's survival and success: the extraordinary creative talent on which Gianni had built Versace. She had to change this perception, not only in the eyes of the company employees and industry executives, but also in her own mind. But who could champion and help her? Whom should she have leaned on? Other women in the company and beyond? Or the men who wielded—and still wield[29]—the greatest power in the fashion industry?

Stereotypes about how women relate to one another in the workplace point in opposite directions.[30] The negative stereotype portrays women as rivalrous, even hostile toward one another. This pessimistic but widely held view was on display during a 2018 concert in Las Vegas, when Donatella's friend Lady Gaga told her audience that she'd need fewer than the fingers of one hand to count the number of supportive women in the music industry.[31] Many would agree. The stereotype of the cat fight is alive and well, as is the persistent image of the queen bee who can be lethal to junior women coming up the ranks.

The positive counterview is that women find colleagues in one another, and that their common experience paves the way for meaningful bonds of solidarity and mutual support. For an illustration, consider the "amplification" strategy women in the Obama Administration devised to help one another get heard during the president's first term in office. After one woman offered an idea, if it wasn't acknowledged, another woman would repeat it and give her colleague credit for suggesting it.[32]

Which view of women's working relationship is true? When she builds her network of professional contacts, whom should a woman prioritize: Other women or men? We set out with colleagues Bill McEvily and Evelyn Zhang to answer these questions by collecting data on more than five thousand middle managers—40 percent of them women—in a large North American bank.[33] Supervisors, subordinates, and peers rated the middle managers along several criteria, including how energizing, trustworthy, competent, reliable, and willing to share networks and resources a manager was. We had 23,648 evaluations to analyze, and clear patterns emerged.

On average, men rated other men more positively than they rated women *on all criteria*—including competence, trust, and how much a colleague enabled them to get their job done. How about women, you ask? Women rated other women more positively than they rated men *on all criteria, too.* The evidence for gender solidarity was so stark that we initially questioned it. Perhaps the relatively large number of women employed at this bank made it unusual in some way? Did conducting the study in 2017, when women's rights issues were more in the news than they had been, skew people's answers? To check, we resurrected data we collected in 2006 in a technology corporation headquartered in the United States. Even in this male-dominated environment, we found the same pattern of gender solidarity across the 9,452 work relationships we measured. On average, men are good to other men in the workplace, and women are good to other women.

When we share this finding with professionals and academics, surprise is the most common response. "Really?" they say. Women are generally just as surprised as men.

A notable exception? Donatella Versace. "I'm not surprised at all," she told us. "I have found enormous strength in the solidarity of women." Being the only woman on Versace's Board at the time of Gianni's death had made a difficult situation even more challenging and painful. "None of these men listened to me, had confidence in me; none gave me the support I needed. And I struggled mightily for years. I had such self-doubt that I put on a mask—literally, a mask of dark makeup, intimidating all-black outfits, a stern expression that never gave way to a smile—to hide my weaknesses from everyone around me."

Over time, Donatella found ways to build the support she needed to be effective. "I met strong, determined women, the kind you don't mess with." Some were fashion insiders, while others were executives and leaders in other industries. Four of them became allies, sounding boards, and constructive critics who joined Donatella on Versace's Board. "Finally, I had people who had full confidence in my ability and pushed my thinking to make me better, not to take me down. Deep inside, I always knew I was capable, but these women gave me the belief in myself that had eluded me for years after Gianni's death."

Donatella's insight aligns with research on the networks that help newly minted MBAs land leadership positions. Unsurprisingly, both male and female graduates achieve higher-level job placements when they have many connections in their MBA student network. But to get executive positions with the highest levels of authority and compensation, women need one more thing: an inner circle of close ties with other women.[34] Women who have both many connections *and* a female-dominated inner circle have an expected job placement level that is 2.5 times greater than women with few connections and a male-dominated inner circle. Because of their strong bond, these fellow women are highly motivated to share tacit knowledge and gender-specific information about employers and opportunities with each other, as well as new connections important for women's job market success. Without a tight-knit group of women who go out of their way to support one another, women don't score prestigious leadership positions at nearly the same rate, even when they have the same qualifications as their male counterparts.

The implications of these findings are both exciting and worrisome. For women struggling to make it in a man's world, being able to count on the understanding and support of other women—as opposed to having to fend off their undermining, as is often assumed—is a relief and a source of strength. But does this also mean we ought to engage in gendered networking to build our power bases at work? Should we uncritically flock to people like ourselves in the quest for safety and self-esteem? And what about differences other than gender? What about Aakash? Should other social groups who face challenging political landscapes—racialized groups, the LGBTQ+ community, or people with disabilities, for example—network with one another before engaging with others in the workplace?

Connecting with people who are similar to us is appealing because we understand them better than people who are different from us, and we see ourselves reflected in them and validated by them. This is a fundamental law of human relationships: Birds of a feather do flock together.[35] Yet, it calls for caution about relying on demographic similarity in your network building. For one, the power of solidarity can only be harnessed if your social group exercises a degree of control over valued resources through all the means we've uncovered so far. And when your social group is a small minority in your work environment, the likelihood of people like yourself occupying powerful positions in it is low.

Even more important, when we fail to build connections with people different from us, we are the losers. The breadth of our networks—the diversity of backgrounds, perspectives, and experiences of the people we connect with, and their ability to connect us to different social groups—opens us up to all kinds of knowledge, opportunities, and innovative insights that can help us succeed.[36] It also helps us draw more accurate power maps: by giving us a wider vantage point from which to observe the network, and by protecting us from the confirmation bias that comes from being exposed to people with the same point of view all the time. Confining ourselves to people like ourselves is terribly limiting and, in the long run, detrimental. That's why Donatella Versace, even while realizing the unique strength she could derive from the solidarity of women, was careful to maintain a healthy mix of men and women with diverse backgrounds and experiences on Versace's Board of Directors.

In fact, nearly the entire world is represented on her creative team. "I scout for designers far and wide. We have Chinese, Indian, English, Italian, American, and Filipino designers. And I love how they relate to each other. They all bring different worldviews, incredible stories, and the most fascinating conversations emerge and change our thinking," Donatella told us. The purposeful breadth in her network gives Donatella access to her most valued resource: creativity.

FINDING SIMILARITY IN UNLIKELY PLACES

But, you might object, embracing diversity is easier for the decision makers at the top of the food chain like Donatella, who gets to choose who's on her team. How can you build a strong, diverse network when you're not at the top *and* the people who have power differ profoundly from you? Many people face this daunting challenge every day. The odds of success may seem dismal because you are asked to connect with others in meaningful ways despite gaping differences in culture and life experience. Similarity is a huge determinant of interpersonal rapport. We naturally connect with people like ourselves because they validate who we are (boosting our self-esteem)[37] and they are more predictable (giving us safety). But similarity takes many forms.

We all organize our networks around what sociologists call *social foci*.[38] These are shared activities, interests, and affiliations that give people opportunities to build relationships with like-minded others. For the big-shot business executives and investors Aakash needed to connect with to be effective at his new job, relevant *foci* might include the golf club or the alumni network of the private school they attended, circles from which Aakash was excluded. But many professionals have told us of other shared interests and affiliations that have given them meaningful ways to establish an authentic connection with people important to their success but otherwise quite distant from their social milieu.[39] For example, many people in the business world engage deeply in humanitarian efforts and social causes. We have seen professionals like Aakash join such efforts and through them find a foundation of shared interest around which to bond with people quite different from themselves. This also applies to joining—or, better yet, launching—employee-led initiatives in their organizations, where an extracurricular activity gives participants a chance to forge networks across functional boundaries, up and down the chain of command. And sometimes the *social foci* are simply personal passions and idiosyncratic interests that two people unexpectedly find they share, bringing them closer.

To find similarities in unlikely places you must ask questions and listen carefully to someone else's stories. Pay close attention and you will often find a common experience, a shared interest, or a passion that unites you. It's not always easy, and some people face overwhelming obstacles; yet almost everyone can carve out a bit of common ground to create genuine connections with those who control access to valuable resources.

But suppose you want to do more than connect with the powers that be? What if you want to change who the powers that be are? This was Aakash's deepest concern and greatest frustration: the sense of unfairness for being judged not as an exceptionally competent professional, but as a brown man with an accent. And imagine how people with even more disadvantages than Aakash feel. What if we changed the system at its root? What if we transformed the way we ascribe value to people and the resources they can contribute? Can we realistically challenge these power hierarchies? Yes—all of us acting in concert can—and in chapter 6 we'll see how. But learning how to disrupt entrenched hierarchies of power requires that we first understand them: How do they come about? Why are they so hard to break? And when is it that people have both the motivation *and* the opportunity to change them? We turn to these questions next.

Chapter 5

Power Is Sticky,
But It Can Be Disrupted

If a person cannot "own" power, and power isn't reserved only for those at the top, why do we so often see it steadily accrue to some groups while continually eluding others? The stability of power hierarchies is mysterious but undeniable: Dynastic rule defined China for millennia and hereditary monarchies dominated Europe for centuries. The caste system, with origins in ancient times, remains a challenge to Indian democracy today. And, throughout history, men have held disproportionate power in societies around the world.

Slavery is perhaps the most egregious example of a power hierarchy. There is no power differential starker or more unjust than the "ownership" of other human beings. Yet in the United States, chattel slavery lasted for generations, ending only after the Civil War nearly tore the country in half. Even the resounding military defeat of the South did not dismantle the racial hierarchy that privileged White people over Black people. The Thirteenth Amendment may have banned slavery, but four hundred years after the first enslaved Africans set foot in Virginia, the myth of White supremacy still shapes American institutions, from the overrepresentation of Black people in the criminal justice system to their underrepresentation in corporate boardrooms. Black people in the United States are more likely to be politically disenfranchised, economically impoverished, and casually brutalized at the hands of the police. The murders of Breonna Taylor and George Floyd in the spring of 2020 were a stark reminder of the long history of violence, injustice, and trauma that Black people continue to suffer in the United States.

Slavery, dynastic rule, systemic racism, and gender inequality: All are supported by the same kind of scaffolding, power hierarchies that have proven resistant to change. These structures are so durable because power is sticky. It has inertia. Once power is distributed in a certain way, over time the resulting hierarchy acquires a patina of legitimacy. It becomes the natural order of things, and we forget that other human beings created it in the first place.[1] Fortunately, what human beings have created, human beings can change.[2] Sticky is not the same thing as stuck.

Before we can learn how to disrupt power hierarchies, though, we need to understand the forces that cement them.

WHAT IT TAKES TO CREATE A POWER HIERARCHY

Jane Elliott was an elementary school teacher like no other. On April 4, 1968, she turned on her television and learned that Martin Luther King Jr., had been assassinated. Overwhelmed with sadness and despair, Elliott then decided she had to do something. How, she wondered, could she give her classroom of White third-graders in a small town in Iowa even a glimpse of the injustice that Black people endured daily?

The next day, when her students arrived at school, she divided them by eye color. "The brown-eyed people are the better people in this room. They are cleaner and they are smarter," she said, explaining that intelligence was determined by the level of melanin in a person's body. The more melanin, the darker a person's eyes were, and therefore the smarter the person was. She then gave her brown-eyed students preferential treatment throughout the day. They were allowed to drink from the water fountain, while the blue-eyed students had to use paper cups. When a girl asked, "Why?" and a brown-eyed boy chimed in, "Because we might catch something," Elliott nodded in agreement. At recess, she gave the brown-eyed children five more minutes of playtime, and she praised them more often.[3]

The children's behavior changed quickly, Elliott observed. The brown-eyed children, at the top of the power hierarchy she had randomly created, became more confident throughout the day. They soon became condescending, even insulting toward their blue-eyed classmates. By contrast, the children with blue eyes became more timid and despondent. They started making silly mistakes in exercises that they usually performed successfully. Brown-eyed children started ganging up on blue-eyed kids. At the end of the day, Elliott asked her students to write about what they had learned. Third-grader Debbie Hughes wrote: "The people in Mrs. Elliott's room who had brown eyes got to discriminate against the people who had blue eyes. I have brown eyes. I felt like hitting them if I wanted to."

The next school day, Elliott flipped the script and told her students that people with blue eyes were, in fact, better than people with brown eyes. The same dynamics unfolded, this time in reverse. About that second day, Debbie Hughes wrote, "I felt like quitting school . . . I felt mad. That's what it feels like when you're discriminated against."

The exercise wasn't meant to suggest that racial hierarchies are easily reversible—obviously, they are not—but rather to highlight that being born into a particular racial group, socioeconomic class, or sex influences one's experience in uncontrollable ways. Some faulted Elliott for what they saw as unethical behavior in failing to obtain parents' permission in advance and doing "great psychological damage" to the students.[4] Yet many—including the children themselves—praised her, both at the time and later in life, for teaching them a critical lesson.

Elliott's experiment emphasizes two levers that can be used to create and legitimize a power hierarchy: authority and narrative. She created the hierarchy by using the power that stemmed from her authority as a teacher, and then she justified and reinforced it with a "legitimizing story": the supposed correlation between melanin and intelligence, which tapped into the students' respect for science. Elliott made up this pseudo-scientific relationship, of course; but the episode shows how easily authority figures can create power hierarchies. While we would like to think that as adults we'd be less susceptible than Elliott's students were, her experiment gives us a taste of how deeply power hierarchies can affect us when we experience them for years, decades, or even centuries.

BEWARE OF OBEDIENCE TO AUTHORITY

One of the chief reasons power hierarchies persist is our tendency to obey authority. How far are we willing to go in doing so? Shockingly far, as a French TV show demonstrated in 2010.[5] Two contestants would compete as a team, with one contestant posing questions to the other. The questions, twenty-seven in all, would relate to pairs of words which the respondent had to memorize at the beginning of the game (e.g. tame-animal, cloudy-sky). The game had all the usual quiz show ingredients: a well-known host, lights and cameras, and a chanting audience. Yet the setting was unusual: The contestant asking questions was seated in front of a set of electric levers, while the respondent was seated on an electric chair, inside a large, closed box, next to the levers.

Before the game started, the host announced the game's only rule: Every time the respondent gave an incorrect answer, their teammate would have to administer an electric shock to him or her. With every wrong answer, the intensity of the shock would increase until it reached a level that could cause serious physical harm. To win, all the contestants had to do was get through the full set of twenty-seven questions. As long as the shocks were administered, it wouldn't matter how many mistakes the respondent made. The additional caveat was that because the show was still in the pilot stage, the contestants would not receive any money beyond a small stipend for participating, but future pairs could together win up to one million euros.

As the game progressed, and the electric shocks became stronger, sounds of discomfort from the contestant on the electric chair turned into screams of pain. Some of the players hesitated as they heard their teammate saying they wanted to stop and demanded to be let out. Yet the host insisted the questioner continue: "The rules say you must go on." "Go on, we are taking all responsibility for this." Clapping and chanting, the audience urged that the game go forward, too. What neither the audience nor the contestants asking the questions knew was that this wasn't a real TV show. The player in the box was an actor, and no electric shocks were administered. This was an experiment, staged to examine how far people would be willing to go in obeying the orders of the TV host. It was inspired by another famous and controversial study that Stanley Milgram, a twenty-eight-year-old, newly appointed psychology professor at Yale University, launched in 1961.

That year, television was saturated with live coverage of the war trial of Adolf Eichmann, who had played a leading role in implementing Hitler's "Final Solution." Professor Milgram, the son of Jewish immigrants, had closely followed the fates of Nazi leaders after the war, noticing that the accused, like Eichmann, often justified their actions by saying they were simply carrying out the orders of superior officers. How much, he wondered, could that basic dynamic—obedience to authority—explain the behavior of Eichmann and others who were complicit in the Holocaust's atrocities. So Milgram set up an experiment in the psychology lab at Yale: Participants, who thought they were taking part in a study on memory and learning, were asked by a scientist to administer an electric shock when the person they were paired with made a mistake. At the time, the majority of the study participants—a full 65 percent—complied with the experimenter's instructions and administered the maximum 450-volt shock.[6] "With numbing regularity," Milgram concluded, "good people were seen to knuckle under the demands of authority and to perform actions that were callous and severe."[7]

What do you think happened with the French TV show? This time the authority figure wasn't a scientist at a top university. Is the power of TV comparable to that of science? The results of the experiment surprised even the social psychologists who had designed it: 72 percent of the contestants ended up administering the maximum electric shock![8] Nor were the participants all young men as was the case at Yale. Of the seventy-six participants, the gender divide was almost fifty-fifty and the mean age of the group was 39.7 years old. Still haunted by the experience, one of the contestants reflected, "I wanted to stop the whole time, but I just couldn't. I didn't have the will to do it. And that goes against my nature."[9] This is what obedience to authority can do: lead us to violate our values.[10]

Would we dare to disobey if we were in Milgram's experiment, or a contestant on the French TV show? Would we have denounced the power hierarchy that the Nazis established if we had been born into a middle-class German family circa 1920? We like to think so, but these experiments call for humility. When political philosopher Hannah Arendt attended Eichmann's trial to see for herself the so-called architect of the Holocaust, she found a man who was "terribly and terrifyingly normal."[11] She concluded that he was less an ideologue than a bureaucrat, following orders with no regard for their consequences. "The banality of evil," as Arendt famously described it, is the ease with which authority can transform someone like Eichmann into an instrument of unspeakable harm. Banality does not excuse evil. As Arendt wrote, "in politics, obedience and support are the same." The lesson for us is that we need to acknowledge the lure of authority, remain alert to its temptations, and summon the courage to disobey when necessary. Power is sticky in no small part because authority can be difficult to resist.

AN INFERNAL TRIO

Power hierarchies are also sticky because those in power actively work, sometimes unconsciously, to maintain the status quo. Social psychologists have identified several mechanisms that lead the powerful to protect and reinforce their position.[12] Three are particularly important: a lack of empathy, an enhanced sense of agency, and a tendency to see one's own actions as legitimate.

We saw in chapter 2 that people who feel more powerful tend to become more self-focused, and therefore less empathetic.[13] Being unaware of or indifferent to another person's feelings and thoughts makes it easier to care only for oneself, hoarding resources instead of sharing them with others. Power persists, therefore, because the powerful lose sight of their interdependence with others, who need resources just as they do.

Power also gives us a greater sense of control, encouraging us to act. In one experiment, psychologists told participants to write about either a time when they felt powerful, or a time when they felt powerless.[14] Here's the trick: While they were writing, every participant was seated alone, at a desk, with a fan blowing directly onto their face. The experiment wasn't about what they were writing, it was about that annoying fan. Would they move it? Turn it off altogether? Or continue to let it blow while they tried to hold down the paper so that they could write? It turns out that those who were writing about feeling powerful were much more likely to turn the fan off or move it out of the way than those responding to the powerlessness prompt, who continued to work with the fan blowing at them. Though the example may seem trivial, the insight is not. People who feel powerful are more likely to disrupt the status quo in order to make themselves comfortable. This study is just one of many showing that those who feel powerful are more prone to acting in response to affronts and to implementing plans and taking risks. Those who feel powerless, by contrast, are more apt to accept the situation, unpleasant as it may be.

Finally, when they do act, powerful people are more likely to consider their actions legitimate even when they are unethical or illegal.[15] They convince themselves that they have earned their position—despite evidence to the contrary[16]—and, therefore, since their power is justified, they are entitled to keep it and use it as they see fit. In one experiment, participants were shown a graph that portrayed changes in average U.S. family income over the last thirty years. Asked why the average income for households in the top 5 percent had skyrocketed, while that of every other household flatlined, participants who considered themselves of higher status were more likely to attribute this income gap to their ability and hard work; they had rightfully earned their privileged position![17]

In sum, power increases people's propensity to act, as well as their sense of entitlement, while decreasing their ability to empathize with others. This is a risky trio, as it makes the powerful particularly adept at justifying their actions to themselves and others, and behaving in ways that give them greater control over valued resources, which in turn reinforces their power.[18]

WHY THE DISADVANTAGED REPRODUCE THE STATUS QUO, TOO

Those at the top are not the only people who contribute to keeping power hierarchies solidly in place. Counterintuitive as this may seem, just as the powerful defend the status quo, research finds that those harmed by the status quo tend to do the same, often unconsciously.[19] This in no way means that the power-disadvantaged are to blame for their situation; but it does help explain how these disparities are reproduced and reinforced.

Powerlessness, by definition, deprives people of control over valued resources. For the disadvantaged, then, life is rife with uncertainty and deprivation, which undermine their sense of safety. The psychological effect of this precariousness and lack of control is to seek order, predictability, and stability. Paradoxically, this motivates the powerless to see the current system as good, fair, inevitable, even desirable, because for those in a situation of dependence, there is comfort in seeing the world as predictable and the power distribution as legitimate. This is why the powerless, consciously and unconsciously, tend to rationalize and justify the system as it stands, even if it goes against their interests.[20]

The justification of the status quo as legitimate manifests itself in many ways. Employees who feel more financially dependent on their job tend to accept the decisions and instructions of their supervisor as more legitimate, regardless of their supervisor's fairness. In the lab, participants who are experimentally induced to feel powerless are more likely to think that society is fair and people usually get what they deserve.[21] In U.S. national survey studies, low-income respondents were more likely than high-income respondents to believe that large differences in pay are needed to foster motivation and effort.[22]

Not only can the power disadvantaged come to believe that the current system is the natural order of things, but others' perception of them can reinforce their belief that they are not "good enough," leading them to behave in ways that confirm this perception. This self-fulfilling prophecy is what happened in Jane Elliott's exercise — and what happens in classrooms and workplaces everywhere.[23] When the blue-eyed students were at the bottom of the hierarchy, they struggled to perform tasks that they usually completed with ease. They had quickly internalized the legitimizing story about brown-eyed superiority and their own inferiority in ways that negatively affected their performance. This behavioral confirmation response, whereby people adapt their behavior in ways that end up fulfilling the expectations others hold about them,[24] further contributes to maintaining power hierarchies.

This dynamic can fuel a vicious cycle as those in power subsequently use the poor performance of the powerless to legitimize their position, making the status quo even stickier. The powerless then come to expect they will remain powerless and align their behavior accordingly. Hopelessness and disempowerment lead to paralysis or inaction, conspiring to maintain the status quo.[25]

THE POWER OF STORIES

We can now understand why both the power-advantaged and the power-disadvantaged reproduce the status quo; but we are still missing a critical factor in the persistence of power hierarchies: the stories we tell to justify the status quo. Look back in time, and you will notice that those who placed themselves at the top didn't simply declare that they were at the top. They came up with narratives that justified their position.[26] Stories are one of the most effective vehicles of persuasion because they appeal not only to reason, but also to our emotions.[27]

Taking on different shapes and forms, legitimizing stories have observable similarities throughout history and across the world. Leaning on religious beliefs is one consistent feature.[28] In the eighteenth century BCE, King Hammurabi created the Code of Hammurabi, a set of 282 laws governing everything from theft and trade to incest and family life.[29] Proclaiming that the gods had called him to spread justice in the land of Babylon, Hammurabi made sure that he and the code were imbued with uncontested legitimacy. While the exact details of the code's distribution are lost to history, it is thought to have been spread via clay tablets and stone slabs, or steles. One of these steles—found in Susa and the source of most of what we know about the code—makes Hammurabi's special connection with divinity clear: At the very top of the stele, before the text with the laws begins, we see him receiving the code from the Babylo-nian god Shamash.[30] One of the oldest bodies of law in the world, Hammurabi's Code created clear power hierarchies between men and women, as well as between the rich, the (poor) free people, and the enslaved.[31] Legitimized by the story of the king's godly connec-tions, this social order was enshrined in laws that perpetuated these hierarchies long after Hammurabi's death.

Hammurabi was hardly alone. Julius Caesar claimed he was a descendant of the goddess Venus, while the kings of France and En-gland justified their absolute power over their subjects for centuries by citing its divine source. Monarchs used stories of miracles—like the "royal touch," reputed to cure scrofula—to add to their mys-tique.[32] News of these healing miracles spread throughout the mon-archs' respective regions as part of propaganda campaigns, which included written reports, sermons, and public ceremonies, all rein-forcing the divine origins of their power.[33] Paintings and engravings were also used to demonstrate rulers' benevolence and power. Im-ages of the monarch dressed in imposing robes and laying divine hands on your compatriots afflicted with a disfiguring disease might make you think twice before avoiding your taxes or, God forbid, openly rebelling.

Myths about physical or biological differences among human beings have also provided fertile ground for stories justifying power hierarchies. The belief that women are not as capable as men, for example, has been spread and reinforced by stories that were made up to justify patriarchal systems for millennia.[34] The English classi-cist Mary Beard opens the manifesto *Women & Power* with a story that is the "first recorded example of a man telling a woman to 'shut up'"—the beginning of Homer's *Odyssey*, when Odysseus's son Telemachus tells his mother, Penelope, to "go back up into your quarters" because "speech will be the business of men."[35]

As scientific knowledge rose to prominence, some fueled these stories with pseudo-scientific findings. In the early 1900s, to cite but one example, biologists Sir Patrick Geddes and Sir John Arthur Thomson concluded that since male sperm were small and active, while female ova tended to be big and relatively inert, men were naturally "more active, energetic, eager, passionate, and variable," while females were "more passive, conservative, sluggish, and stable."[36] Today, the scientific community rejects such claims as absurd, while research finds that cognitive differences between females and males, if they exist at all, are small and not a function of biology.[37]

In fact, decades of research on behavioral differences across genders have shown that many of these differences are related to differential access to power.[38] As we've seen, when existing power hierarchies exclude a group from power, its members tend unconsciously to behave in ways that reproduce these hierarchies. For women, this has meant accepting inferior treatment and adjusting their behaviors accordingly, while men, who have been in power for centuries and whose behavior is shaped by the "infernal trio," have also contributed to reinforcing the status quo. The observed behavioral differences between men and women are thus the result not so much of biological differences as of the stories that have shaped our perceptions and, in turn, our behaviors. As Simone de Beauvoir put it, "One is not born, but rather becomes, a woman."[39]

Stories using pseudo-scientific evidence to justify differential treatment are particularly pernicious and hardly limited to women. English polymath Sir Francis Galton coined the term "eugenics" in 1883, and his ideas spawned a movement across the world that was particularly vibrant in the United States.[40] Eugenicists claimed that "feeble-mindedness," supposedly endemic in the poor and immigrants, was a problem of heredity. This legitimizing narrative, which was never backed by any rigorous science, was then used to justify the position of the poor at the bottom of the social hierarchy, not to mention the sterilization of people considered inferior, lest their defective genes degrade humanity's gene pool. Even though science has since established that poverty is largely a societal problem, not a genetic one, the narrative that the poor are lazy and not as smart as others, and therefore deserve to be where they are, continues to be used to justify inequality.

More recently, another legitimizing myth has become dominant: that of meritocracy.[41] In a meritocracy, power supposedly accrues to the most talented and the hardest-working, irrespective of, say, demographics, family connections, or inherited wealth—thereby implying that those who fail to rise lack the necessary ability or elbow grease.[42] The myth of meritocracy conveyed through stories of self-made men and, lately, women, who started from nothing but ascended the power hierarchy entirely on their own through their extraordinary abilities and courage, has become especially prevalent in many capitalist societies.[43] Books, movies, and the media reinforce this narrative in their portrayals of people whose financial worth often serves as a proxy for success.

Of course, a person's competence and effort make a difference and deserve to be recognized; but the issue with meritocracy is the assumption that the rules of the game are the same for everyone, when they are not. As economists and sociologists have long established, the reason some people are poor is not because they are inherently less able or less intelligent.[44] Instead, they are constrained primarily by the unequal distribution of society's resources. They cannot access the quality schools, networks of influence, or résumé-building extracurricular activities that those at the top easily access. Society's emphasis on individual blame is thus often incorrect. And yet, as philosopher Michael Sandel remarked, "when the meritocratic sorting machine has done its work, those on top find it hard to resist the thought that they deserve their success and that those on the bottom deserve their place as well."[45] This is how the myth of meritocracy contributes to justifying and reinforcing current power hierarchies.

Be they rooted in religion, pseudoscience, the belief in meritocracy, or some other legitimizing myth, the stories we tell ourselves to justify the status quo can become so ingrained that eventually we take the existing hierarchies for granted.[46] They become invisible, like the air we breathe. We come to think of them as "business as usual," when it would in fact be more accurate to think of them as "politics as usual."[47] Embedded in our cultural norms, from what the media cover and how, to what is taught in schools and makes it into the history books, they seep into our social norms and into our policies, influencing what is acceptable and legal. As a result, power hierarchies effectively rig the game against those at the bottom. Even when myths are disproven, they do not instantly evaporate. Rather, they can morph into patterns of discrimination that insidiously shape and bias the expectations we have of others, without ever having met them. They become, in a word, stereotypes.

THE WEIGHT OF STEREOTYPES

To different degrees, we've all been on the receiving end of some sort of bias and, consciously or not, we all hold some biases too. In the 1990s, a team of psychologists devised the Implicit Association Test[48] to gauge a person's unconscious tendency to associate certain groups of people with stereotypes and to evaluate them positively or negatively on that basis. Millions of people have taken Implicit Association Tests on topics as varied as age, race, weight, and disability, shedding light on the pervasiveness of unconscious biases.[49] The effects of these perceptions on people's actions are subtle but can be consequential, and for some of us, they can constrain our ability to access valued resources.

Cheryl Dorsey knows firsthand the discrimination that comes with being a Black woman in the United States. She vividly remembers the day her mother interrupted her Saturday afternoon dance-in-front-of-her-mirror session for "real talk." Seven or eight at the time, she had covered her hair with a T-shirt to mimic the long, straight hair of the famous pop singers of the day. Her mom yanked her still, removed the shirt from her head, and said, "You are a young

Black girl in the United States, and you need to figure out how you are going to navigate through this reality." A teacher by profession, her mom did everything in her power—including being direct about sexism and racism—to give Cheryl the best chance to develop her full potential.

Cheryl proved to be a gifted student, one of the best in her class at her Baltimore high school. Nevertheless, a guidance counselor's advice for "a girl like her" was to focus on applying to state universities, not the Ivy League schools she had put on her list. "This is what happened to so many of my Black friends," Cheryl told us. "They could not express their full potential. They were advised to aim lower." But her parents pushed back. They encouraged their daughter to apply to her original list, and a few months later she was accepted into Harvard College, where she graduated in 1985 with a BA in history and science. That would not be her only Harvard degree; by 1992, she had graduated with an MD and a master's in public policy as well.

Throughout her time at Harvard, though, Cheryl felt like she didn't belong. "I got all the messages in the world that women weren't as good as men and that people of color weren't as good as White people. What in the world was I doing in these environments? For a long time, I felt like I was an accidental participant, that I got lucky." Nor did racism and sexism disappear when she became a doctor. As one of four Black female pediatric residents in a class of twenty-five, she noticed that employees at the medical center constantly referred to each of them by the same first name. And if she wasn't wearing her white doctor's coat, even her colleagues would barely recognize her in the hallway and often confused her with an administrative assistant. "That was a reminder of, 'Oh, I see how I fit into this larger system.'"

Cheryl, whose commitment to fight social and racial injustice grew even stronger with time, went on to serve in the late 1990s as a White House fellow and special assistant to the U.S. Labor

Department. While bouts with prejudice continued, she realized that in addition to her academic pedigree, her six-foot stature and her relatively deep voice helped her assert her presence and competence in high-profile meetings—to a point. She also recognized that over-used, these assets could become liabilities. Attuned to how stereo-types can hold people back, she was well aware of the double-bind women in the workplace face. Perceived as too warm, they break with the image of leaders as strong and masculine, and they run the risk of being perceived as incompetent. But viewed as too strong and competent, they break with the image of women as warm, maternal figures, and run the risk of being seen as cold and insensitive.[50]

As a Black woman, Cheryl felt that she had to be especially cau-tious not to appear too aggressive. "I am a self-described social jus-tice warrior, but I am always careful not to be the angry Black woman in the room." Professional women, in general, tend to be penalized when they display anger.[51] But gender stereotypes do not affect all women and men in the same way. In the United States, as Cheryl rightly pointed out, the stereotype of the angry Black woman— dominant, strong, aggressive, ill-tempered, loud, and hostile—finds its roots in the harrowing experience of female slaves in Antebellum America, and is still prevalent today.[52] Cheryl worried that sounding angry would backfire on her, as people might then view her as "too emotional and erratic."

Stereotypes also constrain or favor men. When Black men in the U.S. display strength and assertiveness—qualities normally as-sociated with leadership—they trigger the stereotype of the Black man as a threat rather than as a leader. And displaying anger has radically different consequences for White and Black men: Research has found that White male executives who express anger tend to be conferred higher status, and even a higher salary, than those who do not. For Black men, in contrast, displaying anger is likely to back-fire, limiting their access to resources. But Black men with disarming, rounder, baby-like faces tend to lead more prestigious companies, make more money, and be perceived as warmer than White and Black leaders without such features.[53]

In accounting for how stereotypes affect our access to valued resources, we need to consider how our identities, like race, ethnicity, gender, sexuality, age, abilities, and socioeconomic class, intersect and interact. As we just saw, racial and gender identities come together in ways that are distinct for women and men, Black and White people. The dynamics differ for other racial groups, too. For example, in North America, East Asian men and women are stereotyped as cold, competent, and nondominant. When they violate these stereotypes, by appearing more dominant for instance, they are subjected to more racial harassment at work than other employees.[54]

In addition to constraining people's access to valued resources, stereotypes also affect their behaviors in ways that further limit this access. Being on the receiving end of negative stereotypes can lead to increased anxiety and worse performance, a phenomenon called "stereotype threat."[55] In one experiment, for example, women underperformed in a math test when told that the test had shown gender differences in the past.[56] In another study, Black participants primed to think about their race before beginning what they were told would be a difficult exam performed worse than participants who weren't primed to think about their race.[57] Another series of experiments found similar evidence of the damage of stereotype threats on performance for Latinx college students, with a stronger effect for Latinx women who had to deal with both gender and race stereotypes.[58]

Cheryl, who went on to become the CEO of Echoing Green, one of the world's most influential social entrepreneurship fellowships, has experienced the devastating effect of such stereotype threats in her own life. Over time, she learned that thinking about what motivated her was the best way to cope with such feelings: "Whenever I feel threatened, when I doubt whether I can succeed, I remind myself of why I do what I do: that it's about fighting inequalities and creating a fairer society." Psychologists observed the same dynamic in a group of female MBA students who were stereotyped as weaker performers. When they were asked to complete a short assignment on their personal values, their performance improved significantly, eliminating the gender gap in performance.[59] The simple act of affirming your own values can help interrupt the process of stereotype threat, just as Cheryl experienced. Yet, as she also pointed out, "individual interventions are not the solution. They are only a way to cope with existing inequalities. What is at stake is changing the whole system."

Effecting such a change seems daunting, now that we have a better understanding of the processes that conspire to make power hierarchies so sticky. The cultural beliefs conveyed by the stories that authority figures tell us, and that we tell ourselves, to justify who has power, combined with the psychological and behavioral effects of having power (or not), reinforce power differences across groups. The more these stories become embedded in a society's collective psyche, the more they permeate the policies and practices that mediate who gets access to what resources, further fossilizing the existing hierarchies.[60] As a result, they end up shaping not only the laws and norms we take for granted, but also our perceptions and misperceptions of others. This cyclical process is forceful, yet often invisible, which makes it difficult to resist. This is why, in our research, we see how terribly difficult it is to effect changes that challenge established power hierarchies and norms.[61]

CAN POWER HIERARCHIES BE DISRUPTED?

If this were the end of the story, the powerful would accrue ever more power forever, the status quo would perpetuate itself, and change would be impossible. Yet history tells a different tale. Power hierarchies may span centuries, but they can be challenged and disrupted. No empire lasts forever. Political regimes are toppled and replaced. New systems of social values replace old ones. Twentieth-and twenty-first-century social movements have chipped away at longstanding hierarchies that have subjugated women, people of color, LGBTQ+ people, religious groups, people with disabilities, and Indigenous communities.[62] Sometimes hierarchies shift gradually over years, decades, or centuries; at other times, radical changes seem to happen in a matter of days. The question is, how?

Research reveals three conditions that facilitate change. The first is crisis: Natural disasters, wars, economic collapses, and technological innovation can all provide an opportunity to challenge the way power is distributed.[63] Consider how World War II unlocked the world of work outside the home for women, as they became crucial to sustaining the economy. The second condition concerns the degree to which a power hierarchy is entrenched: The newer the hierarchy, the more malleable it is, because the reinforcing mechanisms we have described have not yet made power so sticky as to seem immutable.[64] The regimes that emerged from the Arab Spring, for example, were fragile, and the result was political instability. Finally, to challenge established power hierarchies, would-be disruptors need an alternative view of how power should be distributed, not just trenchant criticism of the existing power structure.[65] Popular accounts may stress the speed with which the French Revolution came to a climax in 1789, but the Enlightenment ideals that fueled it—equality, religious tolerance, and the consent of the governed—were developed over a century. These alternatives to the divine right of kings poked holes in the legitimacy of the stories and cultural beliefs that justified and upheld the status quo, making a new reality possible.

Yet these three conditions alone cannot disrupt power hierarchies. For that to happen, people must be motivated to take action against the status quo *and* have the opportunity to act on that motivation. When motivation and opportunity meet, people rise up.[66]

To see how the convergence of motivation and opportunity can disrupt a power hierarchy, let us take you back to the late 1800s and early 1900s, when steel was the lifeblood of much of the U.S. industrial Northeast and Midwest. Working conditions in the steel mills were horrendous: Men labored twelve hours a day, seven days a week, 363 days a year (Christmas and July Fourth being the exceptions). Every two weeks, the mills would switch the men from day to night shifts (and vice versa) by working them for twenty-four hours straight. Heavy, unrelenting work in hot, dangerous conditions made maiming and death commonplace. The very act of leaving home for work carried a substantial risk that you would not make it back at the end of the workday.[67] At the same time, industrialists like Andrew Carnegie and Henry Frick amassed fortunes through their control of the means of production. Their enormous power ensconced them in the upper echelons of American society, with lavish residences in New York City and vacation homes in places like Newport, Rhode Island, that have today become magnets for tourists curious to discover the opulence of America's first mega-rich. The new industrialists and their bankers accumulated so much wealth that they quickly became the most powerful people in America.

Inhumane working conditions and stark inequalities between workers and the owners of capital were not unique to steel mills or to the United States. News of worker revolts in Europe began to cross the ocean, as did new ideas, including the writings of the German philosopher Karl Marx. *Capital*, his new narrative of class identity and class struggle, published in 1867, challenged the legitimacy of the status quo in industrialized nations around the world.[68] Just as stories are critical to justifying and rationalizing the status quo, they can be equally potent in strengthening the resolve of the power-disadvantaged to rise up.

But, individually, the steelworkers were powerless. With millions of immigrants arriving in America, they were eminently replaceable. If one worker died or lost an arm, another was readily available to take his place. Their employers thus had absolute power over them, and they did not hesitate to abuse it. Under these circumstances, workers had only one way to push back: band together and strike—a classic consolidation strategy to shift the balance of power. By presenting a united front, the workers could increase the dependence of Carnegie and other industry captains on them.

The steel mill captains did their best to quash the workers' capacity for collective action. They set pay rates at subsistence levels to deprive workers of savings and minimize their endurance during strikes. They used their political connections to summon police forces to disperse strikers. And they could still fire workers and hire replacements. During the Homestead Strike at Carnegie's main steel plant in 1892, at least ten people died and more than one hundred were injured when a private security agency was called in to end the standoff.[69] But over time, by joining forces, the Pennsylvania steel workers gained more power, and unions there and around the world were able to secure better working conditions and create a somewhat more equitable balance of power between business and labor.

The steelworkers had both motivation and opportunity to push back on the status quo. The motivation came from extreme power imbalance. Why? Because the more unequal the distribution of rewards becomes, the harder it is for the disempowered to justify the status quo as legitimate. As the rewards to the powerful surge, other psychological responses counterbalance the tendency of the power-disadvantaged to justify the current system: People also have a preference for fairness, and blatantly unfair treatment can lead them to perceive the powerful as using their power illegitimately.[70] The exploitation and brutality the steelworkers endured angered them and motivated them to protest and resist. Certain emotions, such as sadness, sorrow, and shame, are associated with helplessness and can even be paralyzing. These are the emotions that underlie the powerless rationalizing the legitimacy of the status quo. But once the assumption of fairness and legitimacy cracks, anger sets in. And anger leads people to act against injustice.[71] That's why the leaders who instill and reinforce in the disadvantaged the idea that they are being treated unfairly and that those in power are illegitimate, can turn the power-disadvantaged into an angry force eager to challenge the status quo.

But until they acquired some measure of power—small though it might have been—over the mills' owners, the workers had no opportunity to act on their discontent. By joining forces, they found a way to control access to a resource—their own labor—that was essential to keeping the mills in operation. While the balance of power still favored the owners and their surrogates, the workers had gained enough leverage to strike and to keep on striking until their demands were met. Motivation and opportunity had met, and the workers rose up.

As always, gaining power opens the door to power abuse, if not downright corruption, and worker unions are not immune.[72] But every time you tell someone on a Friday afternoon, "Have a nice weekend" or, come Monday, ask, "How was your weekend?" you have unions to thank. Without their fighting back as one, individual workers would have remained utterly replaceable and completely powerless. When considering the effects of workers' consolidation strategies on an economic system as a whole, unions remain one of the most effective tools for keeping power imbalances from widening wildly, and therefore help to prevent deleterious consequences for everyone's prosperity in the long run.[73]

WHEN POWER IMBALANCE BACKFIRES

Too great a power imbalance is dangerous, not only for the disadvantaged, but also for those at the top because it motivates action against the status quo, as we just saw. The disadvantaged don't always have an opportunity to act on their motivation, of course. A small company that sells its products on Amazon might resent the terms Amazon imposes, but lacking alternative sales channels, and with millions of sellers reliant on Amazon's platform, it has no way to push back.[74]

But when the disadvantaged gain a measure of power over those who impose unfair terms on them, pushback is likely, and it can be costly for both the powerless and the powerful. To illustrate, consider the war that Tim Sweeney, the founder and CEO of game maker Epic Games, has waged against Apple and Google to fight what he sees as their abuse of power over computer game developers. Sweeney's pushback escalated as the popularity of Epic's flagship game, *Fortnite*, grew, giving him leverage over the tech companies. In 2018, he launched *Fortnite* outside Apple's App Store and the Google Play store to get around what he saw as their disproportionate app fees. In 2020, Apple and Google responded in kind by banning *Fortnite* from their stores. in retaliation for Epic Games' avoiding their payment systems. A legal battle started, with costs for both parties.[75]

Our research on industry profits in the U.S. economy shows this dynamic across an entire economic system. As the power imbalance between two companies grows, the power-advantaged firm imposes more exploitative economic terms, which frustrates their disadvantaged business partners. The moment the latter get a measure of power over the advantaged party, they refuse to do business. The deal doesn't close, and both parties in the failed transaction end up with lower profits than what they would have achieved in a more balanced relationship, where the powerful would have been less tempted to abuse its advantage.[76]

These dynamics are also evident in society at large. Think about the wave of populist movements that swept countries all over the world throughout the 2010s.[77] When economic and social inequality skyrocket, people get angry because in their eyes the disparity in rewards undermines the fairness and legitimacy of the system.[78] Societies then experience more social unrest as well as economic and political instability. Why? Because in such situations the power-disadvantaged will use any means at their disposal—whether a revolution (as in eighteenth-century France and America) or a referendum (as in modern-day Britain)—to reject a system that they perceive as blatantly rigged against them, even when such a rejection may be to their own detriment.

Allowing power imbalances to become so great that they undermine the legitimacy, the stability, and the sustainability of our social and economic systems is not only morally objectionable, but also unwise on the part of the powerful. In the long run, inequality results in less productive economies and lower rates of economic growth.[79] As Nobel Prize–winning economists Abhijit Banerjee and Esther Duflo point out, it would be in the interest of the rich "to argue for a radical shift toward real sharing of prosperity."[80] Yet, the short-term attraction of making an extra dollar (or an extra billion) often blinds the powerful to the long-term consequences of reinforcing massive imbalances in a social system in which we are all mutually dependent.

A few millionaires and billionaires, including Bill Gates, Melinda French Gates, Warren Buffett, MacKenzie Scott, and Abigail Disney, have called for changes to the very system that got them to their position of economic dominance.[81] But many ultra-rich and ultra-powerful seem to worry more about the survival of capitalism in its present form than about disrupting systemic inequities. As Anand Giridharadas has bitingly put it, "Today's titans of tech and finance want to solve the world's problems, as long as the solutions never, ever threaten their own wealth and power."[82]

Sometimes, a wake-up call reminds the powerful of the many forms of mutual dependence that weave people together, and the risks that growing inequality poses for everyone in an interdependent system. In the aftermath of the Great Depression and World War II in the United States, for example, industry captains and corporate executives accepted compensation packages that look like a pittance compared to what American CEOs are paid today. They also accepted (perhaps reluctantly, but still) the role of government regulations, and even unions, to guard the system from the excesses of completely free markets. By the same token, elected officials passed laws to provide good living standards and opportunity to

many, though decidedly not all since segregation was still firmly entrenched. Partly because of these political and economic restraints,
U.S. middle-class incomes rose at roughly the same rate as incomes
at the top in the 1950s and 1960s.[83] Wake-up calls can have a short
shelf-life, however: By the 1970s, the tide had turned, and deregula-
tion, anti-union sentiment, and inequality all began to rise quickly.[84]
The devastation of the Great Depression and World War II had
faded from memory, and with them the awareness of interdependence and impermanence that makes the powerful less selfish and
arrogant.

If it is so rare for the powerful to voluntarily relinquish some
of their power, then change must be driven by those lower in the
hierarchy. But how can people who have less access to resources
build enough power over the higher-ups to make change a reality?
In many situations, such as unionization movements, past and present, collective action has proven an effective way to shift the power
balance by enabling individuals in the power-disadvantaged group
to pool the resources they each control. Yet, for every story of successful collective action to achieve change, there are many stories
of failure. *How* the power-disadvantaged use the resources at their
disposal to influence others to disrupt the status quo is just as critical
as their decision to join forces.

What exactly must collective movements do to pull off a seemingly impossible feat and successfully disrupt the power hierarchy?
We turn to that question next.

Chapter 6

Agitate, Innovate, Orchestrate

B
lack Lives Matter, the Hong Kong protests, #MeToo, the French Yellow Vests, the Arab Spring: These are just a few of the social movements that have risen to prominence in the past decade, propelled by the sustained commitment of large numbers of people seeking social change.[1] Perhaps because they were amplified by the ascent of social media they may seem like a novel phenomenon.[2] They are not.

Collective movements have allowed nations to free themselves from the grasp of empires, citizens to topple dictators and monarchs, and people of different races, ethnicities, religions, and gender identities to assert their right to equality. Time and again, history has taught us that movements which combine the power of many can become a force strong enough to prevail over entrenched power hierarchies and transform society.[3] No matter who we are or where we live, we owe much of our freedom and rights to movements such as those that fought against apartheid in South Africa, and British rule in India and for the civil rights of women, racialized groups, and LGBTQ+ people around the world. Their members suffered gut-wrenching defeats, often over generations, on the way to finally changing the status quo.

Yet, not all collective movements succeed. Why, then, do some triumph, while others do not?

AGITATION ALONE ISN'T ENOUGH

In July 2011, Micah White, an editor at *Adbusters*—a counterculture magazine in Vancouver, Canada—and his boss Kalle Lasn, the magazine's founder, released a six-hundred-word tactical briefing urging "redeemers, rebels, and radicals" to pack a tent and occupy Wall Street. They released this call to arms at the tail end of the global 2008 financial crisis and the bailout of the big banks; on the heels of the Arab Spring and Spain's anti-austerity *Indignados* movement; and one year after the U.S. Supreme Court's *Citizens United* decision, which canceled campaign spending limits designed to curb the political influence of corporations. Many who had lost their homes and jobs saw the system as utterly unfair; and they started to sense that they were not alone in their misery and anger. Messages condemning the greed and corruption of "the 1 percent" resonated. The *Adbusters* brief took off, spreading on blogs, the dark web, and in activist circles across the country and the world.

Inspired by the encampments in Tahir Square during the 2011 Egyptian revolution, Occupy protesters held demonstrations in an estimated 950 cities across the globe over the course of three weeks. "The thing about Occupy is that it really brought together the wildest mix of people. I think that's part of what drew people in, too. It felt like you were part of something that was so refreshing," Micah told us.[4] General assemblies, venues for democratic and consensual decision-making in the camps, reinforced these diverse participants' self-esteem by giving them a sense of autonomy and belonging. But the leaderless movement did not generate clear demands; and the general assembly voted out the initial *Adbusters*' ask for a presidential commission on money in politics.[5] While the movement remained vibrant for three months, little concrete change came of it at the time. Micah, Kalle, and so many others who occupied their cities had hoped that this would be the protest that led to the rise of a radically new social and economic system. Yet, the capitalist system did not change much, if at all, in the following months. What went wrong?

Some may jump to the conclusion that the movement came short because it lacked an exceptionally charismatic leader, like Mahatma Gandhi, Martin Luther King Jr., or Nelson Mandela. But a single iconic change maker, no matter how remarkable, rarely changes the course of organizations or society on their own, because an isolated individual's call to action is far too easy to disregard. These iconic figures used their power to inspire and influence thousands, sometimes millions of individuals to step out of their routine and join a movement to bring about the changes they envisioned. Collective movements make change possible by making it impossible for public opinion and public authorities to ignore the problem at hand.

Occupy Wall Street succeeded in galvanizing a movement to agitate against the status quo—a critical role in social movements. Agitators articulate the grievances of specific individuals or groups and bring them to the forefront of public awareness so that others will become indignant, too, and want to push for change. Occupy's actions, including its media and social media coverage, helped put inequality and the influence of money in politics on the agenda. But it fell short on the other two requisites of effective social change: innovation and orchestration.

Movements need innovators and orchestrators as well as agitators.[6] Innovators are the ones who create actionable solutions to address the grievances identified by agitators. They are able to think out of the box to come up with an alternative to the status quo. Orchestrators are the pollinators of social movements. They coordinate action across diverse parties to put in place the changes that allow the solution envisioned by the innovators to be adopted at scale. Without them, the final act never comes.

Although all three roles are critical for the success of a social movement, the same person need not play all three; nor do the parts follow a set timeline or sequence of activities. Social change is a complex and at times messy process. Movement participants often need to perform each of the three roles multiple times, switching among them depending on what the situation requires. Sometimes the division of labor among participants is strategic, with individuals or allied organizations taking on different roles in the public eye—some adopting more radical stances to agitate, for instance, and others behaving more moderately to innovate or orchestrate.[7] But ultimately all must work together toward a shared agenda.

To illustrate the process of social change and the role of power in it, we will draw on the experiences of three activists who are playing or have played pivotal roles in contemporary movements. For narrative purposes, we will consider each of the three roles independently. But remember, agitation without innovation means complaints without ways forward, and innovation without orchestration means ideas without impact.[8]

PUTTING AN ISSUE ON THE PUBLIC AGENDA

In August 2018, Greta Thunberg, the teenager who has since become the face of the youth climate movement, drew the now-famous words *"Skolstrejk för Klimatet"* (School Strike for Climate) onto poster board and started skipping school, first every day and later every Friday, to protest her government's inaction on climate change on the steps of the Swedish Parliament. Two months later, the UN Intergovernmental Panel on Climate Change (IPCC) published a report stating that, without major steps to reduce greenhouse gas emissions, the Earth's temperature would increase by 1.5 degrees Celsius between 2030 and 2052, causing extreme weather events unlike anything we'd ever seen before.[9] Emboldened by Greta, and alarmed by the IPCC report, teenagers around the world were inspired to participate in

Fridays for Future, the international coalition started by Greta and other students. Xiye Bastida, a sixteen-year-old student at Beacon High School in New York City and the president of the school's environmental club, was among them.[10]

Xiye had moved to New York when her parents' work as advocates for the values and wisdom of Indigenous people brought them to the United States. She had witnessed the effects of climate change in her hometown of San Pedro Tultepec in Mexico, where floods had wiped out people's homes and sent the price of food skyrocketing. Now, two years later, she was working for environmental justice with young organizers across the city. She joined the core organizing committee of Fridays for Future NYC, and these initial organizing efforts would become Xiye's training wheels for co-leading, only months later, one of the largest environmental protests in the United States: the September 20, 2019, global climate strike in New York City.

The youth involved in Fridays for Future had to build power, effectively from scratch. They had no easy access to financial resources or mainstream media that could capture the public's attention and convince them that the status quo was unacceptable. Nor were they old enough to vote, which meant they lacked a key source of power to convince public representatives to act. How, then, did these teenagers pull off one of the largest environmental protests in history and galvanize a movement of millions worldwide? They did what movements must do when they lack formal authority and resources: identify what the people they are trying to influence value and find creative ways to control their access to it.

In this case, the teenagers wanted to push adults to act. To enlist them, they called the adults out for doing little or nothing about climate change for decades;[11] and they highlighted the cost of their inaction: endangering the safety and the survival of future generations, their own children and grandchildren. This public shaming took adults down a peg on the self-esteem ladder. To restore their self-esteem, and to protect their offspring from harm, they had to redeem themselves and act—although some adults preferred to restore their self-esteem by disparaging sixteen-year-old Greta, the movement's public face. As we saw in chapter 3, we don't like to think of ourselves as bad people, which can push us to either become more virtuous or turn the shame on others.

The next challenge was one all agitators face: being heard and standing out in the constant stream of news and noise. The youth organizers systematically documented and shared their progress on social media, just as Occupy had relied on memes and social media, from Twitter to Reddit, to recruit and spread its messaging years earlier. Social media is effective enough at mobilizing people that autocrats have taken to shutting down the internet to suppress popular uprisings and dissent.[12] But the activists of Fridays for Future knew they could not limit themselves to social media if they wanted their message to be heard by the members of every generation. So, they partnered with "adult environmental organizations," as they refer to them, to gain media lists they could use to promote the global climate strike.

In the days leading up to September 20, Xiye and her co-organizers were excited to see growing online momentum and press coverage around the event. By then, Xiye had drilled down her key messages. "We all knew the key statistics off the top of our head. But we also knew that people are twenty-two times more likely to remember what you said if you weave in a personal story. So we trained our activists in how to tell their personal story to the media." Indeed, in a textbook act of organizing, Xiye ran weekly training sessions on a range of topics to equip her peers with the tools to be effective activists, including storytelling and media training. Without knowing it, she was using what the scholar and organizer Marshall Ganz has called "public narrative," a leadership practice that motivates others to join a movement and act.[13] Public narrative combines a story of self (where my values come from), a story of us (how these values tie our community together), and a story of now (why action now is urgent). The framework has helped organizers around the world translate their personal convictions and values into stories that mobilize people to take action. In the previous chapter, we explored the intricate ways in which stories are used to uphold, justify, and legitimize power hierarchies. So, it only makes sense that a critical part of a social movement's work revolves around deconstructing these myths through counter-narratives.

Xiye's "story of self" shared her experiences in Mexico, where she had witnessed firsthand the effects of extreme weather events and society's dependence on fossil fuels. Her "story of us" spoke to New Yorkers: "12 percent of adults in the Bronx have asthma, while close to $19 billion dollars of our tax money was spent to rebuild our city after Hurricane Sandy." Finally, her "story of now" framed climate change as a crisis, one that required swift and immediate action.[14] This was her call to youth and adults that change was possible if they joined the march and the movement. Public narratives like this help to trigger outrage, which motivates action and resistance.[15] As we saw in chapter 5, when anger is combined with a measure of power, it elicits a sense that something can be done to effect change.[16]

Xiye and her peers were hoping to rally at least twenty thousand people. On September 20, 2019, organizers estimated more than 200,000 joined them on the streets of New York City, with similar protests organized by youth underway the same day in 163 countries.[17] The protestors used their voices as children, youth, and students to call out adults contributing to climate change: the meat and dairy industries, ExxonMobil, politicians, the UN, the 1 percent, parents who were "stealing [their children's] future right in front of their eyes."[18] No one was spared. Using rigorous science to support their statements about the urgency of acting to address the climate crisis, they positioned themselves as both victims of the status quo and leaders with moral authority.

They were also employing an organizing tactic used to agitate against the status quo long before they were born: nonviolent civil disobedience. The term was first used in an anthology of the works of American essayist, poet, and philosopher Henry David Thoreau.[19] Thoreau believed that it was justifiable and indeed morally necessary for honest citizens to rebel against unjust and oppressive laws. He himself refused to pay a new Massachusetts poll tax to express his rejection of slavery and of the Mexican–American War. Mahatma Gandhi and Martin Luther King Jr. are among the many movement leaders inspired by his writing who have resorted to acts of civil disobedience and nonviolent protests.[20]

To assess the effectiveness of such protests, political scientists Erica Chenoweth and Maria Stephan analyzed data from violent and nonviolent resistance efforts around the globe between 1900 and 2006. They found that peaceable campaigns were effective 53 percent of the time, while violent ones succeeded only 26 percent of the time. Why the disparity? By lowering the barriers for participation, nonviolent resistance campaigns allow the movement's membership to grow.[21] At the September 20 New York City march, teenagers, parents and their toddlers, retirees, teachers, and students came together in solidarity. In addition to expanding the movement's ranks, nonviolence attracts more diverse members, yielding more innovative tactics.[22] Strategic nonviolence plays into our two basic needs: for safety, by shielding participants from violence (at least that's the intention); and self-esteem, by garnering the goodwill of nonparticipants who often perceive the peaceful resisters as both dignified and just.

Fridays for Future and its coalition of allies built the power to put the climate crisis on the public agenda. At the time of the protest, searches for "climate change" reached one of the highest levels recorded by Google.[23] By calling out adults and leveraging the growing body of science that documented the harm global warming had already done, they legitimated their attacks, fostered moral outrage, and seized control of the public narrative. Their words and actions attracted the world's attention and helped shift the frame used to discuss climate change. They also knew that changing behaviors and laws would require much more than protest, however. So they used organizing activities—such as building activist training camps like those Xiye ran and inviting others into the planning meetings for the march—that helped build participants' commitment to one another and to the movement.

Organizing creates the glue that transforms a collection of individuals into a group with a common purpose. It makes people want to come back, contribute, and feel connected to something larger than themselves. Fostering connections that are strong enough to make people feel part of a community they deeply value helps ensure a movement's survival and vibrancy over time.[24] When organizing is interwoven with stories, like those told by Xiye and her peers, it creates a feeling of "oneness" that mobilizes people around a shared identity. This sense of common cause stems not only from the rationale of the story's message, but also from its emotional appeal. As we will see next, the need for communicating and organizing activities never goes away, whatever role participants may be playing, because this is how movements gain supporters and access the valued resources they need to expand their power.

THINKING OUT OF THE BOX

Innovation is essential to offer a viable solution to a social problem or an alternative to the status quo. Without it, a movement has no specific requests, no yardstick of success. The solutions that innovators design may be altogether new and original, or they may use existing, well-tested ideas that they assemble in novel ways or apply to new contexts. Consider women's rights: The concept gained little traction when French playwright and political activist Olympe de Gouges proposed it in 1791 in the *Declaration of the Rights of Woman and of the [Female] Citizen*. Mirroring the first article of the

Declaration of the Rights of Man and of the Citizen, her *Declaration* proclaimed: "Women are born free and remain equal to men in rights." In 1793, de Gouges was sentenced to death by the Revolutionary Tribunal and executed, but her words did not die with her. They influenced and inspired women to fight for equal rights, in France and beyond. Her innovation contributed to the development of the counter-narrative that multiple waves of feminist movements refined and spread in the decades and centuries that followed.

Social innovations come in a variety of forms: They may be ideas, products, services, programs, processes, or laws and policies. But whatever the form, innovators must provide a viable pathway toward addressing the problem at hand and redefining the status quo. The innovator's role is to identify the weaknesses of the current state of things; imagine a solution that is better than the current alternative and will not cause negative unintended consequences; and articulate and justify these solutions to the various groups who will need to adopt or will be affected by the proposed alternative.[25] Their task is daunting: Not only must they envision a new reality, but they must also find ways to legitimize this new approach in the eyes of others. Doing so without having formal authority or access to resources, financial or otherwise, is challenging. This is why innovators tend be problem-solvers who think out of the box and persevere in the face of complexity and adversity.

This is precisely what Jean Rogers did. In 2008, as the financial crisis ripped through Wall Street and shattered the lives of many on Main Street, one foreclosure at a time, she started thinking about how she could help change the rules of the game in the financial markets. An environmental engineer by training, she had spent nearly two decades working as a sustainability consultant, helping companies adopt environmentally responsible practices. "It didn't make sense to me that corporations were largely not accountable for their impact on local communities, the lives of their employees and customers, and the environment," she told us. "Look where that had gotten us."

Jean had watched her friend David Gottfried develop and scale LEED building certification, a rating system for green buildings. Then an idea started brewing: Investors make decisions based on data; but even if an investor wanted to consider a business's social or environmental impact, such data were limited and often reported haphazardly. What if there were a way for companies to consistently and transparently report on more than just their financial performance? The task would be monumental, and she was bound to face resistance from the "business as usual" corporate sector. But with a two-year-old daughter, the need to change the status quo felt more personal and pressing than ever.

Jean began by doing what all innovators trying to solve a social problem must do: She worked hard to gain an in-depth understanding of the problem she was hoping to help solve.[26] She researched the difficulty of tracking companies' social and environmental performance alongside their financial performance. She learned about and became a supporter of the Global Reporting Initiative (GRI), which had developed a standard set of metrics that companies could use, whatever their industry, to create sustainability reports. At the same time, she interviewed corporate executives and investors about their reporting techniques so that she better understood each actor's constraints and challenges. In the process, she discovered why there was no one-size-fits-all answer: Food retailers and distributors have a greater need to report on the use of packaging, for instance, than banks or software companies, for which privacy may be more important. What emerged was the need for a set of rigorous and vetted standards that companies, investors, and public authorities would find reliable to measure and communicate social and environmental performance specifically for each industry.

Jean's research culminated in the publication of a white paper that laid out her innovative idea: a methodology that would lead to the development of appropriate sustainability standards for each industry.[27] Her practice of leading with questions and seeking advice as a newcomer in the space paid off: The response to the paper was overwhelmingly positive, with investors and asset managers reaching out to ask her when the new metrics would be available.[28]

Thinking that once she had put the idea out, the right person would pick it up and run with it, Jean put the project on the back burner for a year. Then, as the Occupy movement gained momentum, she decided she was done waiting. If she wanted to see these sustainability standards developed, she would have to do it herself. With the support of her husband, she quit her job and gave herself a sixth-month deadline to launch the not-for-profit that would become SASB, the Sustainability Accounting Standards Board.[29]

Beyond fundraising to finance the launching of SASB, Jean's first task was to assemble a team of researchers and technical experts who would be working with her to develop the sustainability metrics for each industry. "I can't tell you how many times I heard that I was crazy to think that we would be able to develop metrics for eighty industries in less than eighty years. We had to prove them wrong and show that it was doable. So, after we came up with a rigorous methodology, we developed a huge blueprint of the next eight years up on the wall to make sure that we would reach our goal in eight and not eighty years!"

Creating SASB, recruiting her team, and developing the methodology to create the standards were only the beginning of Jean's journey as an innovator. She and her team now had to transform SASB into a legitimate standard-setting organization with the power to grow a collective movement behind it. She knew from experience that if she wanted SASB to be taken seriously and to attract supporters, she would first need to understand the existing power relationships among business leaders, investors, public agencies, and NGOs involved in corporate sustainability. In short, she needed a power map. She gathered all the information she could, from the names of the top organizations to those with the biggest budgets; she noted the organizations with influential leaders, and those whose papers were cited in the field. She collected every data point she could to understand who was connected to whom and who seemed to rely on whom.

As an outsider in the world of finance, and a fledging organization opposing the status quo, the exercise made it clear: To build its power and transform SASB into a legitimate standard setter, she needed to identify and obtain access to the resources that these key stakeholders in sustainability valued. She started organizing to identify allies who shared her belief that investors needed new metrics with the goal of getting them invested in SASB as fellow innovators in the development process. "My very first Board had former officials of both the U.S. Securities and Exchange Commission (SEC) and the Financial Accounting Standards Board (FASB) on it," Jean told us, and that "created the legitimacy for others to participate." She launched industry working groups, organized conferences in San Francisco and New York, and hosted regular online feedback sessions. Over time, she was able to build a community of supporters who felt committed to SASB, its vision, and its promise to change the face of capitalism.

Through a mentor, Jean built rapport and then began to meet regularly with the U.S. Chamber of Commerce, a lobbying group for businesses, and the SEC. Their involvement bolstered her credibility and that of SASB in the eyes of other key actors, who were now open to meeting with her. In all these conversations, "I always framed our value proposition in terms of things [I knew] they valued—even instigating and making them a bit 'mad' about the status quo . . . The fact that SASB promised to deliver material information for investors, productivity for corporations, and market efficiency for the SEC was the key to getting these disparate and very powerful groups behind us." And as she "did the rounds," as she called them, expanding her circle of collaborators through quarterly meetings with civil society organizations, corporations, and public authorities to provide updates, Jean became a broker on sustainability issues, the in-between, linking groups that were not connected. She now controlled access to a valued resource: information about key organizations and leaders in the field. Jean and the movement for SASB had started building power.

Soon, they leveraged SASB's newly developed network of relationships to attract big-name investors and companies as advisors and Board members, including Michael Bloomberg, who became the chairman of SASB's Board. His presence further bolstered SASB's legitimacy in the eyes of the corporate world, while the organization continued to strengthen its relationships with NGOs and public authorities as well. By 2018, with the input of movement participants, SASB had developed sustainability standards for more than eighty industries and become the leading sustainability accounting standard in the United States—a feat many thought impossible when she first told them about her idea.

The movement Jean created to develop her innovation was part of a much larger movement that aimed to reinvent and change capitalism, a transformation that would require much more than SASB. But the standards were now developed and ready for use; and after years of relentless work, this was the time Jean chose to step down from her role as SASB's CEO. "I have realized that it is the innovation that excites me. I am a person who loves learning, I'm naturally very curious and fascinated by hard problems to solve, things others say can't be done," Jean told us. What remained to be done was orchestrating the change to make SASB sustainability standards and reporting the new normal for corporations and investors. Orchestration does not happen overnight, as Jean and her successors at SASB know well, because what is ultimately at stake is changing not only the law, but also the culture, both of which are deeply entrenched in society. Nevertheless, such change is possible, as we will see.

MAKING CHANGE A REALITY

In 2000 and 2003, the Netherlands and Belgium became, respectively, the first two countries to legalize same-sex marriage. Inspired by these advances, a group of lesbian activists in Argentina started dreaming up their own campaign for marriage equality. They faced tremendous resistance from a mighty force with centuries of experience with power—the Catholic Church. To make matters worse, they confronted fierce opposition from gay activists within the Argentinian LGBTQ+ community who favored civil union legislation. And yet, in less than a decade, something happened that even this small group of visionary lesbian activists never thought would occur so fast.

They won.

In 2010, Argentina became the first country in Latin America and the tenth in the world—ahead of countries like France, Germany, and New Zealand—to legalize same-sex marriage. That's not all. The campaign that succeeded at changing the country's laws was launched and orchestrated by a group that initially had almost no resources. As María Rachid, the founder of a shelter for bisexual and lesbian women in Buenos Aires and one of the leaders of the marriage equality fight, recounted, "We were weak in many of the areas that traditional social movements leverage for power, meaning we couldn't turn out masses of people in the streets nor invest money in ads or fancy communications campaigns since we were broke."[30] But the success of the movement is no story of miracles or good luck. It is a story of perseverance, strategy, and, of course, power.

Their first accomplishment was seeing and seizing an opportunity to act. In 2003, when Nestór Kirchner, a center-left politician, was elected president of Argentina, he and his government knew they had to be careful not to trigger popular ire. Between 1998 and 2002, Argentina had suffered its own Great Depression. When the government announced austerity measures in 2001, including a freeze on bank account withdrawals, panic and political chaos ensued.[31] The economic crisis had given the country's social movements the opportunity to mobilize Argentines to agitate, driving four consecutive presidents to leave office before Kirchner's election. So, the new president reached out to the country's social movements early on, claiming he wanted to take their demands into account and govern peacefully.

María recalled the government's overture: "They said they were developing a plan to fight discrimination, and they wanted to include sexual diversity. They asked us to share a diagnosis of the problems our community endured and to recommend public policies that would help. We were skeptical. Never in Argentina's history had any government collaborated with the LGBT+ community on anti-discrimination policies. The government, for us, had been persecutors, not advocates."

In the meantime, however, Kirchner's government started going after perpetrators of the brutal military dictatorship that had spread terror across the country between 1976 and 1983; so, María and her co-organizers decided it was worth a try. "We thought, it's now or never. We have to go for equal marriage, and we've got to win this with Kirchner, before his government ends." Their recognition of the political opportunity presented to them and their decision to seize the moment were pivotal for the movement.[32] In their case, the innovation was clear: developing a bill on marriage equality that would legalize same-sex marriage. They had been in touch with the activists who had developed such a bill in Spain and succeeded in getting it signed into law, and they were hoping to do the same in Argentina.

But having a window of opportunity and the draft of an innovative policy were no guarantee it would get adopted. To make this change a reality, María and her peers not only had to agitate for change, but also orchestrate its adoption, which requires changing what people deem valuable, desirable, and often altogether legal. And for laws to change, policymakers and elected officials must support the changes. Influencing the behaviors and mental models of so many people—from the public to policymakers—necessitates coalition building at scale.

To begin with, María helped gather five organizations in the LGBT+ movement, and together they founded the Argentine LGBT Federation. Creating a shared identity, a sense of oneness, among the participants was critical.[33] María and her co-organizers designed training workshops and assigned the participants tasks to perform in groups so that they would get to know one another and develop stronger connections. People were sent out in teams, for example, to get a petition in favor of marriage equality signed. These efforts paid off, "the participants developed a real sense of belonging and a strong commitment to our common cause." But the Federation remained fairly small, and they still lacked access to resources they could leverage to expand their ranks. So they started with the same intangible resource the young climate activists deployed: They appealed to people's conscience, in this case, by promoting their ideals of equality.

The framing strategy they chose—advancing their demands as a crusade for human rights (not civil rights, as LGBTQ+ campaigns in countries like the United States focused on)—had been used by previous generations of Argentine LGBTQ+ activists, starting in the 1980s, as the country was reeling from the wounds of its brutal dictatorship.[34] Linking the fight for gay rights to the country's growing human rights community, which emerged in the decades after the dictatorship as a strong political force, was a way to humanize the LGBTQ+ community and legitimize gay rights.[35] By standing on the shoulders of their predecessors, and framing their campaign as a call for marriage equality, María and her peers were appealing to people's need to feel ethical, hoping to attract everyone who cared about defending human rights: How could the gay community that was, like so many Argentines, persecuted during the dictatorship be deprived of a right that others had? This framing enabled María and her peers to agitate against the status quo, trigger outrage, and push people to join their movement, thereby growing their ranks and finding new allies.

In addition to ideals of equality, the activists harnessed another intangible resource to expand their networks: solidarity. Attending community meetings, bringing supporters to protests organized by other movements, advocating for these movements' demands — solidarity is a highly valued resource, especially among activists. The Federation consistently showed up in solidarity with retirees, union workers, migrant groups, people with disabilities, Afro Argentinians, and others. In this way, they not only developed strong relationships with activists in other movements, but also won the support of many people who were initially opposed to gay rights. Additionally, the support of larger, more established social movements gave the Federation leverage over legislators, because they had more control over an invaluable political resource: votes. This strategy paid off, when the head of the country's largest labor union — "a burly truck driver," as María described him — publicly declared his support for marriage equality in the weeks leading up to the Senate's vote.

To change the country's hearts and minds in favor of marriage equality, one more ally was essential: the media. María and her peers enlisted their support by giving them access to a resource they are always hungry for: personal, emotional stories that couples who had been together for decades despite being unable to marry were willing to share publicly. "I remember one of our first couples," María told us. "They were both living with HIV and needed marriage in order to share their social security benefits. Their story showed people why the law for marriage equality mattered." Once a couple thoroughly understood the proposed law and was able to defend it, they would invite the press along with all their family members and friends to the Civil Register, where they would request to be married. They were denied, of course. But the moment provided an opportunity to humanize the struggle by linking the law to the stories of real people who suffered from this injustice.

Neuroscientists Melanie Green and Timothy Brock have studied the role of *transportation*, the extent to which people are engrossed in a story and connect with its characters, in changing their beliefs and perceptions of the story's protagonists. The evidence supported their hypothesis that transportation—characterized by emotional re-actions, mental imagery, connection with the characters, and focus on the narrative—has a persuasive effect. Study participants who were transported into stories about the importance of loyalty and friend-ship, for instance, exhibited stronger belief in loyalty and friendship as well as positive perceptions of the protagonists, even when no such moral was explicit.[36] This insight crystalizes one reason stories can be a source of power for movements: They help to build empathy and support for the cause, expanding its ranks, exactly what María hoped for.

The Catholic Church did not stand by quietly as marriage equal-ity activists launched this historic campaign. The Church used its deep pockets and even deeper network of influence in government, the media, and the population to rally opposition. María and her co-organizers had another detractor as well, one from within their ranks: A subset of gay rights organizations were advocating with leg-islators for the more politically viable option of civil union. "Our own became our biggest adversaries," María fumed. The risk the movement faced was that their demand would be diluted—a risk or-chestrators often face as they try to address the needs and desires of various groups in their coalition.[37] The balance between expanding the ranks of the movement to tip the scales of change, while main-taining the loyalty of the most ardent supporters, is an issue most or-chestrators have to grapple with. María and the Federation overcame this risk by refusing to compromise. They were confident in their ap-proach, because they had been warned of the risk and advised how to deal with it by the activists with whom they had connected in 2005, when Spain won same-sex marriage: Do not settle for civil unions, even when members of your movement try to make you.

The tension between the two factions escalated until the final months before the vote. But the proponents of civil unions could not match the Federation's orchestration prowess, and "when they saw we were gaining momentum, they jumped on board. Not everyone in our team agreed that we should take them back and give them a platform, and our meetings stretched loudly into the night. But ultimately, we were laser focused on passing the law. That's what mattered most." So they welcomed them into the movement, even introducing the law together to the Senate on the day of the vote.

This moment underscores another trap orchestrators must avoid. People who have played the role of agitators, as many in the movement for marriage equality had, can struggle to pivot from raising public awareness and condemning those who uphold the status quo to broadening the coalition and uniting the different parts of the movement. The change in posture from an agitator's "us vs. them" identity to an orchestrator's stance as mediator and unifier is essential, as María understood; but it can be a tricky shift for agitators to make.[38]

The movement's extensive network building positioned the Federation at the center of a growing coalition. A joint letter, signed by the most prominent human rights organizations, was sent to congressional legislators in support of the law. The country's largest unions publicly announced their support in the media. The country's leading university urged legislators, on human rights grounds, to extend the right to marriage to same-sex couples. Spanish LGBTQ+ activists sent a delegation to testify to the importance of the law. Coupled with the media stories, support from telenovela celebrities and other public figures, 70 percent of Argentines supported the law by the time of the vote.[39]

"In 2010, we achieved legal equality," María recounted, "but there is a long way to go for real equality. Women gained legal equality a long time ago, and yet we're still waiting for the day when we will actually be treated equally. It's the same for the LGBT+ community. We need to continue fighting for public policies and we need to keep working to bring about a cultural change. Sustaining the engagement is necessary, but difficult." This is the final hurdle: movement fatigue. After the novelty of being in the media and the urgency of outright injustice fade, sustaining active participation can be challenging, let alone expanding the membership base. Surmounting this hurdle comes down to persevering, so that the movement is ready to respond and drive change whenever opportunities arise. To this end, its members must continue to agitate to stimulate outrage, innovate to adapt to a changing context, and orchestrate change in the status quo.

IS IT GETTING ANY EASIER?

The twenty-first century has ushered in an explosion of online agitation. Following the revelation of sexual abuse allegations against movie producer Harvey Weinstein in early October 2017, the #MeToo movement took off with incredible speed, its hashtag spreading across the world in just a few days. In France and Belgium, it became #BalanceTonPorc, in Spain and Latin America, it was #YoTambien, in Italy #QuellaVoltaChe. Women finally had a powerful channel to voice their stories of sexual harassment and assault, and be heard, as public shame brought previously untouchable men tumbling from their positions. In its first year, the hashtag was used an average of more than fifty-five thousand times a day in at least eighty-five countries.[40] But it is a mistake to think that the #MeToo movement happened online overnight. Sexual assault survivor and activist Tarana Burke launched it a decade earlier to raise awareness of the pervasiveness of sexual abuse and assault. When Hollywood stars and prestigious institutions like the *New York Times* shone a light on the issue, Tarana's essential work was initially overlooked until outraged activists agitated to set the record straight and give her the credit she deserved, propelling her into the spotlight.

There is no question that social media platforms have made it easier for Tarana and other activists to agitate, congregate, and share. But, as a seasoned activist and community organizer, Tarana was quick to point out to us the limits of digital activism.[41] Despite their mobilizing potential, social media can pose risks even for agitators, since messages aimed to enlist others' support for the cause may reach only those who already agree. People's preferences, combined with algorithms and machine learning, tend to reinforce online divides. Knowing how important it is for movements to mobilize broad bases of support and build far-reaching coalitions, the challenge for agitators in the digital era is to share information with new audiences and across groups not connected to one another.

Innovators face risks as well. Though their innovations can be more broadly disseminated and shared in a digital world, technical fixes rarely change deeply rooted power hierarchies.[42] Even when technology is part of the solution, change is always a political matter. Yet the advent of the digital age has led many innovators to overemphasize technological solutions to problems—a trend we've seen among the social innovators with whom we have been working over the past fifteen years.

As for orchestrators, technology offers useful tools for connecting with various constituencies and building coalitions. In particular, social media make it simple for people to engage in "click activism," in which individuals are encouraged to "click," "like," or "share" items on social media in support of change.[43] Yet as sociologist Zeynep Tufekci notes, "Modern networked movements can scale up quickly and take care of all sorts of logistical tasks without building any substantial organizational capacity before the first protest or march . . . However, with this speed comes weakness."[44] Without the long and grueling work of movement building, participants risk having shallow connections and little experience in collective decision-making, strategizing, communicating, and organizing, all of which play a critical role in ensuring a movement's resilience and effectiveness. In *The Purpose of Power: How We Come Together When We Fall Apart*, Alicia Garza, the cofounder of Black Lives Matter, goes to the heart of this challenge: "You cannot start a movement from a hashtag. Hashtags do not start movements—people do. Movements do not have official moments when they start and end, and there is never just one person who initiates them. Movements are much more like waves than they are like light switches. [They] ebb and flow."[45]

Ultimately, the power of movements comes not from merely assembling large numbers of people, but from using their sustained collective action to influence people's beliefs and behaviors and effect change.[46] This requires understanding what these people need and want, and figuring out how to use the power of banding together to control access to those valued resources.[47] The successful movements we analyzed in this chapter were able to do that. As Marshall Ganz eloquently puts it, for movements, "it is the ability to capitalize on opportunities by turning the resources one has into the power one needs, which transforms possibility into results."[48] While the ascent of new technologies has created new opportunities for collective movements to gain and exercise power, in some parts of the world they have also made it much harder for social change-makers to be heard. In the hands of dictators, new technologies have become tools of surveillance and censorship whose effectiveness is unprecedented. Depending on who controls them and what they are used for, new technologies may either enhance the power of collective movements or constrain them.

What is true for collective movements is also true for every one of us. New technologies can empower us or oppress us, depending on who controls access to them and what they are used for. Let's see how.

Chapter 7

Power Doesn't Change— It Just Changes Hands

When everything seems to be changing at breakneck speed, the resulting uncertainty may lead us to believe that power must be changing too. Sure enough, this is a common assumption. In 2013, as traditionally powerful institutions and players were losing clout to nimbler grassroots entities, journalist and scholar Moisés Naím declared that the end of power was upon us: "In the twenty-first century," he wrote, "power is easier to get, harder to use—and easier to lose."[1] In a similar vein, five years later, entrepreneur and political activist Jeremy Heimans and social impact executive Henry Timms argued that connectivity has brought forth a new form of power: networked, informal, collaborative, transparent, and participatory. It is the kind of power that lives through the energy of the crowd, the kind #MeToo and Black Lives Matter have harnessed. Its opposite, the two authors say, is "old power": closed, inaccessible, and mostly hierarchical.[2]

Whether the end of power or the emergence of new power, both analyses aptly describe important shifts in where power is located and how it can be exercised today. But as you will see, power itself hasn't changed. The changes we are witnessing are just another man-ifestation of the power fundamentals that are always at work.

THE FUNDAMENTALS OF POWER ARE TIMELESS

Consider two technological shifts that transformed how humans live and relate to one another. The first occurred about ten thou-sand years ago, when the agricultural revolution—the farming of crops and the domestication of animals—turned our ancestors away from nomadic wandering to permanent settlements.[3] No lon-ger required to spend every waking hour searching for food, a few group members could now engage in activities other than hunting and gathering. The agricultural revolution changed the distribu-tion of power on two levels: geographically, by favoring societies rich in farming resources, like domesticated animals, crops, and farming technology; and within those societies, by liberating a new social class to devote their time to intellectual, technical, commer-cial, and political pursuits that further consolidated their hold on power.[4]

Much later, in the mid-1400s, the course of human society was radically changed again by the invention of movable type. Guten-berg's invention spread like wildfire, with entrepreneurs who had learned to build and operate the new technology opening printing shops in commercial centers across Western Europe. Merchants, lit-erate peasants, and intellectuals alike could now access and share unprecedented amounts of information. Scribes, however, were displeased: For centuries, they had been guardians of knowledge, thanks to their unique ability to read, write, and copy sacred texts. Now that ability was becoming increasingly obsolete. In 1492, the German abbot Johannes Trithemius wrote *In Praise of Scribes* to ex-press his concern that the loss of handwritten transcription harmed the spiritual development of monks, because copying both occupied them and exposed them to constant learning, and to decry the inferior material and aesthetic quality of printed books.[5]

It was a losing battle: In the fifty years following Gutenberg's invention, millions of books were printed in Europe with far-reaching consequences, including the democratization of knowledge and the acceleration of cultural movements like the Renaissance and religious movements like the Protestant Reformation.[6] Even those who opposed the invention, like Johannes Trithemius, couldn't resist its appeal. Some say that even *In Praise of Scribes* was disseminated not through handwritten copies, but by the very machine its author decried in the text!

As each of these waves of technological change dramatically altered people's lives, something else changed too: the power map. For those who experienced these disruptive changes in real time, the shift was both exhilarating and overwhelming. Different as those changes were, they were driven by the same dynamic: What made the farmers, landowners, and printers powerful was their control of access to newly valued resources. From one period to another, the pattern remains the same: Each era of technological change creates new resources that become highly valued. In turn, those who control these new resources—either because they know how to operate them, or because they own them—have tremendous power. This is why technological changes shift the distribution of power.

Power changes hands for other reasons as well, of course. Natural events, for one, have upended the distribution of power on our planet time and again, sometimes in an instant (as when the impact of a massive asteroid sixty-six million years ago annihilated the dinosaurs that had dominated the earth for 135 million years), and sometimes over the course of centuries (as when volcanic eruptions in the late 530s CE darkened Europe's skies[7], causing dramatic cooling that intensified the political and social upheaval following the fall of the Western Roman Empire). But when it comes to human-made changes in the distribution of power, for better or worse, technology is perhaps the biggest power-shifter of all. And that has never been truer than now.

TECHNOLOGY CHANGES POWER MAPS

Nezuma was born on the island of Unguja, off the coast of Zanzibar, in a village with but one road leading in and out. Though she had never planned to leave her community, in 2016, the mother of six moved twenty miles away to Kinyasini, to study to become a solar engineer. After five months of training, she returned to her village bringing a hitherto unavailable and most valuable resource: electricity.

How had Nezuma, who was illiterate, become a solar engineer? The answer can be found more than three thousand miles away, in India, where social activist and educator Bunker Roy founded Barefoot College. Bunker, who recalled having "a very elitist, snobbish, expensive education"[8] in India's private schools, believes that his real education started in 1966, when massive droughts and crop failures led to devastating famines in the provinces of Bihar and eastern Uttar Pradesh. That was when he decided to dedicate his life to helping poor rural communities become self-reliant.

At first Bunker contributed by digging open wells for drinking water. But he was convinced that, given the opportunity, the villagers he was working with could be trained to use even the most sophisticated technologies, and he was determined not to allow illiteracy to get in the way. In 1972, he came up with an idea: suppose there were a special kind of school, focused on educating and training poor, rural people through learning by doing. That same year, he created the non-governmental organization, Barefoot College, to orchestrate the implementation of his vision. Its first training center was established in India, where visionary educator and dedicated teacher Bagewat Nanda Sevedan developed innovative pedagogical tools to enable students to learn by doing. Other training centers followed in Burkina Faso, Madagascar, Liberia, Guatemala, Fiji, Senegal, and Zanzibar, which is how Nezuma got the opportunity to study and become a solar engineer.

Representatives of Barefoot College visited her village, the way they visit similar rural communities every day, all over the world. They invited the villagers to participate in the college's flagship solar program to bring this renewable and sustainable form of energy to their community. There were, however, a few conditions: The villagers would have to designate one of them to go through the training; this person would have to commit to coming back to install and maintain the equipment, which the college would supply; and they had to agree to pay the trained solar engineer to maintain the service. This was all well and good; but there was one more condition that took the villagers, used to men being in charge, by surprise. The person would have to be a woman, ideally middle-aged and a mother or a grandmother, who—Barefoot College representatives knew from experience—would return at the end of the training and not abandon her community.

As the college representatives stated these conditions, many of the villagers intuitively turned to Nezuma. They would often look to her for help and advice when they were in trouble. But at first, joining the college seemed impossible to Nezuma, not only for logistical reasons, but also because her husband would never allow it. He was utterly opposed to her leaving her family and living by herself for five months. With the help of the village's chief, who could see how much the program would benefit the community, and Nezuma's mother, who agreed to help take care of the family during her daughter's absence, the Barefoot College representatives convinced Nezuma's husband to let her participate. The college staff also arranged for him to visit his wife once a week. For the next five months, Nezuma lived on the campus in Kinyasini, learning to install and repair solar electrical systems from other women who had themselves become solar engineers through the program. Because most of these women were illiterate or semiliterate, most of the teaching was done using visual learning tools, such as color-coded pictures and manuals. Nezuma didn't learn only about solar electricity. Meagan Fallone, the social entrepreneur who succeeded Bunker as Barefoot College CEO, enriched the program with training on women's health and rights as well as digital and entrepreneurial skills. "We want our trainees to learn about technology and about their bodies, their rights, and their responsibilities," Meagan told us. "This holistic approach truly transforms them."[9]

Back in her village at the end of the program, Nezuma felt a new sense of power. Bright and hard-working, she electrified the community. And she received help from an unexpected source: her husband. Transformed from a skeptic to a staunch ally, he could now regularly be found stabilizing the ladder while Nezuma was on a neighbor's roof or assisting her with a repair. He had realized how much he and his family had to gain from Nezuma's newfound prominence. In a few months, she had gained control over access to one of the most valuable and sought-after technologies in her village. Her newfound power made her the first woman to participate in the influential village council. This was the genius of Barefoot College's innovation: The middle-aged women who went through its program became not only a literal source of power for their villages, but also powerful themselves.

Bunker and Meagan understood the potential of technology to change the power map for the better. Over the course of history, technological and scientific advances have done more than just greatly improve our daily existence, as psychologist Steven Pinker notes in his book *Enlightenment Now*. They have also brought us closer to becoming "like lords and possessors of Nature," in the words of French scientist and philosopher René Descartes.[10] For Descartes, science and technology were the gateway for people to understand, interpret, and analyze nature, and thereby gain a measure of control over Mother Nature herself.[11]

We have become so astoundingly powerful that we have even developed plans to prevent massive asteroids from hitting Earth and annihilating us.[12]

The digital revolution that reached warp speed at the turn of the twenty-first century has increased our power at a staggering pace.* In 1989, at one of the world's largest physics laboratories, Tim Berners-Lee and Robert Cailliau invented a new network for sharing and searching information. They called their invention the World Wide Web. As they discussed what to do with it, they had a conversation that would have a tremendous impact on the way we live, work, and play. They were debating whether to patent their discovery, which would prevent its replication, use, or improvement by others. As Cailliau recounts it, "[Tim] said, 'Robert, do you want to be rich?' I thought, *Well, it helps, no?* He apparently didn't care about that. What he cared about was to make sure that the thing would work, that it would just be there for everybody."[13]

Their decision to keep the World Wide Web open-source and freely accessible to all embodied their vision of technology as an equalizing force. Berners-Lee believed that it could help liberate human potential through collaboration and knowledge-sharing at unprecedented scale. He imagined that it would, for once, give everyone access to knowledge. And to some extent he was right. Those of us who can access the internet do have a limitless supply of information at our fingertips. This ability to more easily access information and connect with one another online has provided new channels through which grassroots movements can challenge existing power

---

* Changes in both the technology and its regulation and control are coming so fast and furiously that anything said one day might be contradicted by events the next. For things said in writing, like books, this is a particularly acute dilemma. Instead of repeatedly reminding you that what we say is "as we write," we'd like to acknowledge here that we know whatever we have written will likely need revision by the time our book is published.

hierarchies, as we saw with the #MeToo and Black Lives Matter movements.[14]

Taken together, these shifts have given humankind many more ways to satisfy our needs for safety and self-esteem. But more power overall doesn't necessarily mean more power for all. It takes intentional interventions like the one developed by Barefoot College for technology to empower people whose access to valued resources is constrained by existing power hierarchies. In the absence of such purposeful use of technology, the digital revolution has mostly fallen short of the great equalizing force that Berners-Lee and Cailliau envisioned it could be. Like previous technological waves, it changed the distribution of power, but it did not benefit everyone equally.[15] A few have emerged as the digital revolution's big winners, with tremendous power concentrated in their hands.

HOW THE DIGITAL REVOLUTION SHUFFLED THE CARDS

One of the earliest traces of an algorithm was found in Iraq, inscribed on a Sumerian clay tablet dating back to around 2500 BCE. It consisted of a set of instructions for the task of division.[16] At its root, an "algorithm" is just another word for a set of directions.[17] Algorithms have evolved a great deal since their early appearance, and today, the word is most commonly used to refer to "a sequence of instructions telling a computer what to do."[18] These instructions can be input by humans. For instance, a coder might write an algorithm telling the computer to generate the shortest walking route between point A and point B. But in the era of big data enabled by the digital revolution, computers can be made to write their own instructions based on large sets of data inputs and outputs provided by the coders. For example, if the coder feeds the computer a list of divisions, without the computer knowing what division is, the machine will spot the pattern and learn to replicate it on its own. This is what people mean by "machine learning," an application of artificial intelligence (AI) that has tremendously accelerated our ability to process and learn from massive amounts of data, and to optimize and increase the efficiency, precision, and predictive accuracy of machines.[19]

Digital technology is producing astounding progress, improving our lives in countless ways. Coupled with big data, machine-learning algorithms can learn from thousands of medical images to recognize a cancerous mass in human tissue earlier and more accurately than the human eye can.[20] Mobile health technology is improving and reducing the cost of transmitting health-care information, delivering patient care, and monitoring medication adherence, with the potential to democratize access to health solutions in rural areas in low- and middle-income countries worldwide.[21] And technology's benefits go well beyond medicine. With the aid of its innovative tools and processes, we are improving the productivity of natural resources and sources of energy, the safety and performance of motor vehicles and industrial materials, the availability and affordability of information and consumer goods, and myriad other conveniences and opportunities to satisfy our need for safety and self-esteem.

Algorithmic decision-making is improving our lives in large part because it uses vastly greater amounts of data than humans can process, and it is consistent, precise, and reliable in ways that people aren't. As a result, it has the potential to benefit people whom human decision makers, consciously or unconsciously, discriminate against. For example, a study of automated loan underwriting showed that it can be more accurate than human underwriting in predicting defaults, resulting in a higher rate of approved loans, especially for underserved customers.[22]

Alongside this progress and potential for empowerment, however, digital technology and AI have also affected two critical aspects of the distribution of power that require our vigilance and oversight: the control of algorithms and the control of personal information.

First, control of algorithms is critical because they can be biased, and when they are, the scale of their application enabled by digital technology and big data means that even small biases can affect large numbers of people.[23] For example, the U.S. government and its law enforcement agencies are increasingly using machine-learning algorithms to police neighborhoods and identify and monitor criminals. Helpful as technology like facial recognition–enabled cameras in public transit or biometric data collection in airports may be to reduce and prevent crime, the imperfections of the algorithms that power them can be disproportionately damaging to certain segments of the population, oftentimes those that are disadvantaged already. To wit, facial recognition algorithms are five to ten times more likely to misidentify Black faces than they do White ones, increasing the chances of innocent Black men and women being profiled and prosecuted for crimes they have not committed.[24] One reason why facial recognition systems display lower accuracy on darker skin is that many of the datasets used to train and test facial analysis systems are not properly representative. As Joy Buolamwini of the MIT Media Lab put it, "if the training sets aren't really that diverse, any face that deviates too much from the established norm will be harder to detect."[25] It's not hard to see how such bias, unintentional as it may be, contributes to perpetuating and deepening existing power hierarchies.[26]

These unintended consequences of algorithmic decision-making are hard for us to detect and fix, unaware as we often are that algorithms are affecting our lives at all, and accustomed as many of us are to assuming that algorithms are "neutral." Some engineering whiz wrote a set of rules, the thinking goes, and since this is math, the result must be unbiased and factual.[27] But the devil is in the details. "Algorithms are opinions embedded in code," as mathematician Cathy O'Neil put it, and assuming that their output is always "objective" leads us to dissociate it from human responsibility and accountability.[28]

The people making these important choices are coders and computer engineers. Who these people are and how they work can also introduce bias into the algorithms they build. Only a small percentage of the technical employees at companies like Apple and Facebook are women and BIPOC (Black, Indigenous, and People of Color).[29] Yet diverse perspectives are critical to identifying biases and applying critical lenses to testing and tweaking algorithms. Also, for the most part, their employers are corporations, and they are acting on the orders of executives who, in turn, are accountable to investors, who expect profits. As a result, they can't share the code for their company's golden goose, and nobody can access, analyze, or challenge the algorithms. This lack of transparency keeps control in the hands of engineers and companies that develop and profit from the products, free from public oversight and accountability.

The second power shift effected by the digital revolution is the transfer of control over personal information. While digital technologies have given us access to unlimited information online, we have very little control over the information about us available there. Imagine a world in which your every movement could be observed: Every step you took, every meal you ate, and every conversation you had could be monitored. The English philosopher Jeremy Bentham first conceived of such a system as a way to structure prisons, in which a single guard would be both invisible to and have an unobstructed view of every inmate all the time. Bentham called this system a "panopticon." French philosopher Michel Foucault borrowed Bentham's concept in the 1970s and used it as a metaphor to describe how, through the use of surveillance, the few could exercise social control over the many.[30] The result would be a society remarkably ordered and regulated, but completely unfree. Today, whether we know it or not, more and more aspects of our lives unfold under a digital panopticon, and we can't always tell that we are being watched.

As we use our digital devices, millions of data points are recorded, leaving traces of our habits, desires, and needs. Matched with increased data storage capabilities, this information gives those with access to it an unprecedented opportunity to learn about and surveil us. Without oversight and accountability, such surveillance can quickly turn from benign data gathering to ominous control, which is particularly frightening in the hands of authoritarian governments.[31]

Governments are far from the only entities with access to massive amounts of data about us. Companies can use monitoring software to track how much time per day employees spend typing, to take screenshots of their computers at random, to record every website they visit, and to report this information to their managers.[32] Some, especially large tech companies, have access to information not only about their employees, but about all of us. Amazon knows our taste in shopping. Alexa stores snippets of our conversations. Facebook knows what we like and whom we look up to, whom we text and call on WhatsApp, to whom we owe money, and what type of content is more likely to anger us so that we stay on the site longer. Apple Watch captures our heart rates. Through our searches and YouTube views, Google knows what we are interested in. It can even know where we are at a given time, what we sound like, and how we look.[33] Because they know what we need and want, these companies have tremendous power that can benefit or harm us depending on how it is used and by whom.

The temptation to use control over highly valued resources for less than virtuous purposes is ever-present. In her book *The Age of Surveillance Capitalism*, social psychologist Shoshana Zuboff meticulously documented how companies profit from using and selling our personal data.[34] Initially, tech companies captured users' data to improve the services they offered. Then, in the 1990s, some began using this information to generate revenue by targeting us with ads they knew we were likely to respond to. This business model soon spread, and the race for people's attention was on. "Engagement" became the "currency of the attention economy,"[35] while data became "the new oil."[36] Big tech companies didn't stop at targeted ads, when they realized they could flat-out sell our data to interested parties. Their clients are insurance companies, banks, employers, political campaigns, anyone who is willing and ready to pay to know what we want. Their pitch to potential clients is simple: pay us and we can make people do what you want, buy your products, sign up for your services, even vote for you in the next election.

People at YouTube, Apple, Netflix, and Amazon decide how the site will make recommendations on what you should watch next. People at Facebook, LinkedIn, Twitter, and TikTok decide how algorithms select the content that goes in their newsfeeds. They decide what news we see first online, what posts show up in our newsfeeds, what products pop up when we browse a website, and whom we match with on dating applications. As Twitter's cofounder Jack Dorsey acknowledged when he testified in front of Congress in 2018, "Every time someone opens up our service, every time someone opens up our app, we are implicitly incentivizing them to do something or not to do something." He further noted, "I believe we need to question the fundamental incentives that are in our product today."[37]

Thanks to their control over algorithms and personal data, technology companies have become the gatekeepers of commerce and information channels. This is a stunning display of the power of betweenness: Consumers, employees and suppliers often have little choice but to go through Big Tech to buy, sell, and work. With limited alternatives, they cannot easily withdraw from using a technology or a platform, or from working for a company if they disagree with its practices. The tech companies have often used their dominance to build yet more power and abuse it through anti-competitive practices—like predatory pricing, exclusionary agreements, extortionate fees, self-preferences, and the acquisition of hundreds of rivals to squash the competition.[38] As a result, corporations like Google, Amazon, Facebook, and Apple are monopolies or quasi-monopolies with greater economic power than some countries.[39]

Where does this leave us? The big tech companies have a tight grip on the fundamentals of power. First, they know what we value in real-time, with precision, and at scale, and they can use this information to predict our behaviors. Second, they can unilaterally control not only what data are gathered about us, but also how those data are used to influence our beliefs and actions. Third, they can use their power to reduce alternatives for consumers, suppliers and competitors alike, and use their money to influence legislators and law enforcement into giving them a great deal of leeway. As a result of such a large and unchecked power imbalance, the decisions the technical experts who lead and work for these companies make, deliberately or unwittingly, may not account for our interests and well-being. Often, they don't. What is at stake, therefore, is our ability, and our children's, to think critically and decide for ourselves what we want and how to behave.[40] History has taught us that preserving this ability is critical in the face of propaganda and power concentration. In the digital era, it is particularly crucial as we grapple with deep fakes, fake news, and coordinated disinformation campaigns aimed at altering the very basis of reality.

Yet concentrations of power are not immutable. It is always up to us to agitate, innovate, and orchestrate to change the power hierarchy, as many Google employees have shown us.

CURBING THE POWER OF BIG TECH

In March 2018, it came to light that Google had entered into a contract with the U.S. Department of Defense to help build an artificial intelligence tool that could analyze drone footage.[41] Despite the company's claim that the project was "non-offensive," many Google employees were outraged. Realizing that they couldn't do much by themselves to pressure the company to make substantive changes, they turned to collective organizing. They didn't just want to agitate—they wanted to innovate and orchestrate change. "We wanted to build the capacity to make decisions ourselves, not just entreat with those in power," Meredith Whittaker, one of the Google employees involved at the time, told us.[42]

The result of their efforts was the development of an open letter demanding that Project Maven (as it was referred to) be canceled immediately. They also pushed for an innovation: demanding that Google draft and enforce a clear policy reflecting that neither Google nor any of its contractors would ever build "warfare technology."[43] This open letter was ultimately signed by more than 4,600 Google employees.[44] When a month went by after the letter's publication without any substantive reaction from Google's senior leadership, almost a dozen Google employees resigned to protest the company's continued involvement.[45]

In the meantime, the story of Google's involvement in Project Maven and its employees' response had garnered widespread media coverage, which brought further pressure on the company to make a change. In response, the company announced that their eighteen-month contract with the Department of Defense would expire by March 2019 and not be renewed.[46] Google CEO Sundar Pichai also released a statement describing a set of AI principles, which included not pursuing "weapons or other technologies whose principal purpose or implementation is to cause or directly facilitate injury to people."[47] These guidelines asserted that artificial intelligence and its use should be socially beneficial, avoid creating or reinforcing unfair biases, be built and tested for safety, be accountable to people, incorporate privacy design principles, uphold high standards of scientific excellence, and be made available for uses that accord with these principles.

After months of tireless work, organizers at Google began to see their efforts bear fruit. Collective action had given visibility to their demands, and the media coverage that it triggered gave them some power, because it had the potential to damage the company's reputation, a resource that its leadership and shareholders cared deeply about. Yet, soon after this announcement, Google employees turned to collective action once again to push back against the company's misuse of artificial intelligence.

In August 2018, just a few months after the Project Maven protests, a report appeared in *The Intercept*, an online publication, bringing to light another Google initiative: Project Dragonfly.[48] The report described Dragonfly as a prototype of a censored version of Google's search engine being developed for use in China that would blacklist websites and search terms about human rights, democracy, religion, and peaceful protests. Building on their earlier successes, a group of Google employees decided to draft and circulate another open letter, this time calling for the development of an ethics review structure, which included meaningful employee input and participation at all levels as well as an ethical assessment of Project Dragonfly.[49] Within three weeks, this letter had more than 1,400 signatories within the company. Organizers again effectively leveraged the news media to amplify their message. Amnesty International took up the cause too, publishing their own letter asking Google to stop the project, increase transparency about its position on censorship, and guarantee protections for whistleblowers.[50]

As protests against Dragonfly continued, another bombshell exploded: In October 2018, news broke that Andy Rubin, the creator of the Android mobile operating system, had been paid $90 million when he left Google in 2014 after sexual assault allegations against him were deemed credible.[51] Although Google's leadership might well have used the huge payout as a faster and less litigious way to get an unwelcome senior employee out of the company, in the midst of the international reckoning about sexual harassment and gender discrimination spurred by the #MeToo movement, Google employees found the revelation that the company had allegedly protected a predator in their own ranks unconscionable. So once again, a group of Google employees began organizing a response. But this time, they moved beyond an open letter and took the protests from cyberspace into the physical world, too.

On November 1, 2018, in cities around the world, Google employees took to the streets to protest. According to the organizers, more than 60 percent of all Google offices, amounting to thousands of employees, participated in the walkouts.[52] The same day, they published an article in *The Cut* articulating five key demands: an end to forced arbitration; a commitment to end pay and opportunity inequity; a publicly disclosed sexual harassment transparency report; a clear, uniform, globally inclusive process for reporting sexual misconduct; and changes in organizational governance, including shifting the Chief Diversity Officer to report directly to the CEO and appointing an employee representative to the Board.[53]

In February 2019, Google announced that it would meet one of the walkout's key demands by ending forced arbitration for employee disputes.[54] Yet no announcement was made on Project Dragonfly until July 16, 2019, when Google executive Karan Bhatia announced before the U.S. Senate Judiciary Committee that the project had been canceled.[55]

The story of the Google employees is only one example of the many petitions and protests that tech workers have since been organizing to pressure their companies to act more ethically, not only at Google, but also at Amazon, Facebook, Salesforce, Microsoft, and Apple.[56] Many have also proposed innovations and tried to orchestrate their adoption, because they realize that the tools they build are political. As Meredith Whittaker, who left Google in 2019, put it, what these employees want is nothing short of "a say and control over the products they build."[57] After decades that saw the pursuit of profit take an outsized role, they have mobilized to push Silicon Valley, and high-tech culture more broadly, toward emphasizing other dimensions, as well, like protecting democratic values and human rights in business decisions and making their workplaces more inclusive. It is this aspiration that, in 2021, led more than four hundred Google employees to create a union.[58] Called the Alphabet Workers Union, after Google's parent company, Alphabet, it strives "to

protect Alphabet workers, our global society, and our world. We promote solidarity, democracy, and social and economic justice."[59]

This movement for change led by tech employees from the inside and activists from the outside is as important as it is challenging,
in the face of these companies' inordinate power. To provide citizens,
consumers, and smaller companies with more information and more
alternatives to the services these giant corporations offer, regulation
is necessary too.

REGAINING CONTROL

If we are to rebalance power in the digital era, we need to gain
some measure of control over our personal data and the algorithms
that affect so many aspects of our lives. But where do we start? As
individuals, we have some ways to protect our privacy and data,
for example, using features that allow us to browse incognito and
delete our browsing histories when we close our computers, or
using alternative browsers and apps that better protect personal
information. Yet these features are useful only up to a point, as our
IP addresses are still visible, which means that our internet service
providers, our employers, and/or the government can still track our
activity online.

Ultimately, protecting ourselves from bias in the algorithms and
lack of control over personal data requires changing the laws and
then making sure they are enforced. Addressing the 2021 Computers,
Privacy and Data Protection conference, Apple's CEO, Tim Cook,
forcefully called for far-reaching data privacy reforms to "send a universal, humanistic response to those who claim a right to users' private information about what should not and will not be tolerated."[60]
Sundar Pichai has also called for such regulation. In an op-ed published in the *Financial Times* in 2020, he insisted that regulation was
needed and suggested that existing "rules such as Europe's General
Data Protection Regulation can serve as a strong foundation."[61]

In 2016, the European Union passed the General Data Protection Regulation (GDPR). This landmark legislation gives every European citizen free access to the information companies collect about them, forces companies to seek explicit consent for data collection, limits what data can be collected, and gives citizens the right to seek compensation for privacy breaches.[62] The law's passage did not mark the end of the work for activists who had been tirelessly pushing for it, however. On May 25, 2018, the day the regulation came into effect, Austrian lawyer and privacy activist Max Schrems and his organization, noyb (short for "none of your business"), filed legal cases against Facebook and Google, specifically targeting their now illegal take-it-or-leave-it privacy policies.[63] In February 2020, noyb filed an additional complaint against Amazon on their data security practices.[64]

Activists like Schrems and noyb see their role as that of a watchdog, bringing important cases and privacy issues to the attention of legal and regulatory agencies. In addition to changing the laws, the action of activists and organizations—a movement, in short—continues to be essential to leverage the new legislation and force companies as well as public authorities to comply with it. As legal scholar Lina Khan has noted, relevant laws are often already in the books, but they aren't applied consistently and sometimes languish unused for decades, as is the case for antitrust legislation in the United States.[65]

Voices like Khan's are helping revive governmental oversight of Big Tech, with U.S. lawmakers and attorney generals at both state and federal levels beginning to challenge companies that operate as monopolies in many markets for their anti-competitive practices.[66] So while European legislators have been the most aggressive thus far in fining technology corporations for behavior they consider an abuse of their market domination,[67] governments around the world have been waking up to the threat of these extreme power imbalances, and legislative proposals are increasingly under consideration.[68] Antitrust legislation is not the only domain in which there has been movement. In 2021, Australia passed a law requiring social media companies to pay for the journalism appearing on their platforms, despite their protestations—a landmark step toward restoring a measure of power for public-interest journalism.[69] Judicial systems are also beginning to hold tech companies to account for algorithmic bias. In a watershed 2021 lawsuit brought by delivery riders against food app Deliveroo, a court in Bologna, Italy, ruled that even if an algorithm discriminates against workers unintentionally, a company can still be held liable and be forced to pay damages.[70]

It isn't easy to regulate complex technologies that tend to evolve rapidly, however. Aware of the critical role that activists with technical expertise can play in crafting effective regulation, Meredith, in her new position as the head of the AI Now Institute that she cofounded, has continued her advocacy to make the tech industry more inclusive and for the responsible and ethical use of artificial intelligence in relation to issues of race, gender, and power.[71] In her 2019 testimony before the U.S. House Committee on Science, Space, and Technology, she outlined key priorities related to AI, including the need to halt both governmental and commercial use of facial recognition in sensitive social and political contexts until the risks are fully studied and adequate regulations, such as biometric privacy laws and assessments to vet algorithms for bias, are in place.[72]

The latter will be particularly challenging, not only in terms of deciding where responsibility for assessing algorithms for bias should rest, but also because what constitutes a fair algorithm is a complex question, one that engineers, computer scientists, and legal scholars on the front lines of ethical AI development are asking with increasing urgency.[73] But we do know some things about how algorithms function and where we are better equipped to exercise oversight. Computer scientists have a saying: "garbage in, garbage out," meaning that if you feed an algorithm biased inputs, you will get biased outputs.[74] Although those who develop these algorithms may not directly choose what the output of an algorithm will be (AI algorithms usually include too many input variables for anyone to control directly), they do control its parameters. Critically, they decide what data to "feed" the algorithm, and they fine-tune and tweak it to modify how it learns. In facial recognition technology, for example, the disproportionate misidentification of Black faces compared to White faces can partly be addressed by feeding the algorithm a disproportionate number of images of Black faces, and then measuring the accuracy of the algorithm's output.[75] Requiring transparency about the training data that are fed to the algorithm and the measurement of its outputs is an attainable goal for regulatory intervention.

As we take action to regain control over technology, the kind of inclusive mindset that Bunker Roy had when he created the Barefoot College will be increasingly important. As his successor Meagan told us: "It is only when women in the developing world are able to sit at the table with engineers, designing technology that better meets human needs, that we will be on the way to creating a technological revolution that is inclusive to all." Nezuma's experience is a testament to the positive impact that technology can have on people's lives when its design and implications are carefully thought through, and the time is taken to train people in its use.

Such training is becoming more important by the day, as automation increasingly replaces human workers with computers and machines.[76] The Organization for Economic Co-operation and Development (OECD) now puts 22 to 45 percent of existing jobs at risk of vanishing across its member countries.[77] Some of the resistance to the technology companies stems not only from legitimate concern about their outsized power, but also from the loss of autonomy and sense of achievement that workers and professionals in many fields are experiencing as the resources they have to offer lose value in the marketplace. It's a scary place to be, one that deprives people of their safety and self-esteem and can turn them into Luddites. But while automation can make humans increasingly irrelevant for tasks that can be codified and repeated, it also makes people increasingly indispensable in performing tasks that require creativity and social skills.[78] The power of human workers over digital machines hinges on the execution of non-routine tasks, physical dexterity and versatility, ideation and originality, social perception, persuasion and trust, as well as the design of human-machine partnerships.

Investing in people's (re)training will require providing points of entry to education and skills development tailored to both adults and youth and adjusted to people's level of literacy.[79] This requires educational systems capable of developing not just people's technical skills, but also their cultural, moral, artistic, scientific, and critical capabilities. These capabilities are what differentiates us from machines and what our unique value — and thus our power — depend on.

PUTTING POWER IN THE HANDS OF MANY

Humankind's pursuit of safety and self-esteem has driven us to develop technologies that have enabled us to explore, control, and leverage our environment. We have learned to master new tools, from water purification and wind energy to smartphones and robots. And scientists have now embarked on the journey to modify the very essence of life itself: our DNA and that of other species. Advances in gene editing technology, like CRISPR,[80] have the potential to cure many crippling diseases and modify forms of life to secure food supplies for all, while curbing deleterious human impacts on the environment. Yet, for all our mastery, the persistence of vast inequalities and the frequency of ecological crises from hurricanes to wildfires have taught us two critical lessons.

The first is that with each wave of technological change, power changes hands but doesn't necessarily become more equally distributed. The digital revolution is one example among many of how new technologies can result in the concentration of power and wealth in the hands of a few individuals and organizations. Social entrepreneur Greg Brodsky put it this way: "Technology has disrupted almost every part of the economy: the gig economy, gaming, shopping, and how to book hotels. But the one thing the technology sector has not been willing to touch is ownership itself. In some ways, the tech sector is just recreating the wealth inequality in every other part of the economy."[81]

The second lesson is one in humility: Even the most sophisticated technologies will never allow us to control everything, as Mother Nature keeps reminding us. Some of the advances we have engineered have backfired. Our exploitation of the world's resources has accelerated anthropogenic climate changes that risk transforming life on Earth as we know it. While coal and oil have literally powered modern industries and economies, the global warming resulting from greenhouse gas emissions is altering the natural equilibria that have made our climate predictable and allowed human civilizations to develop for the past twelve thousand years.[82]

Although we cannot control everything, we do control how we choose to organize ourselves as a society. And we can control when, how, and for what purposes we use technology. Some will argue that markets are the solution to difficult decisions about whether a technology should be used. Yet the mere demand for a product does not warrant its existence. Investors lining up to get their share of a bustling surveillance technology market is no justification for its widespread use. Such unrestrained markets—free from political and moral oversight—powered the transatlantic slave trade that deported more than ten million Africans to America over three hundred years.[83] Undiscerning reliance on markets also prompted the corporate world's radical shift to the mantra of shareholder profit maximization. Corporate leaders and investors lost sight of the environmental and societal implications of their activities, exacerbating environmental destruction and socioeconomic inequalities. Leaving control of technology to the market alone will make the world less safe, less humane, and even more unequal and conceivably doom humanity to extinction.

If not the market alone, then who: The technical experts who have built these technologies and know more about them? At best, they may demand moral accountability, as many tech employees have, and remain faithful to their higher purpose. At worst, however, we risk losing the moral compass of our social systems because, as Renaissance writer François Rabelais presciently observed, "science without conscience is only ruin of the soul."[84] Leaving control over new technologies to *any* small group is dangerous, as it gives them permission to use them for their own benefit and thus free rein to concentrate ever more power in their own hands. It's not hard to imagine the rich and powerful leveraging technologies like CRISPR to pay for genetic enhancements, longer and healthier lifespans, and what they consider to be genetically superior offspring.[85] This is the kind of dystopia depicted in many books and movies, from Aldous Huxley's 1932 novel, *Brave New World*, to the more recent movie *Gattaca*, and we are not immune to transforming it into reality.

Technological change always presents us with a choice between two paths: one leads to power for a minority, with dangerous consequences for everyone else; the other leads to shared decision-making about how to organize access to newly valued technologies. The only way for us to navigate this crossroads is to grasp what we can do to regain control over technology, assess its value in terms of its usefulness for society, and democratize access to it. Though their track records are far from perfect, both public policy and private enterprise initiatives have shown us that it is eminently possible to deploy technology not to maximize profits, but to optimize access, fairness, privacy, and usability.[86] This is how power falls in the hands of many. And we can achieve and sustain such a democratization of power if we proactively keep it in check.

Chapter 8

Power in Check

P alazzo Pubblico offers stunning views of Siena's shell-shaped Piazza del Campo, best known for the Palio horse race held there every summer since 1633. Visitors who manage to pull themselves away from Piazza del Campo's hypnotic beauty and venture into Palazzo Pubblico are rewarded with another memorable sight: *The Allegory of Good and Bad Government* by Ambrogio Lorenzetti, an extraordinary oeuvre of political art of medieval Italy.

When Lorenzetti painted the series of frescoes in 1338 and 1339, the Republic of Siena was one of the most powerful and prosperous Italian city-states. It was governed by nine elected citizens, the Government of the Nine, who remained in office for only two months, before giving way to another nine.[1] The citizens of Siena commissioned the frescoes for the Sala della Pace (or Hall of Peace), where the nine governors met, to inspire their work and remind them of the momentous consequences of their decisions. The first two frescoes— one filled with allegorical figures of virtue and the other with symbols of evil—compare Good Government with Bad. The second pair provides contrasting views of a city, intended to be Siena: one showing citizens living together in safety, order, harmony, and prosperity; the other showing the city in ruins, its citizenry overcome by violence and destitution. Thousands of citizens were part of the Government of the Nine in its sixty-eight years of existence, when Siena enjoyed a period of splendor in urban architecture and cultural advances.[2] During a politically turbulent century, marked by violent party struggles and constant governmental upheaval, the contrast between good and bad governance was vivid and stark.

Why do systems of governance matter so much? The answer is simple: No matter how hard we human beings try, we cannot rely solely on our good intentions to keep power's hubris and egotism in check. History and personal experience teach us to be wary of excessive power in any form.[3] Give any individual enough power for enough time and the risk of abuse inevitably increases. Even Vera Cordeiro, the Brazilian doctor we met in chapter 2, who was animated by a noble purpose, risked falling into this trap as her own fame and that of her NGO grew.

Although the risks of excessive power concentration can never be fully eradicated, social science has taught us a great deal about how to contain it. As the citizens of fourteenth-century Siena intuited, keeping power in check requires setting structural limits that ensure two things: first, that power is shared rather than concentrated in the hands of an individual or small group; and second, that those who are in power are held accountable. When family members and colleagues helped Vera recognize the deleterious effects power was having on her, she understood intuitively that she had to institute new practices that shared power and enabled others to hold her accountable in team meetings. As we will see, these two levers—sharing power and power accountability—apply not only to an individual leader of a team or to the governors of a medieval city-state, but to any workplace and any society. We have proven tools that we can all use to keep our power and that of others in check at work and in society.

SHARING POWER AT WORK

In 2013, Ellen Ochoa became the director of the Johnson Space Center (JSC), the home of NASA's mission control and astronaut training program. The first Latina astronaut to have gone to space, she had worked tirelessly to accomplish her dreams. She knew firsthand that for someone like her, being the most qualified for a job was no guarantee of getting it. "If you are a White male engineer, people are just going to assume that you're a good engineer unless proven otherwise; whereas if you come in as a woman engineer, or a Black engineer, or a Latinx engineer, you don't get the benefit of the doubt. You're going to have to prove yourself before anybody will pay attention to you."[4]

Ellen's experience was neither unique nor limited to the world of engineering. Organizational power in Western countries remains largely concentrated in the hands of White men, despite the growing number of qualified people from other demographic groups in the workplace. These same groups also continue to be disadvantaged in compensation and access to resources compared to groups with long-standing power differentials in their favor.[5] Organizations have thus contributed to reproducing gender and racial inequalities that stem from the power hierarchies we dissected in chapter 5.[6]

This realization was what led Michael Coats, Ellen's predecessor as JSC's director, to make diversity and inclusion one of the priorities of his tenure. A former astronaut, his experiences in both the public and private sectors had made him "a firm believer in the power of diversity," as he put it.[7] Michael didn't just talk about the need to make the JSC more inclusive, he worked closely with Ellen, then his deputy director, to make it more inclusive. "He said that he wanted women and racial minorities to have the same opportunities men like him had. At first, I was surprised," Ellen recalled, "but we got to work, and it was clear this was not just discourse; he was committed to making change happen."

Diversity, they advocated, could contribute to innovation. "Both Mike and I believed that if we failed to make every single person at JSC feel valued at work so they could be the best version of themselves, we were limiting the organization's potential," Ellen explained. That was not their only rationale, though. "It's not only the right thing for the organization, it's the right thing, period. My personal experience made that clear. After all, I was a Latina in STEM! From my days as a PhD student in physics . . . I was made to understand women weren't 'supposed to be engineers,' [and to feel] like an outsider who didn't belong."

Michael's and Ellen's belief that making the Johnson Space Center a more inclusive place could help the organization thrive aligns with research on diversity that has found that it can lead to increased organizational effectiveness.[8] Demographic diversity alone will not make an organization more inclusive, however. For that to happen, power has to be shared more equally across all demographic groups, instead of remaining concentrated in the hands of the usual suspects.[9] The question for Michael and Ellen, and one that organizations continue to grapple with today, was how to orchestrate such a shift.

For some time, public attention had concentrated on encouraging women to "lean in"[10] and climb the organizational ladder. Ellen had learned the hard way, though, that as important as it is to put your hand up, voice your opinion, and insist on being heard and considered, "leaning in" wasn't enough to change the distribution of power in an organization. Instead of playing the game better, what was needed was changing the rules of the game.

Ellen's experience had also taught her that while getting a few people from underrepresented groups into senior roles could help break down barriers and inspire others, it would barely change the distribution of power. While such token representatives are visible, their heightened visibility creates more pressure for them to perform at higher levels. They are also likely to feel—and be—isolated, and their opinions may be marginalized. In her pioneering research,

Rosabeth Moss Kanter pointed out that the psychological consequences of tokenism—unsatisfactory social relationships, miserable
self-imagery, frustration from contradictory demands, inhibition of
self-expression, and feelings of inadequacy and self-hatred—take an
enormous toll, even if the person's work performance is exemplary.[11]
Yet many companies have indulged in just this sort of tokenism, appointing a small number of people from underrepresented groups
to leadership and Board positions, as symbols of gender and racial
equality.[12] Not only does this practice fail to enable real power redistribution, it can be a real obstacle to it.

Together with Alicia DeSantola and Lakshmi Ramarajan, we
studied the composition of the Boards of more than two thousand
entrepreneurial ventures over two decades and found that while
they were likely to add a woman to the Board at the time of an IPO
if they had none, they were unlikely to add a second woman if one
was already serving.[13] Having one woman has seemed sufficient to
be regarded as doing the right thing. But it is certainly not enough to
change power dynamics. Research on Boards has found that a critical mass (set at around 30 percent by some) must be reached for the
Board environment to become more receptive to meaningful contributions in terms of oversight, new ideas, and divergent thinking.[14]

What else, then, could Ellen and Mike do to change the distribution of power? Diversity training meant to make employees aware
of their unconscious biases and readjust their behavior to overcome
them is a popular tool; and its popularity makes sense because, as we
saw in chapter 5, biases rooted in entrenched stereotypes are major
obstacles to changing the distribution of power. So, Ellen and Mike
made diversity training mandatory for all employees at JSC. They
knew, however, that such training, on its own, doesn't alter behavior
or change the workplace,[15] because it typically does nothing to give
those who are discriminated against access to valued resources. From
that standpoint, diversity training doesn't fundamentally change or
even challenge who has power in the organization. In fact, when

people who go through it believe that the mere existence of diversity training makes their organization more meritocratic, it might even be counterproductive. Such complacency opens the door to even more discrimination.[16]

The problem is not diversity training, per se—it's thinking that it alone solves the problem. Researchers who have studied what it takes to make an organization's culture more inclusive have reached the same conclusion: Real change requires multipronged interventions that enable the redistribution of power.[17] In addition to focusing on people's individual attitudes and biases, such change efforts require reconsidering all the organization's existing processes and systems—from recruiting to promotion, compensation, and access to plum professional opportunities—in order to understand how they contribute to unequal access to resources for different groups in the organization.[18]

To undertake these very tasks, Michael and Ellen established an Innovation and Inclusion Council, a committee of senior leaders, human resources representatives, members of the Office of Diversity and Equal Opportunity, and employee representatives who rotated for two-year terms. Entrusting these tasks to a committee enables both data-driven decision-making and in-depth diagnosis of organizational practices.[19] Absent such diagnosis, the risk is that the most visible inequalities are denounced, but their causes are never tackled.[20]

The council systematically tracked who applied to jobs and who was promoted. It led them to realize that JSC needed to expand its recruiting channels and involve not just one senior person per department, but a diverse group of team members in the recruiting process. The objective was to cut off network-based recruitment in favor of recruiting through broader, more diverse channels. Doing so requires proactively reaching out to, and investing in, organizations that work with underrepresented groups[21] and then, ideally, adhering to blind résumé reviews, whereby information on a candidate's age, gender, race, and socioeconomic background is hidden as much as possible.[22] The goal is to conduct a recruitment process that is systematic and equitable for all candidates, rather than relying on an interviewer's gut feel or a candidate's cultural fit, which so often excludes high-potential candidates who don't have the same profile as the people in charge of hiring.[23]

A fairer recruiting process is no guarantee that the new hires will succeed, however. So, the council turned to the Center's employees to better understand the challenges they faced and how the organization could help address them. "If you want to address a problem, you need to talk to those who are experiencing it," Ellen told us. Management scholars Laura Morgan Roberts and Tony Mayo agree, underscoring the importance of engaging in this kind of dialogue to build trust, foster empathy, and enable perspectives-sharing.[24] Listening to those who are discriminated against and giving them a say in redesigning the organization's policies and procedures, can reduce the risk of discrimination, while also redistributing power within the organization.[25]

These conversations provided a critical insight for Ellen when she became JSC's director and continued the work she had started with Michael and the council members. They had been paying scant attention to another way in which people gain power in organizations: through the host of informal opportunities that give employees access to networks, plum assignments, visibility, and other valuable resources. Deciding who would stand in for a manager on leave, participate on a center-wide team, or give a tour of the center to an influential guest—like a member of Congress or the director of the White House Office of Science and Technology Policy—typically fell to the department heads. And, as is common across many workplaces, they would typically turn to their "go-to" person. Hence the virtuous (or vicious) cycle of opportunity (or exclusion) would continue. To disrupt this pattern, Ellen piloted and then launched the Transparency Opportunity Program (TOP), which posted internally all informal opportunities (coined "TOPportunities" by the staff), so that people who might have been overlooked, but were eager and ready to contribute had a chance to volunteer. The system was designed to ensure that everyone at the Center knew about existing opportunities and to encourage underrepresented groups to seize them.

Then, Ellen went a step further, one that is crucial for changing a culture: She made the implementation of TOP part of managers' performance evaluation. Going forward, managers' reviews would be linked, in part, to their ability to foster this cultural change and distribute resources more fairly within their teams. Ellen's strategy paid off. Opportunities were more fairly distributed across employees by the time she left her position. Vanessa Wyche, who worked at the JSC at the time and went on to become the center's deputy director a year after Ellen's departure, recalled, "Ellen didn't just climb up the ladder by herself; she climbed, and she brought other people along. And it's a lasting legacy. I would not be in the chair that I am in today if Ellen Ochoa had not made it such that I could have the visibility and the opportunities to be able to be selected. She did that not only for me, but for so many of us women and minorities. She helped redistribute and share power."

Ellen was proud of the organization's progress, but, as she told us, "this work isn't about reaching a destination. It requires constant vigilance, creativity, and renewed commitment." While the route to power sharing remains long and winding, we now have a roadmap for orchestrating this shift. As the social psychologist and diversity scholar Robert Livingston puts it, "The real challenge for organizations is not figuring out 'What we can do,' but rather, 'Are we willing to do it?'"[26]

Once we achieve a more equitable power distribution in organizations, the challenge is to hold those with power to account. Everything we have learned about power and its effects on human psychology makes it clear that those who have power need to be held accountable, no matter what their demographic characteristics and aspirations may be. None of us is immune to hubris and self-focus—not even Miriam, the Holocaust survivor we met in chapter 2, who was horrified to have felt superior and distant from "the little people" after experiencing power for just one day. Hopefully tomorrow's leaders will be more diverse than they are today, but we will still run the risk of power abuse, unless everyone in power is held accountable.

ACCOUNTABILITY IN ORGANIZATIONS: TO WHOM AND FOR WHAT?

Whenever we entrust someone else with the power to make decisions and take action on our behalf, we run the risk that they will use this power against us. Why? Because the things the decision maker (the agent) prioritizes may run counter to our (the principal's) priorities. This is what economists call a principal-agent problem, and the relationship between corporate management and shareholders in companies is a prime example: When the owners of a company delegate the management of their business to its CEO and other executives, they give those executives a level of power that triggers the need for oversight and accountability. Is this because every executive is a crook? Not at all. It's just that, like every power holder, they are vulnerable to being intoxicated by it, and counting exclusively on their self-restraint in the exercise of that power is unwise.

As far back as 1363, the wool merchants who came together to organize one of the first English trading companies recognized this problem and developed governance structures to keep an eye on power holders. They elected a "mayor" (comparable to a CEO today) who was in charge of governing their affairs. And they counterbalanced this role by inaugurating a twenty-four-member council to govern the company—a feature that would resurface in other organizations, including the Bank of England, which went a step further and barred one-third of its directors from seeking re-election after their one-year term.[27]

These councils were the predecessors of modern-day Boards of Directors, which divide power between a company's top executives and the members of the Board who represent the shareholders' interests and are responsible for monitoring the company's activities and overseeing the top executives.[28] Boards are recognized as one of the most critical levers of oversight, and yet not all organizations have an active Board. Moreover, despite their longstanding history, Boards' ability and willingness to exercise oversight varies considerably from one organization to another.

Experts who study Boards have noted multiple barriers to directors' adequately monitoring management's actions. These include the complexity of the issues that companies face, the reluctance of some Board members to go against the wishes of top management, and the difficulty of working effectively as a team when the members get together only a few times a year. Perhaps most important, because Board members often have many other commitments, they may have neither the bandwidth nor the motivation to delve into their operations with a fine-tooth comb.[29]

Some of these barriers can be addressed by changing Board recruiting practices. Until quite recently, most director searches were conducted within the inner circle of the corporate elite, resulting in directors connected to one another, and to management, through direct and indirect channels.[30] These interlocks were so strong that had a virus infected the Board of Chase Manhattan Bank in January 1999, it could have spread to 97 percent of the largest 600 public firms in the United States by May via their monthly Board meetings![31] Beyond the risk of viral spread, why is this so problematic? Because close ties engender lax oversight, as a series of corporate scandals—of which Enron is the poster child—have highlighted. In response, recruiting practices are changing,[32] and directors who sit on multiple Boards have become less desirable, both because they have less time to dedicate to each of the organizations they serve, and because they are less likely to be fully independent.

Even when directors fulfill their oversight duties, they do so mostly on behalf of shareholders whose capital is invested in the company.[33] However, companies have other stakeholders on whom they depend and who are directly affected by corporate activities—including employees, customers, suppliers, and more broadly, the general public—but who mostly have no say in the company's direction. It is not surprising, then, that in many companies the past decades have been marked by the sole pursuit of shareholder value maximization.

An unmistakable symptom of this concentration of power in the hands of shareholders and top executives is the widening income gap between top managers and workers. The average ratio of highest to lowest salary in U.S. corporations grew from 20-to-1 in 1965 to 320-to-1 by 2019. Likewise, CEO pay in the United States increased by 1,167 percent between 1978 and 2019, while worker pay grew only 14 percent.[34] Beyond increasing inequalities, this power imbalance has had dramatic environmental consequences as some leaders of the fossil fuel industry have intentionally hidden the environmental damage caused by their companies' activities to pursue profit unbridled, as we discussed in chapter 3.[35]

Society has not remained passive: Over the past decades, activists around the world have joined forces to agitate against corporate greed and alert the public to the dangers of capitalism run amok. The environmental battles that have pitted big lobbyists against environmental activists epitomize this tug and pull, and this multigenerational mobilization effort is starting to pay off. Employees have also been pushing for change from within, as we saw in chapter 7, organizing internally to urge executives to stop focusing solely on shareholder value maximization and account for their company's social and environmental impact, too.

In the face of this increased pressure, many corporate leaders have expressed their desire to serve other stakeholders in addition to their shareholders.[36] In August 2019, the Business Roundtable, whose membership includes the CEOs of most major U.S. corporations, issued a statement rejecting the primacy of shareholders in favor of creating value for their employees and stakeholders, including their customers, and society at large. But when it comes to accountability to these groups, as of a year later, at least, not much had changed. A study revealed that when COVID started spreading in the spring of 2020, companies that signed the Business Roundtable statement fired their employees 20 percent more than those that did not sign the statement.[37] They were also less likely to donate to relief efforts, offer customer discounts, or shift production to pandemic-related goods. The takeaway is not surprising: If we leave it to those in power to change, they may change their discourse but rarely their behavior.

The good news is that new structures and systems that hold companies accountable not only for their financial performance, but also for their social and environmental impact, make real change possible.[38] The Sustainability Accounting Standards Board created in 2011 by Jean Rogers, whom you met in chapter 6, is a prime example.[39] The metrics that standard setting organizations like SASB have created are not, in themselves, enough to drive change. But complementary forces are coming into play with new legal forms—such as benefit corporations, or B-Corps, in the United States, Community Interest Companies in the United Kingdom, and *sociétés à mission* in France—paving the way for corporations to embrace the pursuit of a triple (social, environmental, and financial) bottom line and for their Boards to be held accountable for these multiple objectives.[40] The infrastructure that surrounds companies—external auditors, financial analysts, and investors—is also beginning to slowly shift its mindset, as the growing number of impact investors, who seek out companies, organizations, and funds with social and environmental objectives alongside a financial return, shows.[41]

Even with new accountability systems, though, concentration of power is hard to avoid if only shareholders are represented on Boards. Such excessive power imbalance between those who invest their financial capital (the shareholders) and those who invest their labor and intellect (the workers) is problematic, not only because it is unfair, but also because it leaves the power of shareholders unchecked.[42] In a provocative statement, the philosopher Elizabeth Anderson suggests that "bosses are dictators, and workers are their subjects," as they are not represented in the governance of their workplaces.[43] The decision to fire employees in a recession instead of cutting management pay to stay afloat, or to offer paid sick leave in the midst of a pandemic, isn't up to workers. In most companies, representatives of shareholders on the Board of Directors and top management still make all strategic decisions.

Fortunately, there is a simple solution: giving more power to employees.[44]

POWER TO THE WORKERS

Two toddlers at home and six days a week trudging across the city for hours of house cleaning took a toll on Sandra Lopez. There was no overtime if the work took longer than expected. And when, as they often did, clients spontaneously asked for an extra service, like cleaning the windows or the ceiling fan, renegotiating the price was often uncomfortable and, with Sandra's limited English, just plain hard.

These working conditions represent the reality for most domestic workers, today and throughout history. Some sixty-seven million domestic workers worldwide—one out of twenty-five women workers—operate quasi invisibly, many of them as part of the informal economy, in the private confines of people's homes, caring for their children, cleaning their rooms, and tending to the elderly.[45] The work is intimate and mostly unregulated. In the United States, domestic workers, alongside farmworkers, were excluded from New Deal worker-protection laws. As Palak Shah, the social innovations director of the National Domestic Workers Alliance in the United

States, told us, "these labor markets have been informal, invisible, and underground for generations. For the longest time, domestic workers were not protected."[46] Hence, for them, questions of employer power and accountability are both crucial and challenging, as the intimate nature of their work can blur the lines between professional and personal relationships. It prompts a broader question, too: What limits, if any, exist on the power of employers over workers?

For many workers, the response to this question is clear: collective action. In the struggle to achieve worker protections, including the right to unionize, the law has played a key role. Unions, as we saw in chapter 5, have been pivotal in bringing workers together to advocate for legal changes to rebalance power in their relationship with employers.[47] Yet unions are often polarizing. Critics argue that they protect unproductive workers, suppress individual voice, make unreasonable demands insensitive to business imperatives, trigger costly lawsuits and arbitrations, and are vulnerable to corruption. While instances of such behavior certainly exist, unions have proven essential to shared prosperity in industrialized societies. Unionized workers have better benefits and wages than non-union workers. Their gains also lead to improvements for non-unionized workers, as their employment terms set the standard. These benefits give workers a larger share of the prosperity created by a company, without decreases in productivity.[48] In the mid-twentieth century, when unionization rates were at their highest in the U.S., unions helped redirect profits into wage increases and hence decreased overall inequality. But when unions lose power—as has been the case in the U.S. since the second half of the twentieth century—or when workers face legal barriers to unionizing, the power imbalance is such that workers' rights are jeopardized[49] and economic growth stunted.[50]

For some, like domestic workers, collective action is especially challenging, because they don't share a common workplace. But difficult doesn't mean impossible, as Ai-jen Poo, the cofounder of the National Domestic Workers Alliance, told us.[51] In 2003, she became involved in an organizing campaign in which 250 domestic workers from across New York City came together to launch a movement to gain basic rights for their highly decentralized and isolated workforce. After six years of sleepless nights and busing domestic workers to the state capitol to protest and lobby, the organizers achieved a breakthrough: New York became the first state to sign the domestic workers' Bill of Rights, which grants them overtime pay, paid time off, protections from harassment, severance pay, and more.[52] The law isn't perfect, and access to justice to fight delinquent employers remains a barrier; but it has contributed to shift the daily balance of power for workers like Sandra, another testament to the importance of collective organizing.

In today's gig economy, the absence of legal protections against abusive power is an issue that affects many other workers. Consider ride-share drivers and delivery food workers who, as we write, do not qualify as "employees" in many countries. Even though the companies that engage with these purportedly "self-employed contractors" cannot operate their businesses without them, they have unilateral control over their working conditions. So, the health and financial risks of cycling through busy cities or maintaining their cars fall on the workers, while the benefits (from selling highly priced shares) accrue to the owners.

Even with better legal protections for workers in the gig and informal economies, however, true power sharing requires that organizations be redesigned. To see how, let's return to Sandra Lopez. Her working conditions have evolved significantly: She now uses an application called Up & Go that matches her to clients across the city. You might assume that Up & Go, like Uber or DoorDash, holds tremendous power over Sandra because it controls access to her critical resource—her clients. But in this case, the balance of power is the other way around, because Sandra is not only a user of the platform, she is also an owner. In 2018, she came across a flyer in her Brooklyn neighborhood from the Center for Family Life, which was incubating a program for home cleaning cooperatives. Being the boss and the founder of a business sounded great to Sandra, and she launched into the year-long program with gusto, working nights and weekends alongside seventeen other women, most of them, like her, immigrants from Mexico or Central America.

Cooperatives give workers, through their ownership, a real say in the direction of the organization. In Sandra's cooperative, the women voted on what services to offer and how much to charge, doubling her income and allowing her to work fewer hours and spend more time with her children. "People tend to assume that the salary is the best advantage. But for me, it's the flexibility and the gift of time with my family. We work so hard. We tend to forget just how important our quality of life is," she told us. The cooperative is designed to meet the worker-owner's needs. For instance, communications or negotiations are supported by the cooperative's telephone or in-app customer service, which is bilingual and can relay critical information in Spanish. Clients book services through the app, so expectations are clear upon arrival. And the cooperative trains the worker-owners about the New York Bill of Rights. "By coming together, we created a structure that supports all of us. The cooperative protects us and fights for our interests. Alone, I never had the same power." For comparison, in 2019, as Uber prepared to go public, it cut driver pay to make its shares more attractive.[53] Meanwhile, in Sandra's cooperative, all profits go directly back to Sandra and her cofounders, except for the amounts they choose to reinvest in the organization itself. They control the valuable resources, so they have power.

As Sandra shared her story with us, it was apparent that this journey had changed her: "Before becoming an owner, I was terribly shy. I couldn't speak up in front of people, or for myself, really. But as I went through the program and learned so much about my rights and about the cooperative process, I felt my self-assurance gradually blossom. I feel like I know what I'm talking about. I know my work and its value. And that self-confidence has affected my personal life, too."

Cooperatives are neither new nor unique to domestic work. For instance, twenty million homes, workplaces, and schools in the U.S. are electrically powered by energy co-ops, aligning prices with the interests of the users.[54] These differences in governance structure are far from trivial. They define who controls what in the workplace. Economist and sociologist Juliet Schor makes a compelling case for cooperatives and regulatory reforms to constrain the actions of platforms, so that the value generated by the gig economy can be shared more equitably.[55] Once again, it all comes down to power sharing and accountability.

Workplaces other than cooperatives remain both hierarchical and unaccountable to most of their workers; but not all of them. Germany, the Netherlands, and some Nordic countries have introduced codetermination laws, guaranteeing worker representation on Boards, which provides a space for top management, shareholders, and workers to negotiate and collaborate around the direction of the company.[56] Yet even with codetermination, shareholders often have a tie-breaking vote, meaning that workers cannot outvote shareholders.[57] This is why the social scientist Isabelle Ferreras proposes to go further by giving both representatives of the shareholders and the workers real decision-making power.[58] This mutual dependence would force them to work together to decide the future of their company. It remains to be seen whether the best way to achieve this kind of joint decision-making is to create two chambers with equal power (one for each group of representatives) or to have representatives of the employees join the existing Board and be given as much decision-making power as the non-employee representatives. What matters ultimately is for the interests of workers to be represented, for all the parties to debate with one another and make more informed strategic decisions, and for the workers to have the power to influence these decisions—especially the ones that directly affect them. Without such a democratization of firms, workers will never have a real say in companies.[59]

Moral reasons alone would make such power rebalancing necessary. But, critically, our research reveals that organizations with more democratic decision-making processes are often better equipped to pursue social and environmental goals in addition to financial ones.[60] The diversity of perspectives, which comes from allowing shareholders, top executives, *and* workers to make their voices heard, helps ensure that the firm does not focus only on one set of objectives to the detriment of others.[61] So, as we start requiring firms to meet stricter social and environmental standards, we can look to those that have already created spaces for democratic decision-making, such as cooperatives, to show the way. This should come as no surprise: Democracy ensures a more balanced distribution of power, enabling the pursuit of more diverse objectives instead of focusing on the narrower goals of a small group of people.[62] This is as true in organizations as it is in society.

POWER SHARING IN SOCIETY

Solon and Cleisthenes, both born in Athens more than 2,500 years ago, are known for innovative reforms that led to *demokratia*, signifying "rule by the people."[63] To forestall corruption and tyranny, these reforms introduced a system of checks and balances which ultimately included the separation of powers into several major political bodies, including the *ekklesia*, or assembly; the *boule*, a popular council that set the agenda of the *ekklesia*; and the *heliaia*, or the popular courts.[64] This democratic system lasted for more than a century before Athens, like most of Greece, fell under Macedonian hegemony in the fourth century BCE.[65]

The separation of powers in government came back into prominence in 1748, with the publication of *The Spirit of the Laws* by Charles-Louis de Secondat (better known as Montesquieu). In his view, the key to avoiding despotism was to divide the exercise of power across three different bodies of government—legislative, executive, and judicial—all bound by the rule of law. Because "constant experience shows us that every man invested with power is apt to abuse it," he wrote, "it is necessary from the very nature of things that power should be a check to power."[66] His proposition had a profound influence on the men who, a few decades later, wrote the U.S. Constitution, which established the separate powers of the Congress, the president, and the Supreme Court. Such a separation of powers is still at the core of modern democracies—a separation as vital as it is constantly vulnerable to erosion and downright demise,[67] as shifts from democracy to autocracy around the world have demonstrated.

Unlike in Athens, where any male citizen could join the *ekklesia* (which exercised what today we'd think of as legislative power), the Founding Fathers of the United States opted to entrust legislative responsibility to elected representatives, who would stay in office for a limited period of time. With this pivot to representative democracy, which has become nearly synonymous with modern democracy, the critical issue becomes whom we choose to represent us. And while we've probably all been in situations in which candidates we didn't support were elected, we accept their election, as it is our duty as citizens to do, as long as they respect the rules and step down when constitutionally required.

Sophisticated as these institutional designs may be, they do not provide sufficient protection against abuses of power. Enshrining the separation of power and term limits in a country's constitution is no guarantee against the creeping advance of autocracy: 2021 was the fifteenth consecutive year in which democracy regressed globally.[68] The processes that corrode democracies through the demolition of checks on power have been documented across societies and eras.[69] As historian Timothy Snyder reminds us, "The mistake is to assume that rulers who came to power through institutions cannot change or destroy those very institutions."[70] They can.

Often, it isn't a sudden and violent coup that kills democracy, but the slow and steady erosion of rights and freedoms that opens the door to autocracy by habituating the public to their loss. Such a loss is what Tope Ogundipe resisted in her work with Paradigm, a pan-African organization at the forefront of digital rights. Her mission, as the chief operations officer, was protecting Nigerians' freedom online. Safeguarding these rights requires constant vigilance which, she explained to us, is what taught her the importance of civic engagement.[71]

WE ARE ALL RESPONSIBLE FOR HOLDING THE POWERFUL ACCOUNTABLE

In December 2015, Nigerian senator Bala Ibn Na'Allah introduced a new law to limit freedom of expression online. If passed, the law would prohibit any posts made about any group (including all government agencies) that the government deemed false. The law would apply to public sites like Twitter and Facebook as well as to private messaging platforms like WhatsApp. The punishment for breaking it would be two years in prison or NGN2,000,000 (approximately US$10,000, at the time). People risked being jailed or going bankrupt for texting their opinions to friends.

Tope Ogundipe was furious, and she quickly gathered her team of local and international partners: Their priority was to uncover the proceedings surrounding the bill and share the information with the public, so its passage couldn't be cloaked in secrecy as the Senate preferred. Tope herself reached out to digital justice organizations she had been working with, like Freedom House, the Web Foundation, and PEN International. Together, they drafted an official letter to the Nigerian Senate, calling out the bill's "dangerous encroachment upon free expression" and asking for its cancellation.[72] Simultaneously, they launched an online campaign with the hashtag #NoToSocialMediaBill, and Tope reached out to traditional media organizations. To get your message out, nothing quite beats making it onto a prime time radio show in Lagos, where radio still blasts through millions of people's cars at rush hour.

Then Tope and this collection of internet organizations decided to move the campaign offline, too. They reached out to members through phone calls, WhatsApp conversations, and house visits. They attended community events and employed any means necessary to move citizens from the gesture of a retweet to the more risky but necessary act of protesting in the streets. Why did Tope lead this shift from online to in-person? Because she knew that the senators wanted to maintain peace in the streets of Nigeria. They feared protestors would question more than the social media bill and thus provoke further political instability. And she was right. On May 17, 2016, the Nigerian Senate threw out the bill, to the sound of protestors chanting outside the Senate doors.[73] Tope and her team had successfully exercised civic vigilance, preventing the government from taking power away from Nigeria's citizens.

A key piece of the puzzle of public accountability in modern democracies rests with each of us. Civic vigilance enables citizens to hold those in power accountable beyond the periodic ballot box.[74] In addition to voting, therefore, we have a critical role to play in exercising counter-powers and fostering the culture of deliberation without which democracy cannot be sustained.[75]

As Tope's story shows, the media is a critical tool for exercising civic vigilance. At its best it exposes, educates, and challenges citizens to understand the world around them and to scrutinize those in power. At its worst it strives to entertain rather than enlighten, fanning the flames of prejudice, fear and hatred and becoming a propaganda tool *par excellence* for autocratic leaders. This is particularly disturbing because, as philosopher and activist Cornel West put it, "democracy depends, in large part, on a free and frank press willing to speak painful truths to the public about our society, including the fact of their own complicity in superficiality and simplistic coverage."[76] The media contribute to shaping the answer to one of the key questions from the fundamentals of power, namely, "What do we value?"[77] And they play a special role in fueling debate among the population and, ideally, expressing the will—or rather the plurality of wills—of the people.

Journalists who are fighting for human rights across the world, like Yemeni activist and Nobel Prize winner Tawakkol Karman, are deeply aware of just how important freedom of expression is. As she told us, "There is no democracy without press freedom, [but] not just press freedom, because people think expression rights is just press freedom. No. It's more than that. Expression rights are the rights of the press, the right of accessing information, the right of movement of citizens, and that of demonstration. This combination of expression rights is the real gate and the real evidence of a truly democratic state."[78]

A free people must thus be vigilant, bear witness, and watch how the government responds to and solves problems to protect these rights. A free people must evaluate, judge, and, when necessary, denounce and obstruct the government's actions.[79] But this kind of civic engagement does not happen overnight. It has to be taught, nurtured, and passed on from one generation to another.

DEVELOPING ENLIGHTENED CITIZENS

Our ability to exercise civic vigilance relies on what the political scientist Danielle Allen calls "participatory readiness," which is a precondition for true political equality.[80] If citizens cannot understand the workings of democracy, "the people" cannot truly rule. Education is fundamental in understanding and exercising power.[81]

Not just any form of education will equip citizens with the knowledge and critical spirit that democratic engagement requires, however. Political theorist Antonio Gramsci underscored the ways in which traditional educational institutions and systems often perpetuate power hierarchies through exclusionary practices and narratives that keep the hegemony solidly in place. What is required, Gramsci argued, is an education that gives every child—not just those lucky enough to belong in the "right" social class—a formative experience that develops the student into "a person capable of thinking, studying, and ruling—or controlling those who rule."[82]

Such an educational system that develops individuals into citizens who can think for themselves and disagree constructively with respect, self-confidence, mental complexity, and openness to new and different ideas has already proven to be possible. Danish futurist and philosopher Lene Rachel Andersen and Swedish social theorist and entrepreneur Tomas Björkman provide an account of the educational revolution that peacefully transformed Scandinavian societies from poor feudal agricultural countries in the mid-1800s to prosperous industrialized countries starting in the early 1900s.[83]

At the root of this transformation is *Bildung*, an Enlightenment-inspired conception of education that goes beyond mere training and skill acquisition to encompass the lifelong development of a person's cultural and spiritual sensibilities, social and life skills, and intellectual depth and breadth.[84] The result is a thinking, autonomous citizenry capable of self-reflection, critical analysis, and an ever-expanding sense of responsibility beyond oneself toward family, neighbors, fellow citizens, society, humanity, and the planet. *Bildung* is moral and emotional growth that echoes the developmental path to power we outlined in chapter 2.

The Scandinavian countries that pivoted to *folk-Bildung* in the mid-1850s aimed to make such a holistic educational system available to swaths of the population—including peasants in rural communities and, later on, workers in cities—that had traditionally received little education of any kind. The idea of *folk-Bildung* was to give the poorest and least educated people time not just to develop stronger reading and writing skills, but also to engage with ambitious ideas that once would have been beyond their reach. The students in these folk high schools learned the latest farming techniques along

with the constitution and legislation of their country, its history, her-
itage, economics, and system of government. They developed technical skills along with democratic competencies, moral character, and
cultural awareness. What emerged were high-trust societies in which
people took part in authoring their collective future and where disagreement was welcome. Self-organizing community engagement
developed with a thriving peasant movement, workers' cooperatives, local community houses, public libraries, sports associations,
and enlightenment periodicals—one with the slogan "Knowledge
Is Power"—that popularized science, poetry, literature, and politics.
This sort of civic engagement and popular participation in volunteer
organizations and associations persists today.[85]

Far from utopian, *folk-Bildung* is achievable, as the Scandinavian experience demonstrates. This educational foundation allows
citizens to interpret and critique sources of information which is the
basis of a healthy democracy. We may not all agree; indeed, we rarely
if ever do. But at its best democracy pools our diverse opinions,
views, and priorities,[86] allowing our collective intelligence to surface
and making the outcome of our debates and dissention "smarter"
than the sum of our individual ideas.[87]

Sustaining such a culture of deliberation is challenging, however,
because the pressure on democratic engagement is constant and the
risk of harmful polarization ever present, especially when groups
of citizens lose respect for one another. Even the Scandinavian *Bildung* story has experienced cracks and fissures after many decades
of progress. Andersen and Björkman offer a clear-eyed account of
how, at the turn of the millennium, the school curricula of Nordic
countries started to refocus on conventional skills with an emphasis on commercial value at the expense of the connections between
moral development, history, culture, aesthetics, and a robust democracy. Growth stops and regresses when we stop cultivating it. But the
Scandinavian experience tells us that a self-aware citizenry can be
developed if we put our minds and resources to it.

EXERCISING OUR CIVIC MUSCLES

The Athenians' *demokratia* included neither women nor slaves. The Declaration of Independence's self-evident truth that "all men are created equal" did not apply to women, enslaved Africans, or Indigenous people. A few years later, on the other side of the Atlantic Ocean, the French revolutionary project also excluded women from its Declaration of the Rights of Man and the Citizen. To this day, democracy has yet to live up to its promise of equal rights, and two existential threats risk heightening power imbalances in democracies across the world.

The first is the concentration of wealth. Far from being a new threat, it is one that philosophers have warned against throughout human history. The French philosopher Rousseau spoke for many when he advised that, "As for riches, let no citizen be wealthy enough to buy another, and none poor enough to be forced to sell themself."[88] While the level of wealth concentration has varied over the centuries, the neoliberal capitalism of the past decades has given the wealthy few enormous influence over who is elected to positions of power and the decisions they make. The more money citizens give, research has found, the more voice they have. The situation is especially dire in the United States, where the courts have defended political contributions as a form of free speech and even extended this right to corporations. Instead of one-person-one-vote, it seems more accurate to say that we're seeing the rise of a one-dollar-one-vote political system.[89]

Funds for political parties and campaign contributions are only two of the avenues the wealthy have available to impose their will on democratic institutions and change the rules of the game in their favor. Some have also funded multimillion-dollar lobbying campaigns that led to the passage of laws that favored their interests.[90] Others have used the regulatory vacuum surrounding digital technologies to accumulate unparalleled wealth at the expense of citizen privacy. Still others have avoided paying their fair share of taxes by concealing their money in offshore accounts.[91] When just a few can control the most valued resources, they can use their power to sway any political system to serve their interests.[92] Without the ability to participate on an equal basis as citizens, we renounce our power, abandon the possibility of deciding our collective future, and surrender to the will of those more powerful than us.

The second, parallel threat to democracy stems from digital technologies, as we explored in the previous chapter. The asymmetry of control over information undermines citizens' ability to exercise civic oversight in multiple ways. To begin with, increased surveillance can squash protest and dissent, as activists like Tope know all too well.[93] Platform algorithms wired for profits spread controversial, inflammatory content to those most susceptible to engage with it[94]—content that is often blatantly false. By deciding what information we see and what opinions we hear, social media amplifies political polarization, while spreading disinformation and fake news.[95] Unregulated and nascent, hostile and profit-driven, the digital public sphere today falls woefully short of its democratic potential.[96]

Though no simple prescription exists to counter these threats, one element is clear: While the world of business and the global economy have been drastically transformed in the past half-century, our democratic institutions have yet to catch up. We need innovations that put power back in the hands of regular citizens. Working to ensure that everyone is eligible to vote, able to vote, and willing to vote is a critical piece of the puzzle.[97] But we too often fall into the trap of associating democracy with voting, when in reality it is a much more ambitious political project. What is at stake today is ensuring that all citizens—not just a subgroup[98]—actively participate in designing and refining the rules of the game. This is precisely why LaTosha Brown, the founder of Black Voters Matter Fund, has created an institute to give communities the tools to influence their own politics.

"We meet with community members and always start by listening. We want to know what issues they really care about, not just the stuff they hear on the news, stuff that matters to them and affects them."[99] Once LaTosha and her team have identified those key issues, they power map the field to identify key players and levers of change. They start small, with winning a seat on the school board or getting speed bumps installed in the neighborhood. But those small wins set the stage for a string of other actions that build the community's power to act and its citizens' capacity to organize. "A sizable part of what we do is to get people to feel their own sense of power. It's not just about the outcome. It's about human agency. And building that human connection." This work, building human connection to spur collective action, helps strengthen the muscle of democracy, which sorely needs a workout.[100]

Participative democracy initiatives that aim to shift power into the hands of regular people are also emerging across the world. France, Vancouver in Canada, and Ireland, among others, have made use of near-randomly selected representative groups of citizens to deliberate contentious issues, such as abortion and climate change.[101] In 2014, the government of Taiwan started collaborating with a collective of civic hackers called g0v ("gov zero") on making government more transparent and accessible. One example of this collaboration is the creation of the platform vTaiwan that aggregates citizen opinions around points of consensus rather than disagreement.[102] By 2018, twenty-six cases had been deliberated through vTaiwan, 80 percent of which led to government action,[103] highlighting technology's potential to foster deliberation and consensus, not just sow discord and polarization. Innovations like these open the door to what could be a new model of democracy for the twenty-first century.[104]

The remedies to excessive power concentration are clear: power sharing and accountability. The failure to share power and hold the powerful accountable opens the door to abuse and tyranny, be it in organizations or in society at large. The only way to counter this failure is for all of us to realize that it is our collective responsibility to keep power in check. To do so, we first need to understand power and how it works. That is why the fundamentals of power are so important. We also need to use our collective power to safeguard and improve the institutions that ensure power sharing and accountability in organizations and in society. For that collective power to thrive, in turn, we need to choose our leaders wisely, and look for those determined to invest society's resources in the development of all of us—no matter who we are and what social groups we belong to—as free thinkers and civic-minded members of society. Only then will we have the moral character and democratic competencies to exercise our civic muscles. And when a politician or a tycoon undermines our democratic institutions, we will see through the demagoguery and the propaganda, recognize the threat, and fight back to protect our individual rights and freedoms in our daily lives.

Conclusion
It's Up to Us

Imagine the world is a blank slate. You have been chosen to distribute society's rights and power. You will participate in this new society, but you have no idea who you will be. Not your social position or your innate abilities. Not your gender, your race, nor your nationality. You are behind what is called a "veil of ignorance." You could be a farmer, a physician, or unemployed. Young or old, rich or poor, male, female, or nonbinary, highly educated or not, disabled or not. Would you design a democracy or an autocracy? Provide universal access to health care or limit such access to those who can afford to pay? Guarantee a quality education for every child or exclude many? This thought experiment, posed by the political philosopher John Rawls, raises critical questions about the just distribution of power. Through the veil of ignorance, the experiment forces us to consider everyone's well-being and access to opportunities without being biased by our own social status—which is why Rawls believed it would lead to fairer societies.[1]

Philosophers have been debating what constitutes a just distribution of power for millennia,[2] and many people are tempted to think that the philosopher's study is precisely where the topic belongs.

In fact, the opposite is true: The distribution of power affects each and every one of us personally. There are always things we can do to change the distribution of power in a given situation. As we have shown you, it comes down to the fundamentals of power: If you can figure out what the other party needs and wants, and find ways to give them access to these valued resources, you can change the balance of power. How we choose to use this knowledge, in our families, at our workplaces and in society, is up to us, as individuals and collectively.

WHAT IT TAKES TO BUILD POWER

Before you can build your own power, you need to understand who currently holds it, and why. Assessing these dynamics so that you can map them with ever more accuracy is always within your reach. We can all observe the environment we're seeking to influence; and knowing that everyone harbors a deep need for safety and self-esteem, you can gain insight into how the people around you are satisfying these needs in different but predictable ways: through the material accumulation of riches and status, or through psychological feelings of achievement, of being loved and belonging, of autonomy of choice, and of moral character. You can also solicit the observations of others: asking questions of your network to better understand what is valued in your environment, and then expanding your network to include people who can give you a different perspective as well as access to the people who control those valued resources.

Once your power map is as clear as possible, you're ready to decide which of the four strategies for shifting the balance of power you will choose: attraction, offering resources the other party values; withdrawal, decreasing your interest in what the other party has to offer; consolidation, reducing the other party's alternatives to you; and expansion, increasing your alternatives to the other party.

You are also in charge of your own relationship with power. The steps you need to take to map power and the strategies you can use to rebalance it are the same, whether you intend to use power to pursue evil ends or just purposes. Power itself is not dirty; the potential to misuse it lies within all of us, depending on what we want power for, and how we acquire and use it. You decide whether to embark on a developmental journey toward empathy and humility; whether to equip yourself to put to good use—and not abuse—the power you gain through your mastery of the fundamentals of power and power mapping.

Through the work and life experiences you expose yourself to, the books you read, the media you consume, the practice of self-reflection, you can see the world as a web of interdependencies, such that our power is someone else's dependence, and our actions have consequences beyond our immediate environment. We are in it together, and none of us forever. This knowledge gives you bulletproof criteria to assess who deserves to be entrusted with power: not those who give you the illusion of safety and self-esteem by projecting an air of strength, but those who have shown empathy and humility, along with competence and commitment to pursue a higher purpose. These are your criteria to apply if you choose.

And the power you cannot build by yourself, you can build through collective action. The truth is that we all, collectively, have a say and a responsibility in shaping tomorrow's distribution of power. Not only because we can join forces to agitate, innovate, and orchestrate change, but also because how power will be distributed ultimately comes down to what we all choose to value and how we decide to regulate control over those valued resources. These collective choices will protect and enhance our freedoms and rights or endanger them.

WHAT WILL WE VALUE?

For most of history we humans interacted directly with the people whose hard work went into making the products we needed. But with the rise of industrialization, as the economy and our roles in it changed, human exchanges shifted from being anchored primarily in relationships and reciprocity to being increasingly distanced and motivated by material gain.[3] As the "market" came between us, we learned to think less about the artisan or factory worker's family and economic situation and more about our own cost-benefit analysis. The neo-liberal sense of self-worth, which revolves primarily around the ability to accumulate money, disenfranchises large swaths of the population—the working class, the poor, immigrants, racialized groups, and people with disabilities, among others.[4]

It does not have to be this way. Research suggests that when we feel like winners or losers in a society that evaluates us by "what we have" rather than "what kind of person we are," our well-being suffers.[5] In our very human pursuit of self-esteem, we feel most fulfilled when we are valued for multiple aspects of our being, not just a single facet.[6] And yet, as economic language and assumptions pervade our daily lives, we measure our self-worth based on how self-reliant, financially successful, and on top of the competition we are.[7]

What our times require is nothing short of a major cultural shift—one that will recognize that dimensions other than financial success also matter, both in how we assess our self-worth and in how we assess the behavior of corporations and institutions.[8] The good news is that younger generations aspire to this shift. So many of the young people we work with around the world care deeply not only about making money, but also about helping to address pressing social and environmental issues in their communities. And yet, those who have undertaken such purposeful initiatives—some recounted in this book—often don't receive the esteem (not to mention the income) their combined competence and altruism would earn them in a less materialistic cultural context.

Operating such a cultural shift at scale will require agitation, innovation, and orchestration efforts. And, as we have seen, many such efforts are already underway, from the young people demanding action to address the climate crisis to organizations like SASB developing new ways of measuring corporate worth. These advances open the door to an era in which the criteria used to make decisions will no longer be exclusively financial. If this shift happens, other resources, such as those that enhance our ability to protect our planet, fight poverty, and enhance our collective well-being, will also become more highly valued. And this change, in turn, will open the door to a possible redistribution of power. Whether that results in a more just distribution of power will depend, however, on how we regulate control over access to valued resources.

WHO WILL CONTROL THE VALUED RESOURCES?

Power hierarchies can bring stability and safety to our lives and provide ladders to climb that satisfy our need for self-esteem. But as we have shown you, power is easily abused, and we must have the insight, and the courage, to watch for and challenge abuses whenever and wherever they occur. Failing that, we will continue to reproduce the status quo, while further concentrating power in the hands of a few. And, while some among them may understand that it is in their self-interest to share their power and avoid the perils that come with massive power imbalances, many will lack this wisdom. They will do everything they can to protect and grow their power, even if it is to the detriment of others and ultimately themselves.

We can counteract the concentration of power by increasing our collective ability to deliberate, discuss, and decide on the rules of the game in our workplaces and, more broadly, in society. This is where democracy comes into play. Without the ability to participate as equals in democratic systems, we throw away the ability to decide our future together. We surrender to the will of others who are more powerful than we are. In short, we renounce our power. The bottom line is simple: As we look forward, we must urgently and fervently reclaim our democratic power in our workplaces and in society.

Recall the story of Gyges with which we opened the book. When given the ring that made him invisible, the shepherd used his newly acquired power to kill the king, marry the queen, and gain ever more power. Plato's story is a cautionary tale. If left unchecked in the hands of one or a few individuals, power always risks being used to achieve evil ends. But the way to counter such devious enterprises is not to turn our backs on power. It is to understand, build, and use our power, both individually and as a collective of citizens, to ensure our individual rights and freedoms and to fight unjust power hierarchies. This requires each one of us to recognize that power is everyone's business. Power is for all of us.

Appendix
Definitions of Power
in the Social Sciences

Like all scholars, we are standing on the shoulders of those who have studied and written about power before us. In this note, we have done our best to acknowledge the authors and works that have most strongly influenced our thinking and contributed to our understanding of what we have called the fundamentals of power.

Social scientists define power in multiple ways. They conceive of power as the ability to carry out one's will despite resistance[1]; to coerce desired behavior out of others[2]; to set the boundaries within which discussion and/or decision-making takes place[3]; to impose one's will on others through withholding rewards or imposing punishments[4]; to convince others to believe what one wants them to believe[5]; or to get things done the way one wants them to be done.[6]

There are two common threads across these definitions. The first is that the authors view power as the ability of a person or a group of people to produce an effect on others—that is, to influence their behaviors.[7] This influence can be exercised in various ways, which has led social scientists to distinguish between different forms of power.[8] As summarized by the sociologist Manuel Castells, "Power is exercised by means of coercion (the monopoly of violence, legitimate or not, by the state) and/or by the construction of meaning in people's minds through mechanisms of cultural production and distribution."[9] Therefore, two broad categories underpin the types of power identified in the literature. The first category encompasses persuasion-based types of power, such as expert power that stems from trusting someone's know-how, referent power that stems from admiration for or identification with someone, or power stemming from control over cultural norms. The other category comprises coercion-based types of power that include the use of force (be it physically violent or not) and authority (or "legitimate power") to influence people's behaviors. Building on this large and rich body of work, we define power as the ability to influence another person or group's behavior, be it through persuasion or coercion.

The second common thread is that they all, implicitly or explicitly, posit that power is a function of one actor's dependence on another. Social exchange theory articulates this view clearly in the seminal model of power-dependence relations developed by sociologist Richard Emerson. In this view, power is the inverse of dependence. The power of Actor A over Actor B is the extent to which Actor B is dependent on Actor A. The dependence of Actor B on Actor A is "directly proportional to B's motivational investment in goals mediated by A and inversely proportional to the availability of those goals to B outside of the A–B relation."[10] The fundamentals of power that we present in this book are derived from this conceptualization of power. They posit that the power of Actor A over Actor B depends on the extent to which A controls access over resources that B values and that, in turn, the power of Actor B over Actor A depends on the extent to which B controls access over resources that A values. It follows from the fundamentals of power that power is always relational and that it is not a zero-sum game. The power relationship between A and B may be balanced if A and B are mutually dependent and they each equally value the resources that the other party has access to. It is imbalanced if one of the parties needs the resources that the other party can provide more.

Importantly, the resources that each of the parties value may be psychological as well as material. As Edna and Uriel Foa put it, a resource can be "material objects such as a dress or a bottle of wine, money and equivalent forms of payment, a kiss, a medical or beauty treatment, a newspaper, a congratulatory handshake, a glance of admiration or reproach, a pat on the back, or a punch on the nose. In short, resource is any item, concrete or symbolic, which can become the object of exchange among people."[11] Having control over any of these resources can be a source of power, but it is no guarantee of power. These resources themselves are not power, as Morris pointed out.[12] Furthermore, having control over valued resources is not the same as exercising power. Some people may use this control to influence others, while other people may not. That one has the ability to influence others does not necessarily mean that one will use it.

Understanding that power is the ability to influence others and that it resides in control over access to valuable resources is critical to understanding power relationships across levels of analysis. Research across the social sciences shows that the dynamics that underlie the fundamentals of power apply not only to power relationships between individuals, but also to power relationships between organizations[13] and between states.[14]

In using the fundamentals of power to understand interpersonal relationships and inter-organizational or interstate relationships, one should always consider the context within which these relationships are embedded. Cultural norms shape what is valued in a given context, while the distribution of resources favors some people and organizations and disadvantages others. As Wrong puts it, "The unequal distribution of power is not the result of the unequal distribution of purely individual attributes and capacities, but reflects the workings of the major institutions of a society and legitimations of these institutions."[15] As such, power becomes entrenched in structures that contribute to the reproduction of power hierarchies. In this respect, as Foucault pointed out, "power is everywhere."[16]

While power hierarchies are deeply entrenched, as we discuss in chapter 5, history shows that they can be challenged through the collective power of people banding together to accomplish ends that could not be accomplished alone.[17] Though our definition of power as the ability to influence another person's behavior may connote "power over," it also encompasses this collective dimension of power, as people can join together as part of groups, organizations, or movements to influence others. This kind of "power with" enables people to collaborate and accomplish common goals in organizations,[18] and to change existing power structures in society.[19]

All these conceptualizations—be they focused on "power over" or "power with"—concern "social power," and they are intrinsically relational, as is our approach to power in this book. Complementing these views, in 1973, political theorist Hanna Pitkin introduced a distinction between power over others and power to act. In Pitkin's words, "one may have power over another or others, and that sort of power is indeed relational . . . But he may have power to do or accomplish something all by himself, and that power is not relational at all; it may involve other people if what he has power to do is a social or political action, but it need not."[20] Subsequent analyses have challenged the notion that power to act is not relational, emphasizing that one's ability to act is often contingent on the social context that is inherently relational.[21]

In conclusion, power always concerns the ability of an individual or a group of individuals to affect, or influence, something, someone, or multiple people, be it through persuasion or coercion. This ability derives from control over access to valued resources, as encapsulated in the fundamentals of power that we present in chapter 1.[22]

Acknowledgments

The seeds for this book were first planted by our students at Harvard University and the University of Toronto, and all those we have had the privilege to meet in conducting our research across the world. It is their curiosity about power, their search for answers, and their desire to have an impact at home, at work, and in society, that set us on the journey to writing this book. We are grateful to each and every one of them for their engagement, their support, and for everything they have taught us. We hope that this book will help answer their questions and enable them to further harness their power to make a positive difference in their lives and in the world.

Although only our two names appear on the cover of the book, it took a village to write it.

Elyse Cheney, our literary agent, has guided us since the beginning of our book writing journey with a gentle but steady hand. Her trust in us and belief in the book, as well as her vision for it, gave us the impetus we needed to get started in earnest. Since the day we first met and walked her through the fundamentals of power on the whiteboard of her New York office, Elyse has been by our side with invaluable feedback and advice, helping us shape the book to make it accessible and helpful to our readers. We are also grateful to everyone at Elyse Cheney Literary Associates who has supported our book, especially Allison Devereux, Claire Gillespie, and Isabel Mendía.

The other visionary force behind this book is our editor at Simon & Schuster, Stephanie Frerich. Her enthusiasm for this project has been a constant source of inspiration and encouragement. Stephanie spent countless hours patiently reviewing and editing several versions of our manuscript. Her acumen, wisdom, and wide-ranging perspective have helped us define the architecture of the book, refine its content, and strengthen our writing. We could not have wished for a better partner. At Simon & Schuster, we are also fortunate to have benefitted from the expert work of Stephen Bedford, Kirsten Berndt, Alicia Brancato, Dana Canedy, Alison Forner, Morgan Hart, Elizabeth Herman, Jon Karp, Jillian Levick, Math Monahan, Lewelin Polanco, Richard Rhorer, and Emily Simonson.

We are eternally grateful to the people who shared their experiences, knowledge, and wisdom with us in interviews. Many of their stories are profiled in this book, many more are not, but every one of them has had a lasting impact on us and has informed our understanding of power. We thank Karen Adams, Mohamad Al Jounde, Gabriela Ayala, Xiye Bastida, Mary Beard, David Beatty, Betsy Beamon, Karol Beffa, Essma Ben Hamida, Paola Bergna, Vikas Birhma, LaTosha Brown, Carol Browner, Tarana Burke, Carol Caruso, Lucia Casadei, Srilekha Chakraborty, Sasha Chanoff, Vera Cordeiro, Pendo Daubi, Cheryl Dorsey, Elina Dumont, Omar Encarnación, Cécile Falcon, Meagan Fallone, Jim Fruchterman, David Gergen, Dorothy Greenaway, Lia Grimanis, Claude Grunitzky, François Hollande, Mashroof Hossain, Tatiana Jama, Tawakkol Karman, Christine Lagarde, Sandra Lopez, Françoise Nyssen, Anand Mahindra, Oriana Mambie, Vanessa Matos, Antoine Mindjimba, Sylvia Morse, Nezuma Mjumbe, Tanya Nesterenko, Ellen Ochoa, Tope Ogundipe, Ai-jen Poo, María Rachid, Emily Rafferty, Andrea Reimer, Jean Rogers, Guillaume Roussel, Miriam Rykes, Urvashi Sahni, Palak Shah, Wendy Sherman, Bright Simons, Maria Speck, Dan Taber, Justus Uwayesu, Donatella Versace, Florence Verzelen, Alexandria Villaseñor, Glen Weyl, Micah White, Meredith Whittaker, Claudine Wolfe, and Vanessa Wyche, as well as "Ning" and "Aakash," whose identities we had to disguise, and an executive whose identity we cannot disclose. We also thank the clinicians and managers at the National Health Service in the United Kingdom whom we interviewed as part of the research project that marked the beginning of our joint work fifteen years ago. We cannot name them for confidentiality reasons, but what we learned from them has enriched our understanding of power.

Because we have built on, and interwoven, the insights of many disciplines in this book, we are indebted to all the researchers whose work has given us a better understanding of power across contexts, countries, and academic perspectives. They are too many to list here, but we hope we have done justice to their ideas and insights.

Many of our friends, colleagues, and students generously took the time to discuss the ideas that we present in this book. For stimulating conversations, thanks to Elizabeth Anderson, Michel Anteby, Sophie Bacq, Lauren Bacon, Sivahn Barli, François Bonnici, Christin Brutsche, Suzanne Cooper, Tom D'Aunno, Jerry Davis, Alicia DeSantola, Sofia Gomez De Silva, Stefan Dimitriadis, Frank Dobbin, David Eaves, Alnoor Ebrahim, Doug Elmendorf, Isabelle Ferreras, Archon Fung, Hervé Gbego, Mattia Gilmartin, Mary Ann Glynn, Royston Greenwood, Monica Higgins, Rakesh Khurana, Clayton Kunz, Nicholas Krawies, Michael Lee, Dutch Leonard, Nick Levitt, Michael Lounsbury, Johanna Mair, Joshua Margolis, John Meyer, Victoria Nguyen, Tomasz Obloj, Timothy O'Brien, Anne-Claire Pache, Catherine Paradeise, Jeff Polzer, Woody Powell, Vincent Pons, Kash Rangan, Subi Rangan, Hannah Riley Bowles, Mathias Risse, Christian Seelos, George Serafeim, Jean-Claude Thoenig, Annie Trainque, Brian Trelstad, David Wood, and Evelyn Zhang.

For sharing their advice on different phases of the book writing process, we thank Iris Bohnet, Diana Cafazzo, Mihir Desai, Jim Fisher, Adam Grant, Sarah Kaplan, Marissa King, Chris Marquis, Jerry Meland, Sheba Meland, Gautam Mukunda, Adeline Sire, Greg Stone, Michael Tushman, Marjorie Williams, Henry Timms, and András Tilcsik.

For reading parts of the manuscript in detail and suggesting edits that have sharpened our content, we owe special thanks to Emelie Aguirre, Erica Chenoweth, Michael Fuerstein, Marshall Ganz, Michele Gelfand, Avi Goldfarb, Jon Jachimowicz, Michèle Lamont, Robert Livingston, Mordecai Lyon, Bill McEvily, Julie Mirocha, Swetha Raja, Satwik Sharma, and Tieying Yu.

We are deeply indebted to Benjamin Abtan, Sigal Barsade, Carol Caruso, Cécile Falcon, Caroline Faure, Barbara Lawrence, Matthew Lee, Umaimah Mendhro, Ayesha Nayar, Deepa Purush-othaman, Metin Sengul, Channing Spencer, Elliot Stoller, Aduke Thelwell, Julie Yen, and Marcela Zingerevitz who read the manuscript cover-to-cover and gave us tremendously helpful detailed feedback; to Lakshmi Ramarajan, who did so twice, brainstormed every aspect of the book with us countless times, and somehow never stopped picking up the phone when we called; and to Peter Scoblic, who helped us refine the architecture of the book and revise thorny sections.

We are also grateful to the teams of the Social Innovation and Change Initiative and the Center for Public Leadership at the Harvard Kennedy School and of the Social Enterprise Initiative at the Harvard Business School. We owe special thanks to Brittany Butler, Colleen Kelly, Ingo Michelfelder, Ally Phillips, Alondra Ramirez, and Mu-Chieh Yun, who have helped and championed us throughout the genesis of the book, from introducing us to people who contributed their stories, to reading and commenting on the manuscript, and brainstorming how to best disseminate our ideas. Many thanks also to the Rotman team, especially Karen Christensen, Daniel Ellul, Ken McGuffin, and Suzanne Tobin, for their determination to see this book have an impact.

Several special partners have enabled us to produce this book with their engagement, hard work, support, and enthusiasm for the project. Jason Gerdom helped set up the right kind of IT infrastructure for us to write this book remotely together. Libby Quinn has been part of our team from the very start. From helping us organize interviews to commenting on multiple drafts of the manuscript and pushing us to think about how to disseminate the core ideas of the book, Libby's contributions have been critical. Emily Grandjean, Matt Higgins, Marissa Kimsey, Leszek Krol, Mordy Sabeti, and Alex Ubalijoro worked with us as research associates at different stages in the development of the book. Their commitment was truly remarkable. We are privileged to have had the opportunity to work with such talented, rigorous, and dedicated research associates.

Most of all, we want to thank Kara Sheppard-Jones and Nan Stone for their immensely valuable help in conceptualizing and writing the book. Kara Sheppard-Jones's ambition and passion for this project have been a constant source of motivation. She has been with us through thick and thin every step of the way. The book has benefitted tremendously from her many talents as a writer, researcher, and social change maker. Last but not least, we could not have successfully completed this journey without the wisdom, skill, and unwavering support of Nan Stone. Her superb editorial advice, always dispensed with kindness and generosity, has immeasurably improved the book. What a beautiful writer, and what a friend.

For their constant encouragement over the years, unshakable faith in us, and unconditional love, we thank our parents. For putting up with us and inspiring us to live life fully and celebrate beauty in the world, we thank our siblings: Emilie, and Raffaele. For letting us lean on them anytime we needed them to read yet another chapter, take the kids to yet another appointment, brainstorm yet another title (or subtitle!), and endure yet another evening or weekend with us absorbed in writing, we thank our spouses: Romain, and Ned. For their energy, humor, ideas, pep talks, hugs, kisses, wisdom that belies their age, patience, and the boundless joy they bring to our lives, we thank our children: Noé and Lou, and Sohier and Livia. Our families are our superpower. Without them, nothing would be possible.

Finally, to all the extraordinary change makers who tirelessly use their power to participate in the building of more just, more democratic, and greener neighborhoods, organizations, and societies, you inspired us to write this book. We know how important and difficult your work is. Our gratitude and admiration are limitless. We hope that this book will help you in your endeavors and that it will inspire others to join you.

Notes

INTRODUCTION: POWER IS MISUNDERSTOOD

1 Plato, *Plato's Republic, Book II* (Agora Publications, 2001): 47–48.
2 Niccolò Machiavelli, *De Principatibus/Il Principe* (Antonio Blado d'Asola, 1532).

1. THE FUNDAMENTALS OF POWER

1 Lia Grimanis, Keynote Talk at International Women's Forum, World Leadership Conference, Toronto, November 15, 2017.
2 Grimanis, Keynote Talk.
3 Grimanis, Keynote Talk.
4 The International Coaching Federation (ICF) certifies coaches according to different levels of professional development: associate certified coach (ACC), professional certified coach (PCC), and master certified coach (MCC). Many certified coaches work as executive coaches. All certified coaches follow a codified methodology, much like a certified public accountant (CPA) or a chartered financial analyst (CFA) does. Lia enlisted only ICF certified coaches for the charity.
5 Lia Grimanis in discussion with the authors, June 2019, September 2019, and October 2020.
6 Grimanis, discussion with authors.
7 Certified coaches in discussion with the authors, August 2020.
8 Mary Parker Follett, *Dynamic Administration: The Collected Papers of Mary Parker Follett*, eds. Henry C. Metcalf and L. Urwick (New York–London: Harper & Brothers, 1942), 101; see also Mary Parker Follett, *Creative Experience* (New York: Longmans, Green, & Co., 1924), xiii.
9 Pam Houston, "The Truest Eye," *O, the Oprah Magazine*, November

2003, accessed December 10, 2020, http://www.oprah.com/omagazine /toni-morrison-talks-love/4/.

10 The figure depicts our adaptation of Emerson's power-balancing strategies. See Richard M. Emerson, "Power-Dependence Relations," *American Sociological Review* 27, no. 1 (1962): 31–41.

11 Andrew Francis-Tan and Hugo M. Mialon, "'A Diamond Is Forever' and Other Fairy Tales: The Relationship Between Wedding Expenses and Marriage Duration." *Economic Inquiry* 53, no. 4 (2015): 1919–30.

12 Stefan Kanfer, *The Last Empire: De Beers, Diamonds, and the World* (New York: Farrar, Straus and Giroux, 1995): 270–72.

13 Edward J. Epstein, *The Rise & Fall of Diamonds* (New York: Simon & Schuster, 1982): 125–26.

14 Francis-Tan and Mialon, "A Diamond Is Forever."

15 Social psychologist Robert Cialdini identified six tactics to influence the perceived value of a resource. These tactics range from making us feel that a resource is rare in order to persuade us that we need it (scarcity), to using figures of authority whom we respect and trust to recommend that resource (authority), to doing us a favor or giving us a gift so that we feel the social obligation to reciprocate when they ask us to do something in return (reciprocity), to pushing us to make a public statement that will bound us to do what they want us to do (consistency), to paying compliments to us to get closer to us and thereby more effectively influence our decisions (liking), and finally to using the behaviors of others around us to put pressure on us to do what these other people do and acquire the resources they have (social validation). See Robert B. Cialdini, *Influence: The Psychology of Persuasion*, vol. 55 (New York: Collins, 2007).

16 Anne Bowers, "Category Expectations, Category Spanning, and Market Outcomes," *Advances in Strategic Management*, 32 (2015): 241–276.

17 Alexandra Wexler, "De Beers Diamonds Reflect a Changing Market," *The Wall Street Journal,* November 30, 2019, https://www.wsj.com/articles /de-beers-diamonds-reflect-a-changing-market-11575109800.

18 Robert H. Frank, *Luxury Fever: Why Money Fails to Satisfy in an Era of Excess* (Free Press, 2001); Thomas Biesheuvel, "The Elite Club That Rules the Diamond World Is Starting to Crack," *Bloomberg*, July 29, 2019, https://www.bloomberg.com/news/articles/2019-07-29/the-elite-club -that-rules-the-diamond-world-is-starting-to-crack.

19 Lara Ewen, "Rock Bottom: Tracing the Decline of Diamond Retail," *Retail Dive*, June 18, 2019, https://www.retaildive.com/news/rock-bottom -tracing-the-decline-of-diamond-retail/555795/.

20 Edahn Golan, "De Beers's Market Share Falls in 2019, Hides a Surprise," *Rubel & Ménasché*, October 8, 2020, https://www.rubel-menasche.com /en/de-beers-market-share-falls-in-2019-hides-a-surprise/.

21 Emerson, "Power-Dependence Relations."

22 National Portrait Gallery, "Lyndon Johnson and the 'Johnson Treatment,'" accessed November 18, 2020, https://npg.si.edu/blog/lyndon-johnson -and-johnson-treatment.

23 "Stay Tuned: Campaign 'Spying' & the Ways and Means of Power (with Bob Caro)," *café*, April 11, 2019, https://cafe.com/stay-tuned/stay-tuned -campaign-spying-the-ways-and-means-of-power-with-bob-caro/.

24 Robert A. Caro, *Master of the Senate* (Westminster, MD: Knopf Doubleday Publishing Group, 2009), 153.

25 In their 2008 article in the *Journal of Applied Psychology*, Anderson, Spataro, and Flynn find that, while extroverts attained more influence in organizations that were team-oriented, in organizations where individuals primarily worked alone on technical tasks, it was conscientious people, not extroverts, who attained the most influence. Cameron Anderson, Sandra Spataro, and Francis Flynn, "Personality and Organizational Culture as Determinants of Influence," *Journal of Applied Psychology* 93, no. 3 (2008): 702–10.

26 Raoul Girardet, *Mythes et mythologies politiques* (Seuil, 1986).

27 Lee Ross, "The Intuitive Psychologist and His Shortcomings: Distortions in the Attribution Process," in *Advances in Experimental Social Psychology*, ed. Leonard Berkowitz, vol. 10 (Academic Press, 1977), 173–220.

28 "Pride goeth before destruction, and a haughty spirit before a fall," *King James Bible*, Proverbs 16:18.

2. POWER CAN BE DIRTY, BUT IT DOESN'T HAVE TO BE

1 Robert Greene, *The 48 Laws of Power* (New York: Penguin Books, 2000), 16, 56, 89, 101.

2 Niccolò Machiavelli, *The Prince*, trans. W. K. Marriott (London & Toronto: E. P. Dutton & Co., 1908), 134.

3 Paul Rozin and Edward B. Royzman, "Negativity Bias, Negativity Dominance, and Contagion," *Personality and Social Psychology Review* 5, no. 4 (2001): 296–320.

4 Saul Alinsky, *Rules for Radicals: A Pragmatic Primer for Realistic Radicals* (New York: Vintage Books, 1989), 51.

5 Bertrand Russell, *Power: A New Social Analysis* (Psychology Press, 2004), 12.

6 Miriam Rykles in discussion with the authors, April 2019 and February 2020.

7 For an overview, see Dacher Keltner, *The Power Paradox: How We Gain and Lose Influence* (New York: Penguin Press, 2016). See also Adam D. Galinsky et al., "Power and Perspectives Not Taken," *Psychological*

Science 17, no. 12 (2006): 1068–74; Deborah H. Gruenfeld et al., "Power and the Objectification of Social Targets," *Journal of Personality and Social Psychology* 95, no. 1 (2008): 111–27; Joe C. Magee and Pamela K. Smith, "The Social Distance Theory of Power," *Personality and Social Psychology Review*, no. 2 (May 2013): 158–86.

8   Simon Baron-Cohen et al., "The 'Reading the Mind in the Eyes' Test Revised Version: A Study with Normal Adults, and Adults with Asperger Syndrome or High-Functioning Autism," *Journal of Child Psychology and Psychiatry and Allied Disciplines* 42, no. 2 (2001): 241–51.

9   Michael W. Kraus et al., "Social Class, Contextualism, and Empathic Accuracy," *Psychological Science* 21, no. 11 (2010): 1716–23.

10 Cameron Anderson et al., "The Local-Ladder Effect: Social Status and Subjective Well-Being," *Psychological Science* 23, no. 7 (2012): 764–71.

11 Vanessa K. Bohns and Scott S. Wiltermuth, "It Hurts When I Do This (or You Do That): Posture and Pain Tolerance," *Journal of Experimental Social Psychology* 48, no. 1 (2012): 341–5.

12 Petra C. Schmid and Marianne Schmid Mast, "Power Increases Performance in a Social Evaluation Situation as a Result of Decreased Stress Responses," *European Journal of Social Psychology* 43, no. 3 (2013): 201–11.

13 Cameron Anderson and Adam D. Galinsky, "Power, Optimism, and Risk-Taking," *European Journal of Social Psychology* 36, no. 4 (2006): 511–536.

14 Robert Graves, *The Greek Myths* (Mt. Kisco, NY: Moyer Bell, 1988).

15 Graves, *The Greek Myths*, 313.

16 Dacher Keltner et al., "Power, Approach, and Inhibition," *Psychological Review* 110, no. 2 (2003): 265–84; Nathanael J. Fast et al., "Illusory Control: A Generative Force Behind Power's Far-Reaching Effects," *Psychological Science* 20, no. 4 (2009): 502–8.

17 Fast et al., "Illusory Control," 502–8.

18 David Gergen in discussion with the authors, June 2019. See also David Gergen, *Eyewitness to Power: The Essence of Leadership Nixon to Clinton* (New York: Simon & Schuster, 2000).

19 François Hollande in discussion with the authors, July 2019.

20 "Acton-Creighton Correspondence" (1887), accessed December 9, 2020, https://oll.libertyfund.org/title/acton-acton-creighton-correspondence.

21 Moral purity is a psychological state derived from a person's view of the self as clean from a moral standpoint and through which a person feels virtuous. Research on embodied cognition has shown that people express a greater desire to cleanse themselves physically when feeling dirty because of having behaved in morally questionable ways. The word-filling paradigm to detect unconscious feelings of moral impurity was developed by Chen-Bo Zhong and Katie Liljenquist in "Washing Away Your Sins: Threatened Morality and Physical Cleansing," *Science* 313, no. 5792

(2006): 1451–2. See also Spike Lee and Norbert Schwarz, "Dirty Hands and Dirty Mouths: Embodiment of the Moral-Purity Metaphor Is Specific to the Motor Modality Involved in Moral Transgression," *Psychological Science* 21, no. 10 (2010): 1423–5.

22   William Shakespeare, *Macbeth*, Act 5, Scene 1.

23   Tiziana Casciaro, Francesca Gino, and Maryam Kouchaki, "The Contaminating Effects of Building Instrumental Ties: How Networking Can Make Us Feel Dirty," *Administrative Science Quarterly* 59, no. 4 (2014): 705–35.

24   Tiziana Casciaro, Francesca Gino, and Maryam Kouchaki, "Learn to Love Networking," *Harvard Business Review* 94, no. 5 (2016): 104–7.

25   Casciaro, Gino, and Kouchaki, "The Contaminating Effects," 705–35.

26   Vera Cordero in discussion with the authors, September 2018 and February 2019.

27   Julie Battilana et al., "Associação Saúde Criança: Trying to Break the Cycle of Poverty and Illness at Scale," Harvard Business School Case 419-048, 2018.

28   Battilana et al., "Associação Saúde Criança."

29   Casciaro, Gino, and Kouchaki, "Learn to Love Networking," 104–107.

30   This act of convincing ourselves our behaviors are moral when they are not is one way we overcome cognitive dissonance by adding a consonant cognition. See Leon Festinger, *A Theory of Cognitive Dissonance* (Stanford: Stanford University Press, 1957).

31   "Princess Diana: A 'Modern' Mother Who Ripped Up the Rule Book," *HistoryExtra*, November 3, 2020, https://www.historyextra.com/period/20th-century/princess-diana-mother-parenting-william-harry-mother-son-relationship/.

32   David Eagleman, *Livewired: The Inside Story of the Ever-Changing Brain* (New York: Pantheon Books, 2020).

33   Jamil Zaki, *The War for Kindness: Building Empathy in a Fractured World* (New York: Crown, 2019).

34   C. Daniel Batson et al., "Empathy and Attitudes: Can Feeling for a Member of a Stigmatized Group Improve Feelings Toward the Group?" *Journal of Personality and Social Psychology* 72, no. 1 (1997): 105–18.

35   Fernanda Herrera et al., "Building Long-Term Empathy: A Large-Scale Comparison of Traditional and Virtual Reality Perspective-Taking," *PLOS ONE* 13, no. 10 (2018): e0204494.

36   Christopher J. Patrick, ed., *Handbook of Psychopathy*, 2nd ed. (New York: Guilford Publications, 2019).

37   Harma Meffert et al., "Reduced Spontaneous but Relatively Normal Deliberate Vicarious Representations in Psychopathy," *Brain* 136, no. 8 (2013): 2550–62.

38 Hazel R. Markus and Shinobu Kitayama, "Culture and the Self: Implications for Cognition, Emotion, and Motivation," *Psychological Review* 98, no. 2 (1991): 224–53; Theodore M. Singelis, "The Measurement of Independent and Interdependent Self-Construals," *Personality and Social Psychology Bulletin* 20, no. 5 (1994): 580–91; Serena Chen, "Social Power and the Self," *Current Opinion in Psychology* 33 (2020): 69–73.

39 For an example, see Wendi L. Gardner, Shira Gabriel, and Angela Y. Lee, "'I' Value Freedom, but 'We' Value Relationships: Self-Construal Priming Mirrors Cultural Differences in Judgement," *Psychological Science* 10, no. 4 (1999): 321–6.

40 For an overview of influential psychological models of ego-development, from Jean Piaget's to Lawrence Kolhberg's and Robert Kegan's, see Lene Rachel Anderson and Tomas Björkman, *The Nordic Secret: A European Story of Beauty and Freedom* (Stockholm: Fri Tanke, 2017).

41 Matthieu Ricard, *Altruism: The Power of Compassion to Change Yourself and the World*, translated ed. (New York: Little, Brown & Co., 2015); Thich Nhat Hanh, *The Art of Power* (New York: HarperCollins, 2009).

42 Analayo, *Satipatthana Meditation: A Practice Guide* (Cambridge, UK: Windhorse Publications, 2018).

43 See Peter Sedlmeier et al., "The Psychological Effects of Meditation: A Meta-Analysis," *Psychological Bulletin* 138, no. 6 (2012): 1139–71.

44 Martin Luther King Jr., "A Christmas Sermon on Peace," December 24, 1967.

45 Cem Çakmaklı, Selva Demiralp, Şebnem Kalemli-Özcan, Sevcan Yeşiltaş, and Muhammed A. Yıldırım, "The Economic Case for Global Vaccinations: An Epidemiological Model with International Production Networks," w28395, National Bureau of Economic Research, January 2021.

46 John Vidal and Ensia, "Destroyed Habitat Creates the Perfect Conditions for Coronavirus to Emerge," *Scientific American*, March 18, 2020, https://www.scientificamerican.com/article/destroyed-habitat-creates-the-perfect-conditions-for-coronavirus-to-emerge/.

47 Karin Brulliard, "The Next Pandemic Is Already Coming, Unless Humans Change How We Interact with Wildlife, Scientists Say," *Washington Post*, April 3, 2020, https://www.washingtonpost.com/science/2020/04/03/coronavirus-wildlife-environment/.

48 Mary Beard, *The Roman Triumph* (Cambridge, MA: Belknap Press, 2009).

49 While this image has long been a staple in popular consciousness, the evidence for it is less clear, and contradictions between different sources and interpretations abound. For a summary, see Beard, *The Roman Triumph*, 85–92.

50 Mashroof Hossain in discussion with the authors, May 2019 and June 2019.

51 "Rohingya," *Britannica Academic*, Encyclopædia Britannica, 2020.

52 Hannah Beech, Saw Nang, and Marlise Simons, "'Kill All You See': In a First, Myanmar Soldiers Tell of Rohingya Slaughter," *New York Times*, September 8, 2020, www.nytimes.com/2020/09/08/world/asia/myanmar -rohingya-genocide.html.

53 Amy Edmondson, *The Fearless Organization: Creating Psychological Safety in the Workplace for Learning, Innovation, and Growth* (Hoboken, NJ: Wiley, 2018); Amy Edmondson, "Psychological Safety and Learning Behavior in Work Teams," *Administrative Science Quarterly* 44, no. 2 (1999): 350–83.

54 See also Julia Rozovsky, "The Five Keys to a Successful Google Team," 2015, https://rework.withgoogle.com/blog/five-keys-to-a-successful-google-team/.

55 Bradley P. Owens, Michael D. Johnson, and Terence R. Mitchell, "Expressed Humility in Organizations: Implications for Performance, Teams, and Leadership," *Organization Science* 24, no. 5 (2013): 1517–1538. In *Think Again: The Power of Knowing What You Don't Know* (Viking, 2021), Adam Grant also shines a light on humility as essential to keeping an open mind, learning, and improving decision-making.

56 See Julie Exline and Peter Hill, "Humility: A Consistent and Robust Predictor of Generosity," *Journal of Positive Psychology* 7, no. 3 (2012): 208–18; Jordan Paul Labouff et al., "Humble Persons Are More Helpful than Less Humble Persons: Evidence from Three Studies," *Journal of Positive Psychology* 7, no. 1 (2012): 16–29.

57 For another analysis of the criteria people should use to elect powerful political leaders, see Gautam Mukunda, *Picking Presidents: How to Make the Most Important Decision in the World* (Oakland, CA: University of California Press, forthcoming 2022).

58 Danielle V. Tussing, "Hesitant at the Helm: The Effectiveness-Emergence Paradox of Reluctance to Lead," (PhD diss., University of Pennsylvania, 2018), 1–118.

59 For analyses of the prevalence of authoritarian attitudes and their consequences across place and time, see Bob Altemeyer, *The Authoritarian Specter* (Cambridge, MA: Harvard University Press, 1996); Daniel Stevens, Benjamin G. Bishin, and Robert R. Barr, "Authoritarian Attitudes, Democracy, and Policy Preferences among Latin American Elites," *American Journal of Political Science* 50, no. 3 (2006): 606-620; and Matthew C. MacWilliams, *On Fascism: Lessons from American History* (London: St. Martin's Press, 2020).

60 Anita Williams Woolley et al., "Evidence for a Collective Intelligence Factor in the Performance of Human Groups," *Science* 330, no. 6004 (2010): 686–8.

61 Marko Pitesa and Stefan Thau, "Masters of the Universe: How Power

and Accountability Influence Self-Serving Decisions under Moral Hazard," *Journal of Applied Psychology* 98, no. 3 (2013): 550–8.
62 Amy Edmondson, "The Competitive Imperative of Learning," *Harvard Business Review* 86, no. 7–8 (2008): 60.

3. WHAT DO PEOPLE VALUE?

1 For a comparison and summary of essential views of human nature in Western and Eastern thought, including Confucianism, Hinduism, Buddhism, Plato, the Bible, Islam, and Kant, see Leslie Forster Stevenson, *Thirteen Theories of Human Nature* (Oxford: Oxford University Press, 2018).
2 Mihaly Csikszentmihalyi, *Flow: The Psychology of Optimal Experience* (New York: Harper, 2008), 8.
3 Johannes Gerschewski, "The Three Pillars of Stability: Legitimation, Repression, and Co-Optation in Autocratic Regimes," *Democratization* 20, no. 1 (2013): 13–38.
4 Diego Gambetta, *The Sicilian Mafia: The Business of Private Protection* (Cambridge, MA: Harvard University Press, 1996).
5 United Nations Office on Drugs and Crime, "Global Study on Homicide 2018: Gender-Related Killing of Women and Girls," 2018; Jan Stets, *Domestic Violence and Control* (New York: Springer-Verlag, 1988).
6 Margaret W. Linn, Richard Sandifer, and Shayna Stein, "Effects of Unemployment on Mental and Physical Health," *American Journal of Public Health* 75, no. 5 (1985): 502–6.
7 Michael Grabell, "Exploitation and Abuse at the Chicken Plant," *The New Yorker*, May 8, 2017, https://www.newyorker.com/magazine/2017/05/08/exploitation-and-abuse-at-the-chicken-plant.
8 David Nakamura and Greg Miller, "'Not Just Chilling but Frightening': Inside Vindman's Ouster amid Fears of Further Retaliation by Trump," *Washington Post*, February 8, 2020, https://www.washingtonpost.com/politics/not-just-chilling-but-frightening-inside-vindmans-ouster-amid-fears-of-further-retaliation-by-trump/2020/02/08/7d5ae666-4a90-11ea-bdbf-1dfb23249293_story.html.
9 Thomas Hobbes, *Leviathan*, ed. C. B. Macpherson (New York: Penguin, 1985).
10 Philip Pettit, *Just Freedom: A Moral Compass for a Complex World* (New York: W. W. Norton, 2014), xxvi.
11 Babu-Kurra, "How 9/11 Completely Changed Surveillance in U.S.," *WIRED*, September 11, 2011, https://www.wired.com/2011/09/911-surveillance/. When experiencing uncertainty and threat that undermine their sense of control, people are inclined to defend the legitimacy of the

governmental institutions that offer structure and order. See Aaron C. Kay, Jennifer A. Whitson, Danielle Gaucher, and Adam D. Galinsky, "Compensatory Control: Achieving Order Through the Mind, Our Institutions, and the Heavens," *Current Directions in Psychological Science* 18, no. 5 (2009): 264–268.

12   Toshiko Kaneda and Carl Haub, "How Many People Have Ever Lived on Earth?" Population Reference Bureau, January 23, 2020, https://www .prb.org/howmanypeoplehaveeverlivedonearth/.

13   For classic treatments of people's self-view, see Morris Rosenberg, *Conceiving the Self* (New York: Basic Books, 1979). Self-esteem is a component of self-concept. Self-concept is a person's view of what they are like. Self-esteem is how a person values what they are like. See Jim Blascovich and Joseph Tomaka, "Measures of Self-Esteem," in *Measures of Personality and Social Psychological Attitudes*, vol. 1, eds. John Robinson, Phillip Shaver, and Lawrence Wrightsman (San Diego: Academic Press, 1991), 115–60.

14   A central idea in psychology, self-esteem is also controversial in its relationship with similar concepts, such as existential meaning and mattering. Supporting our view that existential anxiety is linked to the need to have a positive view of our worth, measures of self-esteem are highly correlated with measures of existential meaning, as well as measures of mattering, especially to others. See Andrew Reece et al., "Mattering Is an Indicator of Organizational Health and Employee Success," *The Journal of Positive Psychology* 16, no. 2 (2019): 1–21.

15   This view of self-esteem as a person's superordinate goal finds its roots in Abraham Maslow's famed hierarchy of needs, though Maslow's original hierarchy conceives of esteem as subordinate to self-actualization (Abraham Maslow, "A Theory of Human Motivation," *Psychological Review* 50, no. 4 [1943]: 370–96). Later psychologists would relate self-actualization needs to a person's intrinsic esteem, as opposed to the extrinsic esteem someone derives from others. Clayton Alderfer's ERG theory organized Maslow's model into three categories: *Existence* concerns people's basic physiological and safety needs. *Relatedness* concerns social and status need that correspond to Maslow's social need and the external component of esteem. *Growth* refers to an intrinsic desire for personal development, which includes the intrinsic component from Maslow's esteem category and self-actualization (Clayton Alderfelder, "An Empirical Test of a New Theory of Human Needs," *Organizational Behavior and Human Performance* 4, no. 2 [1969]: 142–75). The evidence for the hierarchical ordering of these needs—such that people pursue a higher-level need only after they have satisfied lower-level needs—is mixed. What is better documented is that people derive self-esteem from

their self-assessment of being personally competent, worthy of love, virtuous, and having high status in a group, as we detail below. In this sense, self-esteem is a superordinate need.

16   Susan T. Fiske and Shelley E. Taylor, *Social Cognition: From Brains to Culture* (Los Angeles: SAGE, 2013), 123–24.

17   For a psychological view of secure and fragile self-esteem, see Michael Kernis, "Toward a Conceptualization of Optimal Self-Esteem," *Psychological Inquiry* 14, no. 1 (2003): 1–26; Jennifer Crocker and Lora E. Park, "The Costly Pursuit of Self-Esteem," *Psychological Bulletin* 130, no. 3 (2004): 392–414. Interestingly, Buddhism, which might be viewed as having nothing to do with self-esteem, given its emphasis on transcending self-concern, can instead be understood to parallel this distinction between fragile and secure self-esteem when it invites us to embark on a path of liberation from negative preoccupation with the self and the need for affirmation from others.

18   This view of secure self-esteem as authentic mirrors modern and contemporary moral philosophy, in which authenticity is a rejection of the blind, mechanical acceptance of an externally imposed code of values justified by recourse to some higher authority. An ethic of authenticity is guided instead by motives and reasons that express a subject's core individuality, who the person is. For key references, see Somogy Varga, *Authenticity as an Ethical Ideal* (New York: Routledge, 2012). For other sources, see Jacob Golomb, *In Search of Authenticity: From Kierkegaard to Camus* (London: Routledge, 1995); Charles Taylor, *The Ethics of Authenticity* (Cambridge, MA: Harvard University Press, 1991). Having secure self-esteem does not mean being uninterested in improving oneself. A failure can be terribly disappointing to someone and motivate them to become better, but it does not infringe on the person's fundamental self-acceptance and sense of worthiness. For philosophical discussions of the pursuit of self-esteem and its societal implications, see also Kwame Anthony Appiah, *The Honor Code* (New York: W. W. Norton, 2010); Geoffrey Brennan and Philip Pettit, *The Economy of Esteem: An Essay on Civil and Political Society* (Oxford: Oxford University Press, 2005). For the link between authenticity and the sense of power, see Sandra E. Cha et al., "Being Your True Self at Work: Integrating the Fragmented Research on Authenticity in Organizations," *Academy of Management Annals* 13, no. 2 (July 2019): 633–1; Muping Gan, Daniel Heller, and Serena Chen, "The Power in Being Yourself: Feeling Authentic Enhances the Sense of Power," *Personality and Social Psychology Bulletin* 44, no. 10 (October 1, 2018): 1460–72.

19   Social psychologist Seymour Epstein theorized a hierarchical model where overall self-esteem is the first-order dimension of a person's

self-assessment, and second-order dimensions relating to general competence, moral self-approval, power, and love worthiness contribute to the
assessment of self-esteem. We develop a similar model here, with safety
and self-esteem as first-level needs, and material possessions, social status, achievement, affiliation, and morality as second-level resources fulfilling first-level needs. See Seymour Epstein, "Self-Concept Revisited:
Or a Theory of a Theory," *American Psychologist* 28, no. 5 (1973): 404–16.

20 Geoffrey Supran and Naomi Oreskes, "Assessing ExxonMobil's Climate
Change Communications (1977–2014)," *Environmental Research Letters*
12, no. 8 (2017): 1–18.

21 M. B. Glaser, "Exxon Primer on CO_2 Greenhouse Effect," Memo to
Exxon Management, 1982; Lisa Song, Neela Banerjee, and David Hase-
meyer, "Exxon Confirmed Global Warming Consensus in 1982 with
In-House Climate Models," *Inside Climate News*, September 22, 2015,
https://insideclimatenews.org/news/22092015/exxon-confirmed-global
-warming-consensus-in-1982-with-in-house-climate-models/.

22 Jane Mayer, *Dark Money: The Hidden History of the Billionaires Behind
the Rise of the Radical Right* (New York: Knopf, 2017).

23 Robert J. Brulle, "Institutionalizing Delay: Foundation Funding and the
Creation of U.S. Climate Change Counter-Movement Organizations,"
Climatic Change 122, no. 4 (2014): 681–94.

24 Amy Lieberman and Susanne Rust, "Big Oil Companies United to Fight
Regulations, but Spent Millions Bracing for Climate Change," *Los Angeles Times*, December 31, 2015, https://www.latimes.com/nation/la-na-oil
-operations-20151231-story.html.

25 Noam Chomsky, *Who Rules the World?* (New York: Henry Holt, 2016).

26 George Marshall, *Don't Even Think About It: Why Our Brains Are Wired
to Ignore Climate Change* (New York: Bloomsbury, 2015).

27 Milton Friedman, "A Friedman Doctrine: The Social Responsibility
of Business Is to Increase Its Profits," *New York Times*, September 13,
1970, https://www.nytimes.com/1970/09/13/archives/a-friedman-doctrine
-the-social-responsibility-of-business-is-to.html.

28 Thomas Piketty, *Capital and Ideology*, trans. Arthur Goldhammer (Cambridge, MA: Harvard University Press, 2020).

29 For a study of status-signaling consumption to boost self-esteem, see
Niro Sivanathan and Nathan C. Pettit, "Protecting the Self through Consumption: Status Goods as Affirmational Commodities," *Journal of Experimental Social Psychology* 46, no. 3 (May 1, 2010): 564–70.

30 See Michael Hughes, *Forging Napoleon's Grande Armée: Motivation,
Military Culture, and Masculinity in the French Army, 1800–1808* (New
York: New York University Press, 2012). According to the biography of
a contemporary French statesman, Napoleon responded to criticism of

the Legion of Honor as merely symbolic, and description of its associated medals as mere baubles by saying, "You call these baubles, well, it is with baubles that men are led . . . Do you think that you would be able to make men fight by reasoning? Never. That is good only for the scholar in his study. The soldier needs glory, distinctions, rewards." Antoine-Claire Thibaudeau, *Mémoires sur le Consulat 1799 à 1804* (Paris: Chez Ponthieu et Cie, 1827), 83–84.

31   Aruna Ranganathan, "The Artisan and His Audience: Identification with Work and Price Setting in a Handicraft Cluster in Southern India," *Administrative Science Quarterly* 63, no. 3 (2018): 637–67.

32   For an overview of the positive association between socioeconomic status and self-esteem, see Jean Twenge and W. Keith Campbell, "Self-Esteem and Socioeconomic Status: A Meta-Analytic Review," *Personality and Social Psychology Review* 6, no. 1 (February 2002): 59–71. The meta-analysis shows that the positive correlation between socioeconomic status and self-esteem is stronger for occupation and education than for income. Social rank therefore feeds our sense of worth more than economic status.

33   While this theory on the relationship between foot-binding and suitability for marriage is popular, it is not without its skeptics. Laurel Bossen and Hill Gates argue and show that the pervasiveness of foot-binding among rural women in the nineteenth century in no way improved their marital prospects, undermining the dominant explanation for the social value of foot-binding. What it did do, however, was create a captive hand-labor workforce, especially in the thriving textile production in imperial China. When the industrial revolution changed the value of hand labor, scholars argue, the custom of foot-binding rapidly declined. See Laurel Bossen and Hill Gates, *Bound Feet, Young Hands: Tracking the Demise of Footbinding in Village China* (Stanford University Press, 2017); Howard S. Levy, *Chinese Footbinding: The History of a Curious Erotic Custom* (New York: Bell, 1967).

34   Appiah, *The Honor Code*, 98–100.

35   Stefan Kanfer, *The Last Empire: De Beers, Diamonds, and the World* (New York: Farrar, Straus and Giroux, 1995).

36   In psychology, there are competing models of people's needs and wants. David McClelland's model focuses on affiliation, achievement, and power as key motivational needs; Edward Deci and Richard Ryan's self-determination theory refers instead to relatedness, competence, and autonomy. See David C. McClelland, *Human Motivation* (Glenview, IL: Scott Foresman, 1985); Edward L. Deci and Richard Ryan, "Self-Determination Theory," in *Handbook of Theories of Social Psychology*, ed. Paul A. M. Van Lange, Arie W. Kruglanski, and E. Tory

Higgins (London: SAGE, 2012), 416–36. Similarly, in their book *Beyond Reason: Using Emotions as You Negotiate* (New York: Viking Penguin, 2005), negotiation experts Roger Fisher and Daniel Shapiro identify five "core concerns" that people bring to negotiations: appreciation, affiliation, status, role, and autonomy. The similarities outweigh the differences, however, and our approach is to synthesize these models to provide an integrated view of what people value in their pursuit of safety and self-esteem as basic needs.

37 George Valliant, *Triumphs of Experience* (Cambridge, MA: Harvard University Press, 2012).

38 Liz Mineo, "Good Genes Are Nice, but Joy Is Better," *Harvard Gazette*, April 11, 2017, https://news.harvard.edu/gazette/story/2017/04 /over-nearly-80-years-harvard-study-has-been-showing-how-to-live-a -healthy-and-happy-life/.

39 For the study's complete dataset, see George Vaillant, Charles McArthur, and Arlie Bock, "Grant Study of Adult Development, 1938–2000," *Harvard Dataverse*, vol. 4 (2010).

40 Christian Jordan, Virgil Zeigler-Hill, and Jessica Cameron, "Self-Esteem," in *Encyclopedia of Personality and Individual Differences*, eds. Virgil Zeigler-Hill and Todd Shackelford (Springer, 2019). Frances Frei and Anne Morriss also explore the importance of leading by fostering trust, love, and belonging in work environments for people to thrive in *Unleashed: The Unapologetic Leader's Guide to Empowering Everyone Around You* (Boston: Harvard Business Press, 2020).

41 Scott Veale, "Word for Word/Last Words; Voices From Above: 'I Love You, Mommy, Goodbye,'" *New York Times*, September 16, 2001, https://www.nytimes.com/2001/09/16/weekinreview/word-for-word-last -words-voices-from-above-i-love-you-mommy-goodbye.html; CNN, "Paris Terror: Survivor: Kept Saying I Love You," July 21, 2016, video, https:// www.youtube.com/watch?v=K5hp6SWXSKg.

42 Daniel Burke, "Coronavirus Preys on What Terrifies Us: Dying Alone," CNN, March 29, 2020, https://www.cnn.com/2020/03/29/world/funerals -dying-alone-coronavirus/index.html.

43 Dominic Abrams and Michael A. Hogg, "Comments on the Motivational Status of Self-Esteem in Social Identity and Intergroup Discrimination," *European Journal of Social Psychology* 18, no. 4 (1988): 317–34.

44 Andreas Schleicher, *PISA 2018: Insights and Interpretations* (Organization for Economic Cooperation and Development, 2019).

45 Kate Wintrol, "Is Mens Sana in Corpore Sano a Concept Relevant to Honors Students?" *Journal of the National Collegiate Honors Council*—Online Archive 291 (2010): https://digitalcommons.unl.edu/nchcjournal/291.

46 Teresa Amabile and Steven Kramer, *The Progress Principle: Using Small*

Wins to Ignite Joy, Engagement, and Creativity at Work (Boston: Harvard Business Press, 2011).

47   Joris Lammers et al., "To Have Control Over or to Be Free from Others? The Desire for Power Reflects a Need for Autonomy," *Personality and Social Psychology Bulletin* 42, no. 4 (2016): 498–512. How our desire for autonomy is manifested can vary based on our cultural context and upbringing. Researchers have found, for instance, that Asian American children performed a task decoding anagrams best when the set of anagrams they decoded were said to have been chosen by their mother, whereas Anglo-American children performed best when they were allowed to select which set of anagrams to decode (see Sheena Iyengar and Mark R. Lepper, "Rethinking the Value of Choice: A Cultural Perspective on Intrinsic Motivation," *Journal of Personality and Social Psychology* 76, no. 3 [1999]: 349–66). Despite the cultural and context contingency inherent in how we approach autonomy, researchers have found evidence that a desire for choice is nonetheless innate and likely biological in both humans and other animals. (See Lauren A. Leotti, Sheena S. Iyengar, and Kevin N. Ochsner, "Born to Choose: The Origins and Value of the Need for Control," *Trends in Cognitive Sciences* 14, no. 10 [2010]: 457–63.) See also Sheena Iyengar, *The Art of Choosing* (New York: Twelve, 2011).

48   Francesca Gino, Maryam Kouchaki, and Adam D. Galinsky, "The Moral Virtue of Authenticity: How Inauthenticity Produces Feelings of Immorality and Impurity," *Psychological Science* 26, no. 7 (2015): 983–96.

49   Paul P. Baard, Edward L. Deci, and Richard M. Ryan, "Intrinsic Need Satisfaction: A Motivational Basis of Performance and Well-Being in Two Work Settings," *Journal of Applied Social Psychology* 34, no. 10 (2004): 2045–68; Jeffery Pfeffer, *Dying for a Paycheck: How Modern Management Harms Employee Health and Company Performance—and What We Can Do About It* (New York: Harper Business, 2018).

50   Fintan O'Toole, *Heroic Failure: Brexit and the Politics of Pain* (London: Head of Zeus Ltd., 2018).

51   Paraphrased from Jennifer Szalai, "Fear and Fumbling: Brexit, Trump, and the Nationalist Surge," *New York Times*, December 18, 2019, https://www.nytimes.com/2019/12/18/books/review-politics-pain-fintan-otoole-case-for-nationalism-rich-lowry.html/.

52   M. Ena Inesi et al., "Power and Choice: Their Dynamic Interplay in Quenching the Thirst for Personal Control," *Psychological Science* 22, no. 8 (2011): 1042–1048; Stefan Leach, Mario Weick, and Joris Lammers, "Does Influence Beget Autonomy? Clarifying the Relationship between Social and Personal Power," *Journal of Theoretical Social Psychology* 1, no. 1 (2017): 5–14.

53 Jon K. Maner, "Dominance and Prestige: A Tale of Two Hierarchies," *Current Directions in Psychological Science* 26, no. 6 (2017): 526–31.

54 Edward O. Wilson, *On Human Nature* (Cambridge, MA: Harvard University Press, 1978), 107–9.

55 R. Todd Jewell, Afsheen Moti, and Dennis Coates, "A Brief History of Violence and Aggression in Spectator Sports," in *Violence and Aggression in Sporting Contests: Economics, History and Policy*, ed. R. Todd Jewell (New York: Springer, 2012), 15.

56 Minda Zetlin, "New Zealand Prime Minister Won't Say Christchurch Mosque Shooter's Name," *Inc.*, March 20, 2019, https://www.inc.com/minda-zetlin/jacinda-arden-dont-say-christchurch-mosque-killers-name.html.

57 Jamil Zaki, *The War for Kindness: Building Empathy in a Fractured World* (New York: Crown, 2019), 52–9.

58 Émile Durkheim, *Sociology and Philosophy* (Glencoe, IL: Free Press, 1953); Émile Durkheim, "Social Facts," in *Readings in the Philosophy of Social Science*, ed. Michael Martin and Lee C. McIntyre (Boston: MIT Press, 1994), 433–40.

59 Thomas Hobbes, *De Cive: The English Version Entitled, in the First Edition, Philosophicall Rudiments concerning Government and Society*, ed. Howard Warrender (Oxfordshire: Clarendon Press, 1983), 49.

60 Judith M. Burkart, Rahel K. Brügger, and Carel P. Van Schaik, "Evolutionary Origins of Morality: Insights From Non-human Primates," *Frontiers in Sociology* 3 (2018). For further exploration of the relationship between morality and evolution, see Todd K. Shackelford and Ranald D. Hansen, eds., *The Evolution of Morality* (Cham, Switzerland: Springer International Publishing AG, 2015).

61 Wilson, *On Human Nature*, 154.

62 Michael Kernis and Brian Goldman, "Stability and Variability in Self-Concept and Self-Esteem," in *Handbook of Self and Identity*, eds. Mark R. Leary and June Price Tangney (New York: Guilford Press, 2003), 106–27.

63 Excerpted from Stephen Greenblatt, *The Swerve: How the World Became Modern* (New York: W. W. Norton, 2011), 77.

64 Aristotle, *Nicomachean Ethics* (New York: Start Publishing LLC, 2013).

65 Immanuel Kant, *Groundwork for the Metaphysics of Morals*, ed. Thomas E. Hill, trans. Arnulf Zweig (New York: Oxford University Press, 2002).

66 Yong Huang, "Confucius and Mencius on the Motivation to be Moral," *Philosophy East and West* 60, no 1. (2010): 65–87.

67 Leon Festinger, *A Theory of Cognitive Dissonance* (Stanford University Press, 1957).

68 Eliza Barclay and Brian Resnick, "How Big Was the Global Climate

Strike? 4 Million People, Activists Estimate," *Vox*, September 22, 2019, https://www.vox.com/energy-and-environment/2019/9/20/20876143 /climate-strike-2019-september-20-crowd-estimate.

69   Wilson, *On Human Nature*, 163.

70   Peter L. Jennings, Marie S. Mitchell, and Sean T. Hannah, "The Moral Self: A Review and Integration of the Literature," *Journal of Organizational Behavior* 36, no. S1 (February 2015): S104–68.

71   Katherine A. DeCelles et al., "Does Power Corrupt or Enable? When and Why Power Facilitates Self-Interested Behavior," *Journal of Applied Psychology* 97, no. 3 (2012): 681.

72   Simon May, *Nietzsche's Ethics and His War on "Morality"* (Oxford: Oxford University Press, 1999).

73   "What Impact Has Activism Had on the Fur Industry?" *Scientific American*, June 15, 2009, https://www.scientificamerican.com/article/impact -activism-on-fur/.

74   Names and places are disguised for confidentiality.

75   Ning in discussion with the authors, November 2019.

76   The psychology of social judgments has developed along overlapping tracks, which agree on the existence of two fundamental dimensions along which people evaluate others but have labeled them slightly differently. Social psychologist Bogdan Wojciszke distinguishes between competence and morality (see Bogdan Wojciszke, "Affective Concomitants of Information on Morality and Competence," *European Psychologist* 10, no. 1 [2005]: 60–70), while social psychologists Susan Fiske, Amy Cuddy, and Peter Glick (Susan Fiske, Amy Cuddy, and Peter Glick, "Universal Dimensions of Social Cognition: Warmth and Competence," *Trends in Cognitive Sciences* 11, no. 2 [2007]: 77–83), as well as Amy Cuddy, *Presence* (New York: Little, Brown & Co., 2016) talk about competence and warmth. The underlying meaning of those two dimensions is similar. In parallel, psychologists of trust distinguish between affect-based trust and cognition-based trust. Affect-based trust refers to emotional bonds between individuals that presuppose genuine care and concern for the welfare of partners. Cognition-based trust is based on knowledge and expectations concerning an individual's competence and performance reliability (see Daniel J. McAllister, "Affect-and Cognition-Based Trust as Foundations for Interpersonal Cooperation in Organizations," *Academy of Management Journal* 38, no. 1 [1995]: 24–59). Similarly, Mayer, Davis, and Schoorman have identified benevolence and competence as primarily affective and cognitive dimensions of trust, respectively (see Roger C. Mayer, James H. Davis, and F. David Schoorman, "An Integrative Model of Organizational Trust: Past, Present, and Future," *Academy of Management Review* 20, no. 3 [1995]: 709–34).

77 Tiziana Casciaro and Miguel Sousa Lobo, "When Competence Is Irrel-
    evant: The Role of Interpersonal Affect in Task-Related Ties," *Adminis-
    trative Science Quarterly* 53, no. 4 (2008): 655–84; Tiziana Casciaro and
    Miguel Sousa Lobo, "Affective Primacy in Intraorganizational Task Net-
    works," *Organization Science* 26, no. 2 (2015): 373–89.
78 Tiziana Casciaro and Miguel Sousa Lobo, "Competent Jerks, Lovable
    Fools, and the Formation of Social Networks," *Harvard Business Review*
    83 (2005): 92–9.
79 Miller McPherson, Lynn Smith-Lovin, and James M. Cook, "Birds of a
    Feather: Homophily in Social Networks," *Annual Review of Sociology*
    27, no. 1 (2001): 415–44; Robert B. Zajonc, "Attitudinal Effects of Mere
    Exposure," *Journal of Personality and Social Psychology* 9, no. 2, Pt.2
    (1968): 1–27.

4. WHO CONTROLS ACCESS TO WHAT WE VALUE?

1 Donatella Versace in discussion with the authors, November 2019.
2 For an example of the limits of formal authority, see Julie Battilana and
   Tiziana Casciaro, "Change Agents, Networks, and Institutions: A Contingency Theory of Organizational Change," *Academy of Management
   Journal* 55, no. 2 (2012): 381–98; and Julie Battilana and Tiziana Casciaro,
   "The Network Secrets of Great Change Agents," *Harvard Business Review* 91, no.7–8 (2013): 62–68. See also Linda A. Hill and Kent Lineback,
   Being the Boss: The 3 Imperatives for Becoming a Great Leader (Boston,
   MA: Harvard Business Press, 2011).
3 Michael Morris, Joel Podolny, and Sheira Ariel, "Missing Relations: In-
   corporating Relational Constructs into Models of Culture," in *Innovations in International and Cross Cultural Management*, ed. P. C. Earley
   and H. Singh (Thousand Oaks, CA: SAGE, 2000), 52–90.
4 Michele Gelfand, *Rule Makers, Rule Breakers: How Tight and Loose Cultures Wire Our World* (New York: Scribner, 2018). See also Erin Meyer,
   *The Culture Map: Decoding How People Think, Lead, and Get Things
   Done Across Cultures* (New York: PublicAffairs, 2016).
5 François Hollande in conversation with the authors, July 2019.
6 Michel Crozier, *The Bureaucratic Phenomenon* (London: Tavistock
   Publications, 1964). For Michel Crozier's in-depth study of the interaction between power relations and bureaucracy, see Michel Crozier and
   Erhard Friedberg, *Actors and Systems: The Politics of Collective Action*
   (Chicago: University of Chicago Press, 1980).
7 David Krackhardt first told the story of Manuel in "Social Networks and
   the Liability of Newness for Managers," *Trends in Organizational Behavior*, vol. 3 (New York: Wiley, 1996): 159–73. The figures of the auditing

department's formal structure and informal network are reproduced from this article.

8 For an analysis of how the visual representation of networks changes how we interpret them, see Cathleen McGrath, Jim Blythe, and David Krackhardt, "The Effect of Spatial Arrangement on Judgments and Errors in Interpreting Graphs," *Social Networks* 19, no. 3 (1997): 223–242.

9 For an empirical study showing the (limited) influence of the formal chart on the advice network of an organization, see Tiziana Casciaro and Miguel Sousa Lobo, "Affective Primacy in Intraorganizational Task Networks," *Organization Science* 26, no. 2 (2015): 373–89; for a review of research on the link between formal structure and networks in organizations, see Bill McEvily, Giuseppe Soda, and Marco Tortoriello, "More Formally: Rediscovering the Missing Link between Formal Organization and Informal Social Structure," *Academy of Management Annals* 8, no. 1 (2014): 299–345.

10 Krackhardt, "Social Networks and the Liability of Newness," 166.

11 Battilana and Casciaro, "Change Agents, Networks, and Institutions," 381–98; Battilana and Casciaro, "The Network Secrets," 62–68; and Debra Meyerson, "Radical Change, the Quiet Way," *Harvard Business Review* 79, no. 9 (2001): 92–100. For a theory of the firm as a political entity, see James G. March, "The Business Firm as a Political Coalition," *The Journal of Politics* 24, no. 4 (1962): 662–78.

12 For a classic study of how people gain influence through their network, see Daniel J. Brass, "Being in the Right Place: A Structural Analysis of Individual Influence in an Organization," *Administrative Science Quarterly* 29, no. 4 (1984): 518–39.

13 For a historical recounting of the power of networks, see Niall Ferguson, *The Square and the Tower: Networks and Power, from the Freemasons to Facebook* (New York: Penguin Books, 2017).

14 William Samuelson and Richard Zeckhauser, "Status Quo Bias in Decision-Making," *Journal of Risk and Uncertainty* 1, no. 1 (1988): 7–59.

15 Battilana and Casciaro, "The Network Secrets," 62–68.

16 David Krackhardt measured reputational power by asking every company employee to rate everybody else in the company for their capacity to get things done despite resistance, and their capacity to influence others based on personal magnetism. See David Krackhardt, "Assessing the Political Landscape: Structure, Cognition, and Power in Organizations," *Administrative Science Quarterly* 35, no. 2 (1990): 342–69.

17 An accurate power map also gives you two-step leverage: you may not be connected to an influential person, but you can reach them by going through someone who is connected to them, as well as to you. See Martin Gargiulo, "Two-Step Leverage: Managing Constraint in Organizational Politics," *Administrative Science Quarterly* 38, no. 1 (1993): 1–19.

18 Evidence that people become increasingly inaccurate in perceiving re-
    lationships farther from their direct connections is presented in Daniele
    Bondonio, "Predictors of Accuracy in Perceiving Informal Social Net-
    works," *Social Networks* 20, no. 4 (1998): 301–30. For how people de-
    fine the social world relevant to them in an organization, see Barbara
    S. Lawrence, "Organizational Reference Groups: A Missing Perspective
    on Social Context," *Organization Science* 17, no. 1 (2006): 80–100; and
    Barbara S. Lawrence, "The Hughes Award: Who is They? Inquiries into
    How Individuals Construe Social Context," *Human Relations* 64, no. 6
    (2011): 749–73.

19 Brent Simpson, Barry Markovsky, and Mike Steketee, "Power and the
    Perception of Social Networks," *Social Networks* 33, no. 2 (2011): 166–71.

20 Tiziana Casciaro, "Seeing Things Clearly: Social Structure, Personality,
    and Accuracy in Social Network Perception," *Social Networks* 20, no. 4
    (1998): 331–51.

21 This famous line is often misattributed to Sun Tzu but in fact comes from
    Machiavelli—for a change! "It is easier for the prince to make friends
    of those men who were contented under the former government, and
    are therefore his enemies, than of those who, being discontented with it,
    were favourable to him and encouraged him to seize it."—Niccolò Ma-
    chiavelli, *The Prince*, trans. W. K. Marriott (London & Toronto: E. P. Dut-
    ton & Co., 1908), 171.

22 Julie Battilana and Tiziana Casciaro, "Overcoming Resistance to Orga-
    nizational Change: Strong Ties and Affective Cooptation," *Management
    Science* 59 (2013): 819–36.

23 Robert B. Cialdini, *Influence: The Psychology of Persuasion*, vol. 55 (New
    York: Collins, 2007).

24 Julie Battilana, "Agency and Institutions: The Enabling Role of Individu-
    als' Social Position," *Organization* 13, no. 5 (2006): 653–76; Julie Battilana,
    Bernard Leca, and Eva Boxenbaum, "How Actors Change Institutions:
    Towards a Theory of Institutional Entrepreneurship," *Academy of Man-
    agement Annals* 3, no. 1 (2009): 65–107.

25 For details on centrality measures in networks, see Linton C. Freeman,
    "Centrality in Social Networks Conceptual Clarification," *Social Net-
    works* 1, no. 3 (1978): 215–39. For analyses of the strengths and weak-
    nesses of different types of networks, see Ronald S. Burt, *Brokerage and
    Closure: An Introduction to Social Capital* (Oxford: Oxford University
    Press, 2005), and Marissa King, *Social Chemistry: Decoding the Elements
    of Human Connection* (New York: Dutton, 2021).

26 "EPA's Budget and Spending," United States Environmental Protection
    Agency, accessed April 9, 2021, https://www.epa.gov/planandbudget/budget.

27 Carol Browner in discussion with the authors, October 2019.

28   Names and organizations are disguised for confidentiality.
29   Marc Bain, "Women's Labor, Ideas, and Dollars Prop Up the U.S. Fashion Industry, but Men Still Run It," *Quartz*, March 23, 2018. To understand the network constraints that women face in male-dominated organizations, see Herminia Ibarra, "Homophily and Differential Returns: Sex Differences in Network Structure and Access in an Advertising Firm," *Administrative Science Quarterly* 37, no. 3 (1992): 422–47.
30   Robin J. Ely, "The Effects of Organizational Demographics and Social Identity on Relationships among Professional Women," *Administrative Science Quarterly* 39, no. 2 (1994): 203–38.
31   "Lady Gaga Praises Céline Dion during Her Show in Las Vegas," YouTube, video, December 31, 2018, 1:28, https://www.youtube.com/watch?app=desktop&v=ZpwPhh91w2Q.
32   Juliet Eilperin, "How a White House Women's Office Strategy Went Viral," *Washington Post*, October 25, 2016, https://www.washingtonpost.com/news/powerpost/wp/2016/10/25/how-a-white-house-womens-office-strategy-went-viral/.
33   Tiziana Casciaro, Bill McEvily, and Evelyn Zhang, "Gendered Evaluations: How Men and Women Assess Each Other in the Workplace," Working Paper, University of Toronto, 2021.
34   Yang Yang, Nitesh V. Chawla, and Brian Uzzi, "A Network's Gender Composition and Communication Pattern Predict Women's Leadership Success," *Proceedings of the National Academy of Sciences* 116, no. 6 (2019): 2033–2038.
35   Miller McPherson, Lynn Smith-Lovin, and James M. Cook, "Birds of a Feather: Homophily in Social Networks," *Annual Review of Sociology* 27, no. 1 (2001): 415–44.
36   Ronald S. Burt, "Structural Holes and Good Ideas," *American Journal of Sociology* 110, no. 2 (2004): 349–99; Lee Fleming, Santiago Mingo, and David Chen, "Collaborative Brokerage, Generative Creativity, and Creative Success," *Administrative Science Quarterly* 52, no. 3 (2007): 443–75; Jill E. Perry-Smith and Christina E. Shalley, "The Social Side of Creativity: A Static and Dynamic Social Network Perspective," *Academy of Management Review* 28, no. 1 (2003): 89–106.
37   Jan E. Stets and Peter J. Burke, "Self-Esteem and Identities," *Sociological Perspectives* 57, no. 4 (December 2014): 409–33.
38   Scott L. Feld, "The Focused Organization of Social Ties," *American Journal of Sociology* 86, no. 5 (1981): 1015–35.
39   For an example of a professional who has overcome systemic racism to build a powerful global network with people profoundly different from him by taking a genuine interest in them and discovering common interests, passions, and causes, see Julie Battilana, Lakshmi Ramarajan, and

James Weber, "Claude Grunitzky," Harvard Business School Organizational Behavior Unit Case 412-065 (2012).

5. POWER IS STICKY, BUT IT CAN BE DISRUPTED

1 Mary Douglas, *How Institutions Think*, 1st ed., The Frank W. Abrams Lectures (Syracuse, NY: Syracuse University Press, 1986).

2 Julie Battilana, Bernard Leca, and Eva Boxenbaum, "How Actors Change Institutions: Towards a Theory of Institutional Entrepreneurship," *Academy of Management Annals* 3, no. 1 (2009): 65–107.

3 Stephen G. Bloom, "Lesson of a Lifetime," *Smithsonian Magazine*, September 2005.

4 Bloom, "Lesson of a Lifetime."

5 Jean-Léon Beauvois, Didier Courbet, and Dominique Oberlé, "The Prescriptive Power of the Television Host: A Transposition of Milgram's Obedience Paradigm to the Context of TV Game Show," *European Review of Applied Psychology* 62, no. 3 (2012), 111–119.

6 Stanley Milgram, "Behavioral Study of Obedience," *Journal of Abnormal and Social Psychology* 67, no. 4 (1963): 371–78. Since the Milgram experiment was conducted, researchers have raised ethical and methodological concerns about it. See Gina Perry, *Behind the Shock Machine: The Untold Story of the Notorious Milgram Psychology Experiments* (London-Melbourne: Scribe, 2012).

7 Stanley Milgram, "Some Conditions of Obedience and Disobedience to Authority," *Human Relations* 18, no. 1 (1965): 57–76.

8 The researchers tested four scenarios: One was the standard re-creation of Milgram's experiment in which thirty-two contestants participated; one "social support" scenario, where a production assistant ran on set midway through asking the host to stop because the game was too immoral, in which nineteen people participated; a "TV broadcast" scenario, where contestants were told that the game show would be broadcast as a pilot, in which eighteen people participated; and lastly, a "host withdrawal" scenario, where the host left the stage after making the conditions clear, in which seven people participated. The percentage of contestants who went all the way varied by condition, with 81 percent of standard condition contestants going all the way, 74 percent of social support contestants, 72 percent of TV broadcast contestants, and 28 percent of host withdrawal contestants. The overall average among all conditions was about 72 percent. (See Beauvois, Courbet, and Oberlé, "Prescriptive Power.")

9 Eleanor Beardsley, "Fake TV Game Show 'Tortures' Man, Shocks France," *NPR*, March 18, 2010, https://www.npr.org/templates/story/story.php ?storyId=124838091.

10 See also Philip G. Zimbardo, *The Lucifer Effect: How Good People Turn Evil* (London: Rider, 2007).

11 Hannah Arendt, *Eichmann in Jerusalem* (East Rutherford, NJ: Penguin Publishing Group, 2006): 276.

12 Dacher Keltner, Deborah H. Gruenfeld, and Cameron Anderson, "Power, Approach, and Inhibition," *Psychological Review* 110, no. 2 (2003): 265–84; Deborah H. Gruenfeld et al., "Power and the Objectification of Social Targets," *Journal of Personality and Social Psychology* 95, no. 1 (2008): 111–27; Adam D. Galinsky et al., "Power and Perspectives Not Taken," *Psychological Science* 17, no. 12 (2006): 1068–74; Cameron Anderson and Adam D. Galinsky, "Power, Optimism, and Risk-Taking," *European Journal of Social Psychology* 36, no. 4 (2006): 511–36; Kathleen D. Vohs, Nicole L. Mead, and Miranda R. Goode, "The Psychological Consequences of Money," *Science* 314, no. 5802 (2006): 1154–6; Jennifer E. Stellar et al., "Class and Compassion: Socioeconomic Factors Predict Responses to Suffering," *Emotion* 12, no. 3 (2012): 449–59.

13 See also Keely A. Muscatell et al., "Social Status Modulates Neural Activity in the Mentalizing Network," *NeuroImage* 60, no. 3 (2012): 1771–7. The experiment tests for neural activity related to mentalizing, i.e., thinking about others' thoughts and feelings, and finds that subjectively lower-status participants had higher levels of neural activity associated with mentalizing, while higher-status participants had the opposite response.

14 Adam D. Galinsky, Deborah H. Gruenfeld, and Joe C. Magee, "From Power to Action," *Journal of Personality and Social Psychology* 85, no. 3 (2003): 453–66.

15 For more on the correlation between higher social class and increased illegal and unethical behavior, see Paul K. Piff et al., "Higher Social Class Predicts Increased Unethical Behavior," *Proceedings of the National Academy of Sciences—PNAS* 109, no. 11 (2012): 4086–91.

16 Bruce M. Boghosian, "Is Inequality Inevitable?" *Scientific American*, November 1, 2019, https://www.scientificamerican.com/article/is-inequality-inevitable/.

17 Michael W. Kraus, Paul K. Piff, and Dacher Keltner, "Social Class, Sense of Control, and Social Explanation," *Journal of Personality and Social Psychology* 97, no. 6 (2009): 992–1004. The powerful can also be willfully blind to their advantages: They justify their privilege by denying it. See L. Taylor Phillips and Brian S. Lowery, "Herd Invisibility: The Psychology of Racial Privilege," *Current Directions in Psychological Science* 27, no. 3 (2018): 156–62.

18 For more on how power and status self-reinforce, see Joe C. Magee and Adam D. Galinsky, "Social Hierarchy: The Self-Reinforcing Nature of Power and Status," *The Academy of Management Annals* 2, no. 1 (2008): 351–98.

19 John Jost, Mahzarin Banaji, and Brian Nosek, "A Decade of System Justifi-
    cation Theory: Accumulated Evidence of Conscious and Unconscious Bol-
    stering of the Status Quo," *Political Psychology* 25, no. 6 (2004): 881–919.

20 Jost, Banaji, and Nosek, "A Decade of System Justification." For an illus-
    tration of this dynamic with regard to landlords, evictions, and poverty,
    see Matthew Desmond, *Evicted: Poverty and Profit in the American City*
    (New York: Crown Publishing Group, 2016).

21 Jojanneke Van Der Toorn et al., "A Sense of Powerlessness Fosters Sys-
    tem Justification: Implications for the Legitimation of Authority, Hierar-
    chy, and Government," *Political Psychology* 36, no. 1 (2015): 93–110.

22 John Jost et al., "Social Inequality and the Reduction of Ideological
    Dissonance on Behalf of the System: Evidence of Enhanced System
    Justification Among the Disadvantaged," *European Journal of Social
    Psychology* 33, no. 1 (2003): 13–36.

23 Dov Eden, *Pygmalion in Management: Productivity as a Self-Fulfilling
    Prophecy* (Lexington, MA: Lexington Books, 1990).

24 Joe C. Magee and Adam D. Galinsky, "Social Hierarchy: The Self-
    Reinforcing Nature of Power and Status," *Academy of Management An-
    nals* 2 (2008): 351–98.

25 For a case study detailing why disadvantaged groups may not challenge
    inequality, see John Gaventa, *Power and Powerlessness: Quiescence and
    Rebellion in an Appalachian Valley* (Urbana: University of Illinois Press,
    1980).

26 Pierre Bourdieu, *Language and Symbolic Power* (Cambridge, MA: Har-
    vard University Press, 1991); Manuel Castells, "A Sociology of Power: My
    Intellectual Journey," *Annual Review of Sociology* 42 (2016): 1–19. See
    also Jim Sidanius and Felicia Pratto, *Social Dominance: An Intergroup
    Theory of Social Hierarchy and Oppression* (Cambridge, UK: Cambridge
    University Press, 2001).

27 Chip Heath and Dan Heath, *Made to Stick: Why Some Ideas Survive and
    Others Die* (New York: Random House Publishing Group, 2007).

28 Etienne de La Boetie, *Discourse on Voluntary Servitude* (Indianapolis:
    Hackett Publishing, 2012).

29 "Code of Hammurabi," *Encyclopædia Britannica Academic*, July 2, 2020,
    https://academic-eb-com.eres.qnl.qa/levels/collegiate/article/Code-of
    -Hammurabi/39076.

30 Iselin Claire, "Work Law Code of Hammurabi, King of Babylon,"
    Louvre Museum, Paris, accessed October 6, 2020, https://web.archive.org
    /web/20201021003238/https://www.louvre.fr/en/oeuvre-notices/law-code
    -hammurabi-king-babylon.

31 Robert Francis Harper, *The Code of Hammurabi, King of Babylon, about
    2250 B.C.* (Illinois: University of Chicago Press, 1904), xii.

32   The specific connection to scrofula, a disease of the lymph nodes of the neck resulting in swelling and usually infection, dates back at least to the reign of Edward the Confessor (1042–1066) in England and Louis VI (1108–1137) in France; monarchs healing by hands dates even further back in France to the reign of Robert the Pious (987–1031). See Marc Bloch, *The Royal Touch: Sacred Monarchy and Scrofula in England and France*, trans. John Anderson (Montreal: McGill-Queen's University Press, 1973).

33   David J. Sturdy, "The Royal Touch in England," in *European Monarchy: Its Evolution and Practice from Roman Antiquity to Modern Times*, eds. Heinz Duchhardt, Richard Jackson, and David Sturdy (Stuttgart: Franz Steiner Verlag, 1992), 171–84.

34   Pierre Bourdieu, *Masculine Domination* (Redwood City, CA: Stanford University Press, 2001).

35   Mary Beard, *Women & Power: A Manifesto*, 1st edition (New York: Liveright, 2017), 4–21.

36   Sir Patrick Geddes and John Arthur Thomson, *The Evolution of Sex* (London: Walter Scott, 1908), 270; see also D. A. Dewsbury, "The Darwin-Bateman Paradigm in Historical Context," *Integrative and Comparative Biology* 45, no. 5 (2005), 831–7.

37   Anne Fausto-Sterling, *Myths of Gender: Biological Theories about Women and Men* (New York: Basic Books, 1985); Cordelia Fine, *Testosterone Rex: Myths of Sex, Science, and Society* (New York: W. W. Norton & Company, 2017).

38   For one instance of this effect, see Brian Pike and Adam D. Galinsky, "The Power Shield: Powerful Roles Eliminate Gender Disparities in Political Elections," *Journal of Applied Psychology* 106, no. 2 (2021): 268–80.

39   Simone de Beauvoir, *Le Deuxième Sexe* (Paris: Gallimard, 1949).

40   American Experience, *The Eugenics Crusade: What's Wrong with Perfect?* (Arlington, VA; PBS Distribution, 2018); Wendy Zukerman, "How Science Created Morons," *Gimlet*, May 25, 2018, https://gimletmedia .com/shows/science-vs/o2ho5g.

41   Felicia Pratto et al., "Social Dominance Orientation: A Personality Variable Predicting Social and Political Attitudes," *Journal of Personality and Social Psychology* 67, no. 4 (1994): 741–63.

42   The term "meritocracy" was first coined in: Michael Young, *The Rise of the Meritocracy* (London: Thames and Hudson, 1958).

43   For an early study of the concept of the "self-made man," see Irving Wyllie, *The Self-Made Man in America: The Myth of Rags to Riches* (New Brunswick, NJ: Rutgers University Press, 1954).

44   Abhijit Banerjee and Esther Duflo, *Poor Economics: A Radical Rethinking*

of the Way to Fight Global Poverty (New York: PublicAffairs, 2012), 256. See also Sendhil Mullainathan and Eldar Shafir, *Scarcity: Why Having Too Little Means So Much*, (New York: Henry Holt and Co., 2013).

45 Michael Sandel, *The Tyranny of Merit: What's Become of the Common Good?* (New York: Farrar, Straus, and Giroux, 2020), 226. See also Daniel Markovits, *The Meritocracy Trap: How America's Foundational Myth Feeds Inequality, Dismantles the Middle Class, and Devours the Elite* (New York: Penguin Random House, 2019).

46 John W. Meyer and Brian Rowan, "Institutionalized Organizations: Formal Structure as Myth and Ceremony," *American Journal of Sociology* 83, no. 2 (1977): 340–63; Paul J. DiMaggio and Walter W. Powell, "The Iron Cage Revisited: Institutional Isomorphism and Collective Rationality in Organizational Fields," *American Sociological Review* 48, no. 2 (1983): 147–60; Cecilia L. Ridgeway, "Status Construction Theory," *The Blackwell Encyclopedia of Sociology*, 2007; Richard W. Scott, *Institutions and Organizations: Ideas, Interests, and Identities*, 4th edition (London: SAGE, 2013).

47 John Rajchman used the expression "politics as usual" in the foreword of Noam Chomsky and Michel Foucault, *The Chomsky-Foucault Debate on Human Nature* (New York: The New Press, 2006), 6.

48 Anthony G. Greenwald and Mahzarin R. Banaji, "Implicit Social Cognition: Attitudes, Self-Esteem, and Stereotypes," *Psychological Review* 102, no. 1 (1995): 4–27; Anthony G. Greenwald, Debbie E. McGhee, and Jordan L.K. Schwartz, "Measuring Individual Differences in Implicit Cognition: The Implicit Association Test," *Journal of Personality and Social Psychology* 74, no. 6 (1998): 1464.

49 For the Implicit Association Test, see https://implicit.harvard.edu/implicit/takeatest.html. For a dive into how to fight bias proactively, see Dolly Chugh, *The Person You Mean to Be* (New York: HarperCollins, 2018); Ibram X. Kendi, *How to Be an Anti-Racist* (New York: Penguin Random House, 2019).

50 Laurie A. Rudman and Peter Glick, "Prescriptive Gender Stereotypes and Backlash Toward Agentic Women," *Journal of Social Issues* 57, no. 4 (2001): 743–62; Madeline E. Heilman and Tyler G. Okimoto, "Why Are Women Penalized for Success at Male Tasks?: The Implied Communality Deficit," *Journal of Applied Psychology* 92, no. 1 (2007): 81–92; Alice H. Eagly and Steven J. Karau, "Role Congruity Theory of Prejudice toward Female Leaders," *Psychological Review* 109, no. 3 (2002): 573–98; Hannah R. Bowles et al., "Social Incentives for Gender Differences in the Propensity to Initiate Negotiations: Sometimes It Does Hurt to Ask," *Organizational Behavior and Human Decision Processes* 103, no. 1 (2007): 84–103.

51 Victoria L. Brescoll and Eric Luis Uhlmann, "Can an Angry Woman Get Ahead? Status Conferral, Gender, and Expression of Emotion in the Workplace," *Psychological Science* 19, no. 3 (2008): 268–75.

52 Deborah Gray White, *Ar'n't I a Woman?: Female Slaves in the Plantation South* (New York: W.W. Norton & Company, 1999); Melissa V. Harris-Perry, *Sister Citizen: Shame, Stereotypes, and Black Women in America* (New Haven: Yale University Press, 2011); Ashleigh Shelby Rosette et al., "Race Matters for Women Leaders: Intersectional Effects on Agentic Deficiencies and Penalties," *The Leadership Quarterly* 27, no. 3 (2016): 429–45. Michelle Obama also recalls this stereotype being used against her in *Becoming* (New York: Crown Publishing Group, 2018), x.

53 Robert W. Livingston and Nicholas A. Pearce, "The Teddy-Bear Effect: Does Having a Baby Face Benefit Black Chief Executive Officers?" *Psychological Science* 20, no. 10 (2009): 1229–36. The results of another study, in which White male participants reviewed résumés that signaled whether the applicant was White or Black and gay or straight, are similarly telling, in that they suggest that Black gay men are offered significantly higher starting salaries than White gay men and Black straight men because they are viewed as less threatening. See David S. Pedulla, "The Positive Consequences of Negative Stereotypes: Race, Sexual Orientation, and the Job Application Process," *Social Psychology Quarterly* 77, no. 1 (2014): 75–94; John Paul Wilson, Jessica D. Remedios, and Nicholas O. Rule, "Interactive Effects of Obvious and Ambiguous Social Categories on Perceptions of Leadership: When Double-Minority Status May Be Beneficial," *Personality & Social Psychology Bulletin* 43, no. 6 (2017): 888–900.

54 Jennifer L. Berdahl and Ji-A Min, "Prescriptive Stereotypes and Workplace Consequences for East Asians in North America," *Cultural Diversity and Ethnic Minority Psychology* 18, no. 2 (2012): 141–52.

55 Claude M. Steele, Steven J. Spencer, and Joshua Aronson, "Contending with Group Image: The Psychology of Stereotype and Social Identity Threat," in *Advances in Experimental Social Psychology*, vol. 34 (Cambridge, MA: Academic Press, 2002): 379–440.

56 Steven J. Spencer, Claude M. Steele, and Diane M. Quinn, "Stereotype Threat and Women's Math Performance," *Journal of Experimental Social Psychology* 35, no. 1 (1999): 4–28.

57 Claude M. Steele and Joshua Aronson, "Stereotype Threat and the Intellectual Test Performance of African Americans," *Journal of Personality and Social Psychology* 69, no. 5 (1995): 797–811.

58 Patricia Gonzales, Hart Blanton, and Kevin Williams, "The Effects of Stereotype Threat and Double-Minority Status on the Test Performance

of Latino Women," *Personality and Social Psychology Bulletin* 28, no. 5 (2002): 659–70.

59 Zoe Kinias and Jessica Sim, "Facilitating Women's Success in Business: Interrupting the Process of Stereotype Threat through Affirmation of Personal Values," *Journal of Applied Psychology* 101, no. 11 (2016): 1585–97. See also Claude M. Steele, "The Psychology of Self-Affirmation: Sustaining the Integrity of the Self," *Advances in Experimental Social Psychology* 21, no. 2 (1988): 261–302.

60 Isabel Wilkerson, *Caste: The Origins of Our Discontents* (New York: Penguin Random House, 2020).

61 Julie Battilana and Tiziana Casciaro, "Overcoming Resistance to Organizational Change: Strong Ties and Affective Cooptation," *Management Science* 59 (2013): 819–36; Julie Battilana and Tiziana Casciaro, "Change Agents, Networks, and Institutions: A Contingency Theory of Organizational Change," *Academy of Management Journal* 55, no. 2 (2012): 381–98; Julie Battilana, Bernard Leca, and Eva Boxenbaum, "How Actors Change Institutions: Toward a Theory of Institutional Entrepreneurship," *Academy of Management Annals* 3, no. 1 (2009): 65–107.

62 Marc Schneiberg and Michael Lounsbury, "Social Movements and the Dynamics of Institutions and Organizations," in *The Sage Handbook of Organizational Institutionalism*, eds. Royston Greenwood, Christine Oliver, Thomas B. Lawrence, and Renate E. Meyer (London: SAGE, 2017), 281–310; Paul Osterman, *Gathering Power: The Future of Progressive Politics in America* (Boston: Beacon Press, 2002). See also *Crip Camp: A Disability Revolution*, n.d., accessed February 28, 2021, https://cripcamp.com/.

63 Neil Fligstein, "Social Skill and the Theory of Fields," *Sociological Theory* 19, no. 2 (2001): 105–25; Royston Greenwood, Roy Suddaby, and C. R. Hinings, "Theorizing Change: The Role of Professional Associations in the Transformation of Institutionalized Fields," *Academy of Management Journal* 45, no. 1 (2002): 58–80; Elisabeth S. Clemens and James M. Cook, "Politics and Institutionalism: Explaining Durability and Change," *Annual Review of Sociology* 25 (1999): 441–66; Petter Holm, "The Dynamics of Institutionalization: Transformation Processes in Norwegian Fisheries," *Administrative Science Quarterly* 40, no. 3 (1995): 392–422; Neil Fligstein, *The Transformation of Corporate Control* (Cambridge, MA: Harvard University Press, 1993).

64 Paul J. DiMaggio, "Interest and Agency in Institutional Theory," *Institutional Patterns and Organizations*, ed. Lynne Zucker (Cambridge, MA: Ballinger, 1988), 3–22; Neil Fligstein, "Social Skill and Institutional Theory," *American Behavioral Scientist* 40, no. 4 (1997): 397–405; Nelson Phillips, Thomas B. Lawrence, and Cynthia Hardy, "Inter-Organizational Collaboration and the Dynamics of Institutional Fields," *Journal of*

Management Studies 37, no. 1 (2000); Pamela S. Tolbert and L. G. Zucker, "Institutionalization of Institutional Theory," *Handbook of Organizational Studies*, eds. S. Clegg, C. Hardy, and W. Nord (London: SAGE, 1996), 175–90.

65 Elisabeth S. Clemens and James M. Cook, "Politics and Institutionalism: Explaining Durability and Change," *Annual Review of Sociology* 25, no. 1 (1999): 441–66; Mustafa Emirbayer and Ann Mische, "What Is Agency?" *American Journal of Sociology* 103, no. 4 (1998): 962–1023; Myeong-Gu Seo and W. E. Douglas Creed, "Institutional Contradictions, Praxis, and Institutional Change: A Dialectical Perspective," *Academy of Management Review* 27, no. 2 (2002): 222–47; William H. Sewell, "A Theory of Structure: Duality, Agency, and Transformation," *American Journal of Sociology* 98, no. 1 (1992): 1–29; Patricia H. Thornton, William Ocasio, and Michael Lounsbury, *The Institutional Logics Perspective: A New Approach to Culture, Structure, and Process* (Oxford: Oxford University Press, 2012).

66 For details on the distinction between motivation and opportunity to rebalance power and its implication for how power relationships change, see Mikołaj Jan Piskorski and Tiziana Casciaro, "When More Power Makes Actors Worse Off: Turning a Profit in the American Economy," *Social Forces* 85, no. 2 (2006): 1011–36; Tiziana Casciaro and Mikołaj Jan Piskorski, "Power Imbalance, Mutual Dependence, and Constraint Absorption: A Closer Look at Resource Dependence Theory," *Administrative Science Quarterly* 50, no. 2 (2005): 167–99. For a complementary view of the distinction between power imbalance and mutual dependence, see Ranjay Gulati and Maxim Sytch, "Dependence Asymmetry and Joint Dependence in Interorganizational Relationships: Effects of Embeddedness on a Manufacturer's Performance in Procurement Relationships," *Administrative Science Quarterly* 52, no. 1 (2007): 32–69. An essential source on measuring such dependence is Ronald S. Burt, *Toward a Structural Theory of Action: Network Models of Social Structure, Perception, and Action.* (New York: Academic Press, 1982).

67 For a memorable account of the lives of the European immigrants to Pittsburgh in the late 1800s and early 1900s, see the historical novel: Thomas Bell, *Out of This Furnace* (Pittsburgh: University of Pittsburgh Press, 1976).

68 Karl Marx, *Capital: A Critique of Political Economy* (London: S. Sonnenschein, Lowrey, & Co., 1887).

69 Contemporary American corporations do not resort to bloodshed to discourage unionization, but often put up a fight using other methods: Jay Greene, "Amazon's Anti-Union Blitz Stalks Alabama Warehouse Workers Everywhere, Even the Bathroom," *Washington Post*, February 2, 2021, https://www.washingtonpost.com/technology/2021/02/02/amazon -union-warehouse-workers/.

70   Magee and Galinsky, "Social Hierarchy." For more on the relationship
     between (il)legitimacy and systems change, see Paul V. Martorana, Adam
     D. Galinsky, and Hayagreeva Rao, "From System Justification to System
     Condemnation: Antecedents of Attempts to Change Power Hierarchies,"
     Research on Managing Groups and Teams 7 (2005): 283–313.
71   For anger as a response to injustice, see Robert C. Solomon, *The Passions:
     Emotions and the Meaning of Life* (Indianapolis, IN: Hackett, 1993); and
     C. Daniel Batson et al., "Anger at Unfairness: Is It Moral Outrage?" *Eu-
     ropean Journal of Social Psychology* 37, no. 6 (November 2007): 1272–85,
     on anger motivating action against injustice. For research on the relation-
     ship between sadness and helplessness, and anger and personal control,
     see Dacher Keltner, Phoebe C. Ellsworth, and Kari Edwards, "Beyond
     Simple Pessimism: Effects of Sadness and Anger on Social Perception,"
     Journal of Personality and Social Psychology 64, no. 5 (1993): 740; and
     on emotions that lead to action or risk-taking, see Jennifer Lerner and
     Dacher Keltner, "Fear, Anger, and Risk," *Journal of Personality and So-
     cial Psychology* 81, no. 1 (2001): 146–59; Nico H. Frijda, "Emotions and
     Action," in *Feelings and Emotions*, eds. Antony S. R. Manstead, Nico Fri-
     jda, and Agneta Fischer (Cambridge, UK: Cambridge University Press,
     2004), 158–73; James Jasper, *The Emotions of Protest* (Chicago: Univer-
     sity of Chicago Press, 2018).
72   See, for example, Michele Masterfano, "Unions: The Good, the Bad, the
     Ugly," *HuffPost*, September 17, 2013, https://www.huffpost.com/entry
     /unions-the-good-the-bad-t_b_3880878.
73   Joseph Stiglitz, *The Price of Inequality: How Today's Divided Society En-
     dangers Our Future* (New York: W. W. Norton, 2012).
74   "Amazon Empire: The Rise and Reign of Jeff Bezos," *Frontline*, Febru-
     ary 18, 2020, https://www.pbs.org/wgbh/frontline/film/amazon-empire/;
     Jay Greene, "Amazon Sellers Say Online Retail Giant Is Trying to Help
     Itself, Not Consumers," *Washington Post*, October 19, 2019, https://www
     .washingtonpost.com/technology/2019/10/01/amazon-sellers-say-online
     -retail-giant-is-trying-help-itself-not-consumers/.
75   Erin Griffith, "To Fight Apple and Google's Grip, Fortnite Creator Mounts
     a Crusade," *New York Times*, August 25, 2020, sec. Technology, https://
     www.nytimes.com/2020/08/25/technology/fortnite-creator-tim-sweeney
     -apple-google.html.
76   Piskorski and Casciaro, "When More Power Makes Actors Worse Off,"
     1011–36.
77   Adam Taylor, "The Global Wave of Populism That Turned 2016 Upside
     Down," *Washington Post*, December 19, 2016, https://www.washington
     post.com/news/worldviews/wp/2016/12/19/the-global-wave-of-populism
     -that-turned-2016-upside-down/.

78   Arlie Russell Hochschild, *Strangers in Their Own Land: Anger and Mourning on the American Right* (New York: The New Press, 2018).

79   Stiglitz, *The Price of Inequality*; Torsten Persson and Guido Tabellini, "Is Inequality Harmful for Growth? Theory and Evidence," *American Economic Review* 84, no. 3 (1994): 600–21; and, for an analysis of the relationship between the pursuit of economic efficiency, inequality, and threats to democratic capitalism, Roger L. Martin, *When More Is Not Better: Overcoming America's Obsession with Economic Efficiency* (Boston: Harvard Business School Press, 2020).

80   Abhijit Banerjee and Esther Duflo, *Good Economics for Hard Times* (New York: PublicAffairs, 2019), 256.

81   Emmie Martin, "Warren Buffett and Bill Gates Agree That the Rich Should Pay Higher Taxes—Here's What They Suggest," *CNBC*, February 26, 2019, https://www.cnbc.com/2019/02/25/warren-buffett-and-bill-gates -the-rich-should-pay-higher-taxes.html; Sheelah Kolhatkar, "The Ultra-Wealthy Who Argue That They Should Be Paying Higher Taxes," *The New Yorker*, January 6, 2020, https://www.newyorker.com/magazine/2020 /01/06/the-ultra-wealthy-who-argue-that-they-should-be-paying-higher -taxes.

82   Anand Giridharadas, "The New Elite's Phoney Crusade to Save the World—Without Changing Anything," *The Guardian*, January 22, 2019, http://www.theguardian.com/news/2019/jan/22/the-new-elites-phoney -crusade-to-save-the-world-without-changing-anything; Anand Giridharadas, *Winners Take All: The Elite Charade of Changing the World* (New York: Knopf, 2018).

83   Chad Stone et al., *A Guide to Statistics on Historical Trends in Income Inequality* (Center on Budget and Policy Priorities, 2020), https://www .cbpp.org/sites/default/files/atoms/files/11-28-11pov_0.pdf.

84   For detailed discussions of the neoliberal turn, see Thomas Piketty, *Capital and Ideology*, trans. Arthur Goldhammer (Cambridge, MA: Belknap, 2020); Paul Adler, *The 99% Economy* (Oxford: Oxford University Press, 2019); Luc Boltanski and Eve Chiapello, *The New Spirit of Capitalism* (London: Verso, 2006); and, for an account of its impact on the lives of Americans, see Nicholas Kristof and Sheryl WuDunn, *Tightrope: Americans Reaching for Hope* (New York: Penguin Random House, 2020).

6. AGITATE, INNOVATE, ORCHESTRATE

1   Charles Tilly, *Social Movements 1768–2004* (London: Paradigm Publishers, 2004). For a review of the literature on social movements, see David A. Snow, Sarah A. Soule, and Hanspeter Kriesi, eds., *The Blackwell Companion to Social Movements* (Hoboken, NJ: John Wiley & Sons, 2008);

David A. Snow and Sarah A. Soule, *A Primer on Social Movements* (New York: W. W. Norton, 2010).

2   For an in-depth analysis of the impact of communication technology on social movements, see Manuel Castells, *Networks of Outrage and Hope: Social Movements in the Internet Age*, 2nd ed. (Malden, MA: Polity Press, 2015).

3   Gene Sharp, *From Dictatorship to Democracy: A Conceptual Framework for Liberation* (Boston: Albert Einstein Institution, 2003).

4   Micah White in discussion with the authors, January and March 2020.

5   Micah White, *The End of Protest: A New Playbook for Revolution* (Toronto: Knopf Canada, 2016).

6   Julie Battilana, "Power and Influence in Society," Harvard Business School note 415-055 (2015); Julie Battilana and Marissa Kimsey, "Should You Agitate, Innovate, or Orchestrate?" *Stanford Social Innovation Review* (online), 2017, https://ssir.org/articles/entry/should_you_agitate _innovate_or_orchestrate.

7   Studies have documented the "radical flank effect" in which the bargaining position of moderate groups is strengthened, rather than weakened, by the presence of more radical ones (see, for example, Herbert H. Haines, "Black Radicalization and the Funding of Civil Rights: 1957–1970," *Social Problems* 32, no. 1 [1984]: 31–43).

8   Battilana and Kimsey, "Should You Agitate?"

9   IPCC, *Global Warming of 1.5°C: An IPCC Special Report on the Impacts of Global Warming of 1.5°C above Pre-industrial Levels and Related Global Greenhouse Gas Emission Pathways, in the Context of Strengthening the Global Response to the Threat of Climate Change, Sustainable Development, and Efforts to Eradicate Poverty*, Valerie Masson-Delmotte et al., (eds.) (2018), https://www.ipcc.ch/sr15/.

10   Xiye Bastida in discussion with the authors, September 2019.

11   For a psychological explanation of our inaction on climate change, see George Marshall, *Don't Even Think About It: Why Our Brains Are Wired to Ignore Climate Change* (New York: Bloomsbury, 2015).

12   See Niall McCarthy, "The Countries Shutting Down the Internet the Most," *Forbes*, August 28, 2018; Zeynep Tufekci, *Twitter and Tear Gas: The Power and Fragility of Networked Protest* (New Haven: Yale University Press, 2017).

13   Marshall Ganz, "What Is Public Narrative: Self, Us & Now," working paper, Harvard University (2009).

14   Research has shown how important it is for movements to master framing, the process through which a social movement attributes meaning to an issue by promoting an interpretation of this issue that shifts how it is understood or perceived in the public consciousness. See Robert D. Benford and David A. Snow, "Framing Processes and Social Movements: An

Overview and Assessment," *Annual Review of Sociology* 26 (2000): 611–39; David A. Snow et al., "Frame Alignment Processes, Micromobilization, and Movement Participation," *American Sociological Review* 51, no. 4 (1986): 464–81; Paul Almeida, *Social Movements: The Structure of Collective Mobilization* (Oakland, CA: University of California Press, 2019).

15 Paul V. Martorana, Adam D. Galinsky, and Hayagreeva Rao, "From System Justification to System Condemnation: Antecedents of Attempts to Change Power Hierarchies," in *Status and Groups* (Bingley: Emerald Group Publishing Ltd., 2005), 283–313; Ernesto Laclau and Chantal Mouffe, *Hegemony and Socialist Strategy: Towards a Radical Democratic Politics* (New York: Verso, 2001).

16 Erika Summers-Effler, "The Micro Potential for Social Change: Emotion, Consciousness, and Social Movement Formation," *Sociological Theory* 20, no. 1 (2002): 41–60; Michal Reifen Tagar, Christopher M. Federico, and Eran Halperin, "The Positive Effect of Negative Emotions in Protracted Conflict: The Case of Anger," *Journal of Experimental Social Psychology* 47, no. 1 (2011): 157–64; Marshall Ganz, "Leading Change: Leadership, Organization, and Social Movements," in *Handbook of Leadership Theory and Practice*, ed. Nitin Nohria and Rakesh Khurana (Boston: Harvard Business Press, 2010). See also Paul Slovic, "'If I Look at the Mass I Will Never Act': Psychic Numbing and Genocide," *Judgment and Decision-Making* 2, no. 2 (2007): 79–95.

17 Eliza Barclay and Brian Resnick, "How Big Was the Global Climate Strike? 4 Million People, Activists Estimate," *Vox*, September 22, 2019, https://www.vox.com/energy-and-environment/2019/9/20/20876143/climate-strike-2019-september-20-crowd-estimate.

18 Greta Thunberg, 24th Conference of the Parties to the United Nations Framework Convention on Climate Change (COP 24), Katowice, Poland, 2018.

19 Henry David Thoreau, *A Yankee in Canada, with Anti-Slavery and Reform Papers*, eds. Sophie Thoreau, William Ellery Channing, and Ralph Waldo Emerson (Ticknor and Fields, 1866).

20 George Hendrick, "The Influence of Thoreau's 'Civil Disobedience' on Gandhi's Satyagraha," *The New England Quarterly* 29, no. 4 (1956): 462–71; Mark Engler and Paul Engler, *This Is an Uprising* (New York: Nation, 2017); Gene Sharp, *The Politics of Nonviolent Action* (New York: Porter Sargent Publishers, 1973).

21 Erica Chenoweth and Maria J. Stephan, *Why Civil Resistance Works: The Strategic Logic of Nonviolent Conflict* (New York: Columbia University Press, 2011).

22 Chenoweth and Stephan, *Why Civil Resistance Works*.

23 "Google Trends Interest in 'Climate Change' and 'Climate Crisis'

2004–2020," Google Trends, 2020; Barclay, "How Big Was the Global Climate Strike?"

24 Hahrie Han, *How Organizations Develop Activists: Civic Associations and Leadership in the 21st Century* (Oxford: Oxford University Press, 2014); Engler and Engler, *This Is an Uprising*; Jane McAlevey, *A Collective Bargain: Unions, Organizing, and the Fight for Democracy* (New York: HarperCollins, 2020).

25 Julie Battilana et al., "Problem, Person, and Pathway: A Framework for Social Innovators," in *Handbook of Inclusive Innovation*, ed. Gerard George et al. (Cheltenham, UK: Edward Elgar Publishing, 2019), 61–74.

26 Cynthia Rayner and François Bonnici, *The Systems Work of Social Change* (forthcoming); Christian Seelos and Johanna Mair, *Innovation and Scaling for Impact: How Effective Social Enterprises Do It* (Palo Alto, CA: Stanford University Press, 2017).

27 Steve Lydenberg, Jean Rogers, and David Wood, "From Transparency to Performance: Industry-Based Sustainability Reporting on Key Issues," Initiative for Responsible Investment, Hauser Center for Nonprofit Organizations, Harvard University, 2010.

28 Julie Battilana and Michael Norris, "The Sustainability Accounting Standards Board," Harvard Business School Case 414-078, 2015.

29 Jean Rogers in discussion with the authors, December 2018, December 2020, and January 2021.

30 María Rachid, in discussion with the authors, August 2020.

31 Hector Tobar and Chris Kraul, "Millions of Bank Accounts Are Frozen in Beleaguered Argentina," *Los Angeles Times*, January 11, 2002, https://www.latimes.com/archives/la-xpm-2002-jan-11-mn-21962-story.html.

32 For more on political opportunity, see William A. Gamson and David Meyer "Framing Political Opportunity," in Doug McAdam, J. McCarthy, and M. Zald, eds., *Comparative Perspectives on Social Movements: Political Opportunities, Mobilizing Structures, and Cultural Framings* (Cambridge, UK: Cambridge University Press, 1996): 275–90; Hanspeter Kriesi, "Political Context and Opportunity," in David Snow, Sarah Soule, and Hanspeter Kriesi, eds., *Blackwell Companion to Social Movements* (Oxford: Blackwell, 2004): 67–90; Doug McAdam, *Political Process and the Development of Black Insurgency, 1930–1970* (Chicago: University of Chicago Press, 2010); David S. Meyer, "Protest and Political Opportunities," *Annual Review of Sociology* 30 (2004): 125–45; Sidney Tarrow, "States and Opportunities: The Political Structuring of Social Movements," in *Comparative Perspectives on Social Movements*, eds. Doug McAdam, Joseph McCarthy, and Meyer Zald, (Cambridge, UK: Cambridge University Press, 1996): 41–61; Charles Tilly, *From Mobilization to Revolution* (Reading, MA: Addison-Wesley, 1978).

33   Han, *How Organizations Develop Activists*.

34   Argentina is one of the few countries in the world to have granted the Universal Declaration of Human Rights, along with other human rights–centered international agreements, constitutional status, complementing the other rights guaranteed by the national constitution.

35   Omar G. Encarnación, *Out in the Periphery: Latin America's Gay Rights Revolution* (New York: Oxford University Press, 2016).

36   Melanie C. Green and Timothy C. Brock, "The Role of Transportation in the Persuasiveness of Public Narratives," *Journal of Personality and Social Psychology* 79, no. 5 (2000): 701–21.

37   Ryann Manning, Julie Battilana, and Lakshmi Ramarajan, "Up for Interpretation: How Audiences' Unexpected Responses Threaten Social Movement Identities," *Academy of Management Annual Meeting Proceedings* (October 2014).

38   Manning, Battilana, and Ramarajan, "Up for Interpretation."

39   Encarnación, *Out in the Periphery*, 146.

40   Monica Anderson and Skye Toor, "How Social Media Users Have Discussed Sexual Harassment since #MeToo Went Viral," *Pew Research Center*, October 11, 2018; Benedetta Faedi Duramy, "#MeToo and the Pursuit of Women's International Human Rights," *University of San Francisco Law Review* 54, no. 2 (2020): 215–68.

41   Tarana Burke in discussion with the authors, February 2020.

42   Scholar Ronald A. Heifetz distinguishes between "technical problems," which may be solved through better management or expertise, and "adaptive problems" that require changes in beliefs and values. For more on Heifetz's pioneering concept of adaptive leadership, see *Leadership Without Easy Answers* (Cambridge, MA: Belknap Press, 1994).

43   To further explore the transformation in political participation instigated by the digital age, see Danielle Allen and Jennifer S. Light, *From Voice to Influence: Understanding Citizenship in a Digital Age* (Chicago: University of Chicago Press, 2015).

44   Tufekci, *Twitter and Tear Gas*, 70–1.

45   Alicia Garza, *The Purpose of Power: How We Come Together When We Fall Apart* (New York: One World, 2020), xi.

46   Marshall Ganz, *Why David Sometimes Wins: Leadership, Organization, and Strategy in the California Farm Worker Movement* (Oxford: Oxford University Press, 2009); Tufekci, *Twitter and Tear Gas*.

47   John D. McCarthy and Mayer N. Zald, "Resource Mobilization and Social Movements: A Partial Theory," *American Journal of Sociology* 82, no. 6 (1977): 1212–41.

48   Ganz, *Why David Sometimes Wins*, 252.

7. POWER DOESN'T CHANGE—IT JUST CHANGES HANDS

1 Moisés Naím, *The End of Power: From Boardrooms to Battlefields and Churches to States, Why Being in Charge Isn't What It Used to Be* (New York: Basic Books, 2014), 12.

2 Jeremy Heimans and Henry Timms, *New Power: How Power Works in Our Hyperconnected World—and How to Make It Work for You* (New York: Doubleday, 2018).

3 "The Development of Agriculture," *National Geographic Society*, August 19, 2019, http://www.nationalgeographic.org/article/development -agriculture/; Yuval N. Harari, *Sapiens: A Brief History of Humankind* (London: Harvill Secker, 2014).

4 Jared Diamond, *Guns, Germs, and Steel: The Fates of Human Societies* (New York: W. W. Norton, 1999).

5 David I. Howie, "Benedictine Monks, Manuscripts Copying, and the Renaissance: Johannes Trithemius' «De Laude Scriptorum»" *Revue Bénédictine* 86, no. 1–2 (1976): 129–54.

6 Elizabeth L. Einstein, *The Printing Press as an Agent of Change* (Cambridge, UK: Cambridge University Press, 1980).

7 L. B. Larsen et al., "New Ice Core Evidence for a Volcanic Cause of the A.D. 536 Dust Veil," *Geophysical Research Letters* 35, no. 4 (2008).

8 Greg Williams, "Disrupting Poverty: How Barefoot College Is Empowering Women through Peer-to-Peer Learning and Technology," *Wired UK*, March 7, 2011, https://www.wired.co.uk/article/disrupting-poverty.

9 Meagan Fallone, in discussion with the authors, December 2020.

10 René Descartes, *A Discourse on Method*, trans. John Veitch (London: J. M. Dent, 1912), 49.

11 The scientific method uses observations and rigorous testing of falsifiable hypotheses to acquire knowledge about the world.

12 Meghan Bartels, "How Do You Stop a Hypothetical Asteroid From Hitting Earth? NASA's On It," *Space.com*, May 2, 2019, https://www.space .com/asteroid-threat-simulation-nasa-deflection-idea.html.

13 Keenan Mayo and Peter Newcomb, "The Birth of the World Wide Web: An Oral History of the Internet," *Vanity Fair*, July 2008, https://www .vanityfair.com/news/2008/07/internet200807.

14 Naím, *The End of Power*; Heimans and Timms, *New Power*.

15 Joshua Gans and Andrew Leigh, *Innovation + Equality: How to Create a Future that is More Star Trek Than Terminator* (Cambridge, MA: The MIT Press, 2019): 7.

16 Jean Luc Chabert, *A History of Algorithms: From the Pebble to the Microchip* (Berlin: Springer, 1999): 7.

17 "Coding," *Explained*, Vox Media (Netflix, 2019).

18   Pedro Domingos, *The Master Algorithm: How the Quest for the Ultimate Learning Machine Will Remake Our World* (New York: Basic Books, 2015), 1.

19   "Coding," Vox Media; Ajay Agrawal, Joshua Gans, and Avi Goldfarb, *Prediction Machines: The Simple Economics of Artificial Intelligence* (Boston, MA: *Harvard Business Review Press*, 2018).

20   Sara Reardon, "Rise of Robot Radiologists," *Nature (London)* 576, no. 7787 (2019): S54–58.

21   For an analysis of the opportunities and challenges in this domain, see Miriam Mutebi et al., "Innovative Use of MHealth and Clinical Technology for Oncology Clinical Trials in Africa," *JCO Global Oncology*, no. 6 (2020): 948–53.

22   Susan Wharton Gates, Vanessa Gail Perry, and Peter M. Zorn, "Automated Underwriting in Mortgage Lending: Good News for the Underserved?" *Housing Policy Debate* 13, no. 2 (2002): 369–91. For a pioneering analysis of the debiasing potential of linear models, including their superior accuracy in predicting loan underwriting defaults, see Robyn M. Dawes, "The Robust Beauty of Improper Linear Models in Decision-Making," *American Psychologist* 34, no. 7 (1979): 571–82.

23   Batya Friedman and Helen Nissenbaum, "Bias in Computer Systems," *ACM Transactions on Information Systems* 14, no. 3 (1996): 330–47; also discussed in Agrawal, Gans, and Goldfarb, *Prediction Machines*, and in Marco Ianstiti and Karim Lakhani, *Competing in the Age of AI: Strategy and Leadership When Algorithms and Networks Run the World* (Boston: Harvard Business Review Press, 2020).

24   Tom Simonite, "The Best Algorithms Still Struggle to Recognize Black Faces," *Wired*, Conde Nast, July 22, 2019, https://www.wired.com/story/best-algorithms-struggle-recognize-black-faces-equally/. For more on algorithmic recognition bias see Joy Buolamwini and Timnit Gebru, "Gender Shades: Intersectional Accuracy Disparities in Commercial Gender Classification," in *Conference on Fairness, Accountability and Transparency*, PMLR (2018): 77–91; Yui Man Lui et al., "A Meta-Analysis of Face Recognition Covariates," in *2009 IEEE 3rd International Conference on Biometrics: Theory, Applications, and Systems* (2009): 1–8.

25   Joy Buolamwini, "How I'm Fighting Bias in Algorithms," TEDxBeaconStreet, November 2016, https://www.ted.com/talks/joy_buolamwini_how_i_m_fighting_bias_in_algorithms.

26   Virginia Eubanks, *Automating Inequality: How High-Tech Tools Profile, Police, and Punish the Poor* (New York: Picador, 2019); Ruha Benjamin, *Race After Technology: Abolitionist Tools for the New Jim Code* (Cambridge, MA: Polity, 2019).

27   Cathy O'Neil, *Weapons of Math Destruction: How Big Data Increases*

Inequality and Threatens Democracy (Westminster, UK: Penguin Books, 2017); Safiya Umoja Noble, *Algorithms of Oppression: How Search Engines Reinforce Racism* (New York: New York University Press, 2018).

28 Cathy O'Neil, "The Era of Blind Faith in Big Data Must End," TED, April 2017, https://www.ted.com/talks/cathy_o_neil_the_era_of_blind _faith_in_big_data_must_end.

29 Emily Chang, *Brotopia: Breaking up the Boys' Club of Silicon Valley* (New York: Portfolio/Penguin, 2019).

30 In the eighteenth century, English philosopher Jeremy Bentham designed an influential prison system, the "panopticon." His design delineated space in the prison such that a ring-shape of prison cells surrounded a central tower for guards. While guards could always see all of prisoners' cells, guards remained invisible to prisoners in faraway small windows. French intellectual Michel Foucault went on to see the panopticon as a symbol of social control that could be understood to characterize the everyday life of not only prisoners but actually all citizens. See Michel Foucault, *Discipline and Punish: The Birth of the Prison* (New York: Vintage Books, 1995).

31 Yuval Noah Harari, "Why Technology Favors Tyranny," *The Atlantic*, September 13, 2018, https://www.theatlantic.com/magazine/archive/2018 /10/yuval-noah-harari-technology-tyranny/568330/.

32 Adam Satariano, "How My Boss Monitors Me While I Work From Home," *New York Times*, May 6, 2020, https://www.nytimes.com/2020/05 /06/technology/employee-monitoring-work-from-home-virus.html.

33 Amy Webb, *The Big Nine: How the Tech Titans and Their Thinking Machines Could Warp Humanity* (New York: PublicAffairs, 2020).

34 Shoshana Zuboff, *The Age of Surveillance Capitalism: The Fight for a Human Future at the New Frontier of Power* (New York: PublicAffairs, 2020).

35 Tobias Rose-Stockwell, "This Is How Your Fear and Outrage Are Being Sold for Profit," *Medium*, August 12, 2019, https://medium.com /@tobiasrose/the-enemy-in-our-feeds-e86511488de. See also Tim Wu, *The Attention Merchants: The Epic Scramble to Get inside Our Heads* (Vancouver, B.C.: Langara College, 2020).

36 Agrawal, Gans, and Goldfarb, *Prediction Machines*, 43.

37 *Open Hearing on Foreign Influence Operations' Use of Social Media Platforms (Company Witnesses), Before the Select Committee on Intelligence of the United States Senate*, 115th Cong. (2018) (statement of Jack Dorsey, CEO of Twitter).

38 Jerrold Nadler and David N. Cicilline, *Investigation of Competition in Digital Markets: Majority Staff Report and Recommendations*, United States House of Representatives Subcommittee on Antitrust, Commercial and Administrative Law of the Committee of the Judiciary, 2020.

39 Fernando Belinchón and Moynihan Qayyah, "25 Giant Companies That Are Bigger than Entire Countries," *Business Insider*, July 25, 2018, https://www.businessinsider.com/25-giant-companies-that-earn-more-than-entire-countries-2018-7.

40 Jenny Odell, *How to Do Nothing: Resisting the Attention Economy* (New York: Melville House, 2021).

41 Dell Cameron and Kate Conger, "Google Is Helping the Pentagon Build AI for Drones," *Gizmodo*, June 1, 2018, https://gizmodo.com/google-is-helping-the-pentagon-build-ai-for-drones-1823464533.

42 Meredith Whittaker, in discussion with the authors, September 2020.

43 Scott Shane and Daisuke Wakabayashi, "'The Business of War': Google Employees Protest Work for the Pentagon," *New York Times*, April 4, 2018, https://www.nytimes.com/2018/04/04/technology/google-letter-ceo-pentagon-project.html.

44 Reuters, "Google to Halt Controversial Project Aiding Pentagon Drones," *NBC News*, June 2, 2018, https://www.nbcnews.com/news/military/google-halt-controversial-project-aiding-pentagon-drones-n879471.

45 Lulu Chang, "As Google Continues Its Work on a Military Project, a Dozen Employees Resign," *Digital Trends*, June 2, 2018, https://www.digitaltrends.com/business/google-employees-letter-to-ceo-war/.

46 Davey Alba, "Google Backs Away from Controversial Military Drone Project," *BuzzFeed*, June 1, 2018, https://www.buzzfeednews.com/article/daveyalba/google-says-it-will-not-follow-through-on-pentagon-drone-ai.

47 Sundar Pichai, "AI at Google: Our Principles," Google, June 7, 2018, https://blog.google/technology/ai/ai-principles/.

48 Ryan Gallagher, "Google Plans to Launch Censored Search Engine in China, Leaked Documents Reveal," *The Intercept*, August 1, 2018, https://theintercept.com/2018/08/01/google-china-search-engine-censorship/.

49 Find a copy of the open letter in the *New York Times* archive here: https://int.nyt.com/data/documenthelper/166-dragonfly-letter/ae6267f0128f4facd183/optimized/full.pdf#page=1.

50 "Open Letter: Google Must Not Capitulate on Human Rights to Gain Access to China," Amnesty International, August 28, 2018, https://www.amnesty.org/en/latest/news/2018/08/open-letter-to-google-on-reported-plans-to-launch-a-censored-search-engine-in-china/.

51 Taylor Telford and Elizabeth Dwoskin, "Google Employees Worldwide Walk Out over Allegations of Sexual Harassment, Inequality within Company," *Washington Post*, November 1, 2018, https://www.washingtonpost.com/business/2018/11/01/google-employees-worldwide-begin-walkout-over-allegations-sexual-harassment-inequality-within-company; Ryan Mac, "Disgraced Google Exec Andy Rubin Quietly Left His Venture Firm

Earlier This Year," *BuzzFeed*, October 13, 2019, https://www.buzzfeed news.com/article/ryanmac/andy-rubin-playground-global-google-quiet -departure.

52 Sam Byford, "Google Employees Worldwide are Walking Out Today to Protest Handling of Sexual Misconduct," *The Verge*, November 1, 2018, https://www.theverge.com/2018/11/1/18051026/google-walkout-sexual -harassment-protest.

53 Telford and Dwoskin, "Google Employees Worldwide Walk Out."

54 Daisuke Wakabayashi, "Google Ends Forced Arbitration for All Employee Disputes," *New York Times*, February 21, 2019, https://www.ny times.com/2019/02/21/technology/google-forced-arbitration.html.

55 "Google's Project Dragonfly 'Terminated' in China," *BBC News*, July 17, 2019, https://www.bbc.com/news/technology-49015516.

56 Johana Bhuiyan, "How the Google Walkout Transformed Tech Workers into Activists," *Los Angeles Times*, November 6, 2019, https://www .latimes.com/business/technology/story/2019-11-06/google-employee -walkout-tech-industry-activism. On the importance of paying attention to such employee rebellions, see David Courpasson and Jean-Claude Thoenig, *When Managers Rebel*, 1st ed. (London: Palgrave Macmillan UK, 2010).

57 Beth Kowitt, "Inside Google's Civil War," *Fortune*, January 29, 2020, https://fortune.com/longform/inside-googles-civil-war/.

58 Kate Conger, "Hundreds of Google Employees Unionize, Culminating Years of Activism," *New York Times*, January 4, 2021, https://www.nytimes .com/2021/01/04/technology/google-employees-union.html.

59 "Home," Alphabet Workers Union, December 15, 2020, https://alphabet workersunion.org/.

60 "LIVE: Apple CEO Tim Cook speaks at Brussels' International Data Privacy Day," *Reuters* (video), January 28, 2021, https://www.youtube .com/watch?v=ug6tA6fhhdQ.

61 Sundar Pichai, "Why Google Thinks We Need to Regulate AI," *Financial Times*, January 20, 2020, https://www.ft.com/content/3467659a-386d -11ea-ac3c-f68c10993b04.

62 "What is GDRP, the EU's New Data Protection Law?," gdrp.eu, accessed April 7, 2021, https://gdrp.eu/what-is-gdpr/.

63 "GDPR: Noyb.eu Filed Four Complaints over 'Forced Consent' against Google, Instagram, WhatsApp and Facebook," noyb.eu, May 25, 2018, https://noyb.eu/en/gdpr-noybeu-filed-four-complaints-over-forced -consent-against-google-instagram-whatsapp-and.

64 "Austrian Privacy Activist Schrems Files Complaint against Amazon," *Reuters*, February 19, 2020, https://www.reuters.com/article/europe -privacy-amazoncom/austrian-privacy-activist-schrems-files-complaint -against-amazon-idUSL8N2AJ4ZJ.

65   Kara Swisher, "She's Bursting Big Tech's Bubble," *New York Times*, October 29, 2020, https://www.nytimes.com/2020/10/29/opinion/sway-kara -swisher-lina-khan.html.

66   Lina M. Khan, "The Separation of Platforms and Commerce," *Columbia Law Review* 119, no. 4 (2019): 973–1098; Kari Paul, "'This Is Big': U.S. Lawmakers Take Aim at Once-Untouchable Big Tech," *The Guardian*, December 19, 2020, https://www.theguardian.com/technology/2020/dec /18/google-facebook-antitrust-lawsuits-big-tech.

67   For instance, European regulators investigated Google for seven years, which resulted in a $2.7 billion fine because the web giant was found to favor its own shopping service in search results, stifling competition. In 2019, Germany cracked down on Facebook for abuse of its market power, prohibiting the company from sharing data about users, without their consent, across Facebook-owned platforms such as Instagram and WhatsApp. See Michael A. Corrier, "Big Tech, Antitrust, and Breakup," *Georgetown Journal of International Affairs*, 2020.

68   Sheelah Kolhatkar, "How Elizabeth Warren Came Up with a Plan to Break Up Big Tech," *The New Yorker*, August 20, 2019, https://www.new yorker.com/business/currency/how-elizabeth-warren-came-up-with-a-plan -to-break-up-big-tech; Lina M. Khan, "Amazon's Paradox," *The Yale Law Journal* 126, no. 3 (2017): 710–805.

69   Rod McGuirk, "Australia Passes Law to Make Google, Facebook Pay for News," *AP News*, February 25, 2021, https://apnews.com/article /australia-law-google-facebook-pay-news-959ffb44307da22cdeebdd85 290c0cde.

70   Gabriel Gieger, "Court Rules Deliveroo Used 'Discriminatory' Algorithm," *Vice*, January 5, 2021, https://www.vice.com/en/article/7k9e4e /court-rules-deliveroo-used-discriminatory-algorithm.

71   Shirin Ghaffary, "After 20,000 Workers Walked out, Google Said It Got the Message. The Workers Disagree," *Vox*, November 21, 2018, https://www.vox.com/2018/11/21/18105719/google-walkout-real-change -organizers-protest-discrimination-kara-swisher-recode-decode-podcast.

72   *Artificial Intelligence, Societal and Ethical Implications, Before the United States House of Representatives Committee on Science, Space, and Technology*, 116th Cong. (2019) (statement of Meredith Whittaker, cofounder and codirector of AI Now Institute).

73   For example, Genie Barton, Nicol Turner-Lee, and Paul Resnick, "Algorithmic Bias Detection and Mitigation: Best Practices and Policies to Reduce Consumer Harms," *Brookings*, May 22, 2019, https://www.brookings.edu /research/algorithmic-bias-detection-and-mitigation-best-practices-and -policies-to-reduce-consumer-harms/; Sorelle A. Friedler et al., "A Comparative Study of Fairness Enhancing Interventions in Machine Learning,"

in *Proceedings of the Conference on Fairness, Accountability, and Transparency* (2019): 329–38; Solon Barocas, Moritz Hardt, and Arvind Narayanan, *Fairness and Machine Learning* (fairmlbook.org, 2019).

74 Cynthia Dwork, "Skewed or Rescued? The Emerging Theory of Algorithmic Fairness," Berkman Klein Center, November 29, 2018, https://cyber.harvard.edu/events/skewed-or-rescued-emerging-theory-algorithmic-fairness.

75 Brendan F. Klare et al., "Face Recognition Performance: Role of Demographic Information," *IEEE Transactions on Information Forensics and Security* 7, no. 6 (December 2012): 1789–1801.

76 Jerry Kaplan, *Humans Need Not Apply: A Guide to Wealth and Work in the Age of Artificial Intelligence* (New Haven: Yale University Press, 2015); Morgan R. Frank et al., "Toward Understanding the Impact of Artificial Intelligence on Labor," *Proceedings of the National Academy of Sciences* 116, no.14 (2019): 6531–9.

77 John Hawksworth, Richard Berriman, and Saloni Goel, *Will Robots Really Steal Our Jobs? An International Analysis of the Potential Long-Term Impact of Automation* (PwC, February 2018).

78 For key works in the sprawling literature on the future of work, see Erik Brynjolfsson and Andrew McAfee, *Race Against the Machine* (Lexington, MA: Digital Frontier Press, 2011); Erik Brynjolfsson and Andrew McAfee, *The Second Machine Age* (New York: W. W. Norton, 2014); Kaplan, *Humans Need Not Apply* (2015); Alec Ross, *The Industries of the Future* (New York: Simon & Schuster, 2016); and Richard Susskind and Daniel Susskind, *The Future of the Professions* (Oxford: Oxford University Press, 2017).

79 David Autor, David Mindell, and Elisabeth Reynolds, "The Work of the Future: Shaping Technology and Institutions," MIT Work of the Future, November 17, 2020, https://workofthefuture.mit.edu/research-post/the-work-of-the-future-shaping-technology-and-institutions/.

80 The acronym CRISPR stands for "clustered regularly interspaced short palindromic repeats," which refers to a region of DNA that, with various CRISPR-associated proteins, functions like genetic scissors, enabling a cell or scientist to edit DNA or its messenger RNA very precisely. See Jennifer A. Doudna and Emmanuelle Charpentier, "The New Frontier of Genome Editing with CRISPR-Cas9," *Science* 346, no. 6213 (2013).

81 Megan Rose Dickey, "Human Capital: 'People Were Afraid of Being Critical with Me,'" *TechCrunch*, August 28, 2020, https://social.techcrunch.com/2020/08/28/human-capital-it-doesnt-have-to-be-this-way/.

82 Ottmar Edenhofer et al., "Summary for Policymakers," in *Climate Change 2014: Mitigation of Climate Change*, Contribution of Working Group III to the Fifth Assessment Report of the Intergovernmental

Panel on Climate Change (Cambridge, UK: Cambridge University Press, 2014).

83 Ronald Segal, *The Black Diaspora: Five Centuries of the Black Experience Outside Africa* (New York: Farrar, Straus, and Giroux, 1995), 4.

84 François Rabelais and Andrew Brown, *Pantagruel: King of the Dipsodes Restored to His Natural State with His Dreadful Deeds and Exploits* (London: Hesperus, 2003), 34.

85 Yuval N. Harari, *Homo Deus: A Brief History of Tomorrow* (New York: Harper, 2017); Derek Thompson, "Can Science Cure Aging?" *The Atlantic*, September 13, 2018, https://www.theatlantic.com/ideas/archive/2018/09/can-science-cure-aging/570121/.

86 For just two examples, John Koetsier, "Elon Musk's 42,000 Star-Link Satellites Could Just Save the World," *Forbes*, January 9, 2020, https://www.forbes.com/sites/johnkoetsier/2020/01/09/elon-musks-42000-starlink-satellites-could-just-save-the-world/; and Navneet Alang, "As the Robots Arrive, We Have to Remember: Another Future is Possible," *Toronto Star*, February 27, 2021, https://www.thestar.com/business/opinion/2021/02/27/as-the-robots-arrive-we-have-to-remember-another-future-is-possible.html.

8. POWER IN CHECK

1 Simonetta Adorni Braccesi and Mario Ascheri, eds., *Politica e Cultura nelle Repubbliche Italiane dal Medioevo all'Età Moderna: Firenze, Genova, Lucca, Siena, Venezia,* (Rome: Istituto storico italiano per l'Età Moderna e Contemporanea, 2001); William Marvin Bowsky, *A Medieval Italian Commune: Siena Under the Nine, 1287–1355* (Berkeley: University of California Press, 1981).

2 Estimates place the number of Sienese citizens who served in the Government of the Nine between 2,000 and 3,000 from 1287 to 1355, when Siena's estimated population ranged from 62,000 to a peak of 100,000 before the Black Death. Although the Nine were all men (women were excluded from the city's political life) and members of certain social classes and families were elected more often than others, the many rules of exclusion of aristocrats and other privileged citizens from serving as city governors, together with the stringent two-month term limits and twenty-month waiting period before eligibility for reappointment, gave political representation to broad swaths of Siena's citizenry. For a detailed analysis, see Mario Ascheri, "La Siena del 'Buon Governo' (1287–1355)," in Adorni Braccesi and Ascheri, *Politica e Cultura nelle Repubbliche Italiane*, 81–107.

3 Cameron Anderson and Sebastien Brion, "Perspectives on Power in

Organizations," *Annual Review of Organizational Psychology and Organizational Behavior* 1, no. 1 (2014): 67–97; Peter Fleming and André Spicer, "Power in Management and Organization Science," *Academy of Management Annals* 8, no. 1 (2014): 237–98.

4 Ellen Ochoa in discussion with the authors, April 2019 and October 2020.

5 Raj Chetty et al., "Race and Economic Opportunity in the United States," *NBER* working paper 24441 (2018); Cecilia L. Ridgeway, *Framed by Gender: How Gender Inequality Persists in the Modern World* (Oxford: Oxford University Press, 2011).

6 John Matthew Amis, Johanna Mair, and Kamal Munir, "The Organizational Reproduction of Inequality," *Academy of Management Annals* 14, no. 1 (2020): 195–230.

7 Michael L. Coats, "Michael L. Coats—NASA, Johnson Space Center," *Diversity Journal*, March 12, 2012, https://diversityjournal.com/7663 -michael-l-coats-nasa-johnson-space-center/.

8 David Thomas and Robin Ely, "Making Differences Matter: A New Paradigm for Managing Diversity," *Harvard Business Review* 74, no. 5 (1996): 79–90.

9 Robin J. Ely and David A. Thomas, "Getting Serious About Diversity: Enough Already with the Business Case," *Harvard Business Review* 98, no. 6 (2020): 114–22.

10 See Sheryl Sandberg, *Lean In: Women, Work, and the Will to Lead* (New York: Knopf, 2013).

11 Rosabeth Moss Kanter, *Men and Women of the Corporation* (New York: Basic Books, 2010).

12 For more on the cultural contingency of tokenism, see Catherine J. Turco, "Cultural Foundations of Tokenism: Evidence from the Leveraged Buyout Industry," *American Sociological Review* 75, no. 6 (2010): 894–913.

13 Alicia DeSantola, Lakshmi Ramarajan, and Julie Battilana, "New Venture Milestones and the First Female Board Member," *Academy of Management Best Paper Proceedings* (2017).

14 Carolyn Wiley and Mireia Monllor-Tormos, "Board Gender Diversity in the STEM&F Sectors: The Critical Mass Required to Drive Firm Performance," *Journal of Leadership & Organizational Studies* 25, no. 3 (2018): 290–308.

15 Alexandra Kalev, Frank Dobbin, and Erin Kelly, "Best Practices or Best Guesses? Assessing the Efficacy of Corporate Affirmative Action and Diversity Policies," *American Sociological Review* 71, no. 4 (2006): 589–617.

16 Emilio J. Castilla and Stephen Benard, "The Paradox of Meritocracy in

Organizations," *Administrative Science Quarterly* 55, no. 4 (2010): 543–76. For more on how diversity programs, when misused, can undermine racial justice, see Ellen Berrey, *The Enigma of Diversity: The Language of Race and the Limits of Racial Justice* (Chicago: University of Chicago Press, 2015).

17 Frank Dobbin and Alexandra Kalev, "Why Doesn't Diversity Training Work? The Challenge for Industry and Academia," *Anthropology Now* 10, no. 2 (2018): 48–55; Alexandra Kalev and Frank Dobbin, "Companies Need to Think Bigger Than Diversity Training," *Harvard Business Review* (October 20, 2020), https://hbr.org/2020/10/companies-need-to-think-bigger-than-diversity-training.

18 Iris Bohnet, *What Works: Gender Equality by Design* (Cambridge, MA: Belknap Press of Harvard University Press, 2018); Colleen Ammerman and Boris Groysberg, *Glass Half-Broken: Shattering the Barriers That Still Hold Women Back at Work* (Harvard Business Review Press, 2021).

19 Frank Dobbin and Alexandra Kalev, "Why Diversity Programs Fail," *Harvard Business Review* (2016), https://hbr.org/2016/07/why-diversity-programs-fail; see also Kalev and Dobbin, "Companies Need to Think Bigger."

20 Robert Livingston, "How to Promote Racial Equity in the Workplace," *Harvard Business Review* 98, no. 5 (2020): 64–72; see also Robert Livingston, *The Conversation: How Seeking and Speaking the Truth About Racism Can Radically Transform Individuals and Organizations* (New York: Currency, 2021).

21 Tina Opie and Laura Morgan Roberts, "Do Black Lives Really Matter in the Workplace? Restorative Justice as a Means to Reclaim Humanity," *Equality, Diversity and Inclusion: An International Journal* 36, no. 8 (2017): 707–19.

22 For more on racial labor market discrimination, see Marianne Bertrand and Sendhil Mullainathan, "Are Emily and Greg More Employable than Lakisha and Jamal: A Field Experiment on Labor Market Discrimination," *The American Economic Review* 94, no. 4 (2004): 991–1013; Devah Pager, Bart Bonikowski, and Bruce Western, "Discrimination in a Low-Wage Labor Market," *American Sociological Review* 74, no. 5 (2009): 777–99.

23 Lauren A. Rivera, "Go with Your Gut: Emotion and Evaluation in Job Interviews," *American Journal of Sociology* 120, no. 5 (2015): 1139–89; and *Pedigree: How Elite Students Get Elite Jobs* (Princeton: Princeton University Press, 2015). See also Gardiner Morse, "Designing a Bias-Free Organization," *Harvard Business Review* 94, no. 7–8 (2016): 62–7.

24 Laura Morgan Roberts and Anthony J. Mayo, "Toward a Racially Just Workplace," *Harvard Business Review*, November 14, 2019, https://hbr

.org/2019/11/toward-a-racially-just-workplace. See also Laura Morgan Roberts, Anthony J. Mayo, and David A. Thomas, *Race, Work, and Leadership* (La Vergne: Harvard Business Review Press, 2019).

25 Colleen Sheppard, *Inclusive Equality: The Relational Dimensions of Systemic Discrimination in Canada* (Montreal: McGill Queen's University Press, 2010).

26 Livingston, "How to Promote Racial Equity in the Workplace"; Livingston, *The Conversation*.

27 Franklin A. Gevurtz, "The Historical and Political Origins of the Corporate Board of Directors," *Hofstra Law Review* 33, no. 1 (2004); Cyril O'Donnell, "Origins of the Corporate Executive," *Bulletin of the Business Historical Society* 26, no. 2 (1952): 55–72.

28 Richard Mulgan, *Holding Power to Account: Accountability in Modern Democracies* (New York: Palgrave Macmillan, 2014).

29 Steven Boivie et al., "Are Boards Designed to Fail? The Implausibility of Effective Board Monitoring," *Academy of Management Annals* 10, no. 1 (2016): 319–407.

30 Michael Useem, *The Inner Circle: Large Corporations and the Rise of Business Political Activity in the U.S. and U.K.* (Oxford: Oxford University Press, 1992); Mark Mizruchi, *The American Corporate Network* (Beverly Hills, CA: SAGE, 1982).

31 Gerald F. Davis, Mina Yoo, and Wayne E. Baker, "The Small World of the American Corporate Elite, 1982–2001," *Strategic Organization* 1, no. 3 (2003): 301–26.

32 Johan S. G. Chu and Gerald F. Davis, "Who Killed the Inner Circle? The Decline of the American Corporate Interlock Network," *American Journal of Sociology* 122, no. 3 (2016): 714–54.

33 Traditionally, directors have an obligation to act in the best interest of the shareholders. This is their fiduciary duty to shareholders. For more, see Leo Strine, "The Dangers of Denial: The Need for a Clear-Eyed Understanding of the Power and Accountability Structure Established by the Delaware General Corporation Law," SSRN Scholarly Paper ID 2576389, Rochester, NY: Social Science Research Network, https://papers.ssrn.com/abstract=2576389.

34 Lawrence Mishel and Jori Kandra, "CEO Compensation Surged 14% in 2019 to $21.3 Million: CEOs Now Earn 320 Times as Much as a Typical Worker," *Economic Policy Institute* (blog), August 18, 2020, https://www.epi.org/publication/ceo-compensation-surged-14-in-2019-to-21-3-million-ceos-now-earn-320-times-as-much-as-a-typical-worker/.

35 Rebecca Henderson, *Reimagining Capitalism in a World on Fire* (New York: PublicAffairs, 2020); Naomi Klein, *This Changes Everything: Capitalism vs. the Climate* (New York: Simon & Schuster, 2014).

36 Sarah Kaplan, *The 360° Corporation: From Stakeholder Trade-Offs to Transformation* (Stanford, CA: Stanford Business Books, 2019); R. Edward Freeman, Kristen Martin, and Bidhan L. Parmar, *The Power of And: Responsible Business Without Trade-Offs* (New York: Columbia Business School Publishing, 2020). See also Mariana Mazzucato, *Mission Economy: A Moonshot Guide to Changing Capitalism* (Harper Business, 2021).

37 Tyler Wry, Kevin Chuah, and Michael Useem, *Rigidity and Reversion: Why the Business Roundtable Faltered in the Face of COVID* (Wharton School Working Paper, 2021).

38 Alnoor Ebrahim, Julie Battilana, and Johanna Mair, "The Governance of Social Enterprises: Mission Drift and Accountability Challenges in Hybrid Organizations," *Research in Organizational Behavior* 34 (2014): 81–100; Julie Battilana et al., "Beyond Shareholder Value Maximization: Accounting for Financial/Social Tradeoffs in Dual Purpose Companies," *The Academy of Management Review*, in press; Alnoor Ebrahim, *Measuring Social Change: Performance and Accountability in a Complex World* (Redwood City: Stanford Business Books, 2019).

39 Julie Battilana, Anne-Claire Pache, Metin Sengul, and Marissa Kimsey, "The Dual-Purpose Playbook," *Harvard Business Review* 97, no. 4 (2019): 124–33; Julie Battilana, "Cracking the Organizational Challenge of Pursuing Joint Social and Financial Goals: Social Enterprise as a Laboratory to Understand Hybrid Organizing," *M@n@gment* 21, no. 4 (2018): 1278–305; Ebrahim, Battilana, and Mair, "The Governance of Social Enterprises."

40 Chris Marquis, *Better Business: How the B Corp Movement is Remaking Capitalism* (New Haven: Yale University Press, 2020).

41 Cornelia Caseau and Gilles Grolleau, "Impact Investing: Killing Two Birds with One Stone?" *Financial Analysts Journal* 76, no. 4 (2020): 40–52; Abhilash Mudaliar and Hannah Dithrich, "Sizing the Impact Investing Market," *Global Impact Investing Network*, April 2019, https://thegiin.org/assets/Sizing%20the%20Impact%20Investing%20Market _webfile.pdf; Global Impact Investing Network, "Annual Impact Investor Survey 2020," 10th ed., June 2020, https://thegiin.org/assets/GIIN %20Annual%20Impact%20Investor%20Survey%202020.pdf.

42 Isabelle Ferreras, *Firms as Political Entities: Saving Democracy through Economic Bicameralism* (Cambridge, UK: Cambridge University Press, 2017).

43 Elizabeth Anderson, "How Bosses Are (Literally) like Dictators," *Vox*, July 17, 2017, https://www.vox.com/the-big-idea/2017/7/17/15973478 /bosses-dictators-workplace-rights-free-markets-unions; see also Elizabeth Anderson, *Private Government: How Employers Rule Our Lives (and Why We Don't Talk about It)* (Princeton, NJ: Princeton University Press, 2017), 39.

44   Isabelle Ferreras, Julie Battilana, and Dominique Méda, *Le Manifeste Travail: Démocratiser, Démarchandiser, Dépolluer* (Paris: Le Seuil, Paris; forthcoming in English, University of Chicago Press, 2022); Gerald Davis, "Corporate Purpose Needs Democracy," *Journal of Management Studies* (2020).

45   International Labor Organization, "Who Are Domestic Workers," International Labour Organization, accessed April 7, 2021, https://www.ilo .org/global/topics/domestic-workers/who/lang--en/index.htm.

46   Palak Shah in discussion with the authors, April and September 2019.

47   Robert Reich, "Almost 80% of U.S. Workers Live from Paycheck to Paycheck. Here's Why," *The Guardian*, July 29, 2018, http://www.theguardian .com/commentisfree/2018/jul/29/us-economy-workers-paycheck-robert -reich.

48   "Union Membership (Annual) News Release," January 22, 2021, https:// www.bls.gov/news.release/union2.htm#; Matthew Walters and Lawrence Mishel, "How Unions Help All Workers," *Economic Policy Institute*, August 26, 2003, https://www.epi.org/publication/briefingpapers_bp143/. For an analysis of the global evidence from over three hundred studies on the economic impact of unionization, see Hristos Doucouliagos, Richard B. Freeman, and Patrice Laroche, *The Economics of Trade Unions: A Study of a Research Field and Its Findings* (Abingdon-on-Thames: Taylor & Francis, 2017).

49   ILO, *Domestic Workers across the World: Global and Regional Statistics and the Extent of Legal Protection* (Geneva: ILO, 2013).

50   Joseph E. Stiglitz, *The Price of Inequality*, 1st ed. (New York: W. W. Norton, 2012); Torsten Persson and Guido Tabellini, "Is Inequality Harmful for Growth? Theory and Evidence," *American Economic Review* 84, no. 3 (1994): 600–21.

51   Ai-jen Poo in discussion with the authors, October 2019.

52   Lauren Hilgers, "The New Labor Movement Fighting for Domestic Workers' Rights," *New York Times*, February 21, 2019, https://www.nytimes .com/interactive/2019/02/21/magazine/national-domestic-workers -alliance.html.

53   Alexia Fernández Campbell, "The Worldwide Uber Strike Is a Key Test for the Gig Economy," *Vox*, May 8, 2019, https://www.vox.com/2019/5/8 /18535367/uber-drivers-strike-2019-cities.

54   For more data on electricity co-ops in the United States, see the National Rural Electric Cooperative Association's fact sheet at: https://www .electric.coop/wp-content/uploads/2021/01/Co-op-Facts-and-Figures.pdf.

55   Juliet Shor, *After the Gig: How the Sharing Economy Got Hijacked and How To Win It Back* (Berkeley: University of California Press, 2020).

56   "What's American for Mitbestimmung?: Most of the World Has Yet to

Embrace Co-determination," *The Economist*, February 1, 2020, https://www.economist.com/business/2020/02/01/most-of-the-world-has-yet-to-embrace-co-determination.

57 John Addison, *The Economics of Codetermination: Lessons from the German Experience* (New York: Palgrave Macmillan US, 2009).

58 Isabelle Ferreras, *Firms as Political Entities*.

59 Isabelle Ferreras, Julie Battilana, and Dominique Méda, "Let's Democratize and Decommodify Work," *The Boston Globe*, May 2020. The publication was reprinted in more than forty other newspapers in thirty-six countries across the world. It led to the launching of an initiative (www.democratizingwork.org) and to the writing of a book, Ferreras, Battilana, and Méda, *Le Manifeste Travail*.

60 Julie Battilana et al., "Harnessing Productive Tensions in Hybrid Organizations: The Case of Work Integration Social Enterprises," *Academy of Management Journal* 58, no. 6 (2015): 1658–85; Battilana et al., "The Dual-Purpose Playbook"; Sophie Bacq, Julie Battilana, and Hélène Bovais, "The Role of Collegial Governance in Sustaining the Organizational Pursuit of Hybrid Goals," Working Paper, 2020; Battilana, "Cracking the Organizational Challenge."

61 Julie Battilana, Michael Fuerstein, and Mike Lee, "New Prospects for Organizational Democracy? How the Joint Pursuit of Social and Financial Goals Challenges Traditional Organizational Designs," in *Capitalism Beyond Mutuality?: Perspectives Integrating Philosophy and Social Science*, ed. Subramanian Rangan (Oxford, UK: Oxford University Press, 2018).

62 Battilana, Fuerstein, and Lee, "New Prospects for Organizational Democracy?"

63 Sviatoslav Dmitriev, *The Birth of the Athenian Community: From Solon to Cleisthenes* (Abingdon-on-Thames: Routledge, 2018). There is some controversy over whether Cleisthenes himself used the term *demokratia* to describe his new system, with some instead describing it with the term *isonomia*, meaning roughly "equality before the law." See Raphael Sealey, "The Origins of 'Demokratia,'" *California Studies in Classical Antiquity* 6 (1974): 253.

64 David Stockton, *The Classical Athenian Democracy* (Oxford University Press, 1990); George Tridimas, "A Political Economy Perspective of Direct Democracy in Ancient Athens?" *Constitutional Political Economy* 22, no. 1 (2011): 58–82.

65 Ian Worthington, *Demosthenes of Athens and the Fall of Classical Greece* (Oxford University Press, 2012).

66 Charles de Secondat Montesquieu, *The Spirit of the Laws*, Anne Cohler, Basia Carolyn Miller, and Harold Stone (Cambridge, UK: Cambridge University Press, 1989), 155.

67 Hilary Bok, "Baron de Montesquieu, Charles-Louis de Secondat," in *The Stanford Encyclopedia of Philosophy*, ed. Edward N. Zalta (Stanford University, 2018).

68 For the full report, see Sarah Repucci and Amy Slipowitz, *Freedom in the World 2021: Democracy Under Siege* (Washington, DC: Freedom House, 2021).

69 The many sources on this topic include: Steven Levitsky and Daniel Ziblatt, *How Democracies Die* (New York: Crown, 2018); Timothy Snyder, *On Tyranny: Twenty Lessons from the Twentieth Century* (New York: Tim Duggan Books, 2017); Benjamin Carter Hett, *The Death of Democracy: Hitler's Rise to Power and the Downfall of the Weimar Republic* (New York: Henry Holt & Co., 2018).

70 Snyder, *On Tyranny*, 24.

71 Tope Ogundipe in discussion with the authors, July 2019.

72 PEN International et al., *Open Letter to the Nigerian Senate on the Matter of the Frivolous Petitions Prohibition Bill (aka "Social Media" Bill)*, accessed February 26, 2021, https://pen-international.org/print/3985.

73 Segun Olaniyi, "Senate Throws Out Frivolous Petitions Bill," *The Guardian Nigeria*, May 18, 2016, https://guardian.ng/news/senate-throws-out-frivolous-petitions-bill/.

74 The French historian and sociologist Pierre Rosanvallon identifies the importance of civic counterpowers in bridging the preferences of citizens with the actions of representatives on a more regular basis than voting permits. See Pierre Rosanvallon, *Counter-Democracy: Politics in an Age of Distrust*, trans. Arthur Goldhammer (Cambridge, UK: Cambridge University Press, 2008).

75 Joshua Cohen, "Deliberation and Democratic Legitimacy," in D. Estlund, ed., *Democracy* (Malden, MA: Blackwell Publishers, 2002); Jürgen Habermas, *Between Facts and Norms: Contributions to a Discourse Theory of Law and Democracy* (Cambridge, MA: MIT Press, 1996).

76 Cornel West, *Democracy Matters: Winning the Fight Against Imperialism* (New York: Penguin, 2005): 41.

77 Edward S. Herman and Noam Chomsky, *Manufacturing Consent: The Political Economy of the Mass Media* (New York: Pantheon Books, 1988).

78 Tawakkol Karman in discussion with the authors, April 2020.

79 Daron Acemoglu and James Robinson say: "Without society's vigilance, constitutions and guarantees are not worth much more than the parchment they are written on." See Daron Acemoglu and James A. Robinson, *The Narrow Corridor: States, Societies, and the Fate of Liberty* (New York: Penguin Books, 2019), xvi.

80 Danielle Allen, *Education and Equality* (Chicago: University of Chicago Press, 2016), 27.

81   Danielle Allen, Stephen B. Heintz, and Eric P. Liu, *Our Common Purpose: Reinventing American Democracy for the 21st Century* (Cambridge, MA: American Academy of Arts and Sciences, 2020).

82   Antonio Gramsci, *Selections from the Prison Notebooks* (London: Lawrence and Wishart, 1971), 40. See also Paolo Freire, *Pedagogy of the Oppressed* (1970), trans. Myra B. Ramos (New York: Bloomsbury Academic, 2012).

83   Lene Rachel Andersen and Tomas Björkman, *The Nordic Secret* (Stockholm: Fri Tanke, 2017).

84   As Andersen and Björkman detail in *The Nordic Secret*, *Bildung* finds its roots primarily in Kierkegaard's existential philosophy of aesthetic expression and the romanticism of Pestalozzi's pedagogy of ego-development. Subsequent models also see personal and moral development as progressing in stages of increasing mental complexity, most prominently the developmental psychology of Robert Kegan (see Robert Kegan, *The Evolving Self: Problem and Process in Human Development* [Cambridge, MA: Harvard University Press, 1982]).

85   Lars Skov Henriksen, Kristin Strømsnes, and Lars Svedberg, eds., *Civic Engagement in Scandinavia: Volunteering, Informal Help and Giving in Denmark, Norway and Sweden* (Cham, Switzerland: Springer, 2018).

86   Elizabeth Anderson, "The Epistemology of Democracy," *Episteme* 3, no. 1–2 (2006): 8–22.

87   James Surowiecki, *The Wisdom of Crowds* (New York: Anchor Books, 2005); Hélène Landemore, *Democratic Reason: Politics, Collective Intelligence, and the Rule of the Many* (Princeton, NJ: Princeton University Press, 2017).

88   Jean-Jacques Rousseau, *Du contrat social ou Principes du droit politique* (Paris: P. Pourrat Frères, 1839), 93. Translation our own.

89   Julia Cagé, *The Price of Democracy: How Money Shapes Politics and What to Do About It* (Cambridge, MA: Harvard University Press, 2020).

90   Alexander Hertel-Fernandez, *State Capture: How Conservative Activists, Big Businesses, and Wealthy Donors Reshaped the American States—and the Nation* (Oxford: Oxford University Press, 2019).

91   Emmanuel Saez and Gabriel Zucman, "Wealth Inequality in the United States since 1913: Evidence from Capitalized Income Tax Data," *The Quarterly Journal of Economics* 131, no. 2 (2016): 519–78.

92   Wendy Brown, *In the Ruins of Neoliberalism: The Rise of Antidemocratic Politics in the West* (New York: Columbia University Press, 2019).

93   Point made by David Eaves in Janna Anderson and Lee Rainie, "Many Tech Experts Say Digital Disruption Will Hurt Democracy," Pew Research Center, 2020, https://www.pewresearch.org/internet/2020/02/21/many-tech-experts-say-digital-disruption-will-hurt-democracy/.

94 Jeffrey M. Berry and Sarah Sobieraj, *The Outrage Industry: Political Opinion Media and the New Incivility* (Oxford: Oxford University Press, 2013).

95 See Cass R. Sunstein, *#Republic: Divided Democracy in the Age of Social Media* (Princeton, NJ: Princeton University Press, 2017); Jacob L. Nelson and Harsh Taneja, "The Small, Disloyal Fake News Audience: The Role of Audience Availability in Fake News Consumption," *New Media & Society* 20, no. 10 (2018): 3720–37; and for a review of the nuanced literature on social media and democracy: Joshua A. Tucker et al., "Social Media, Political Polarization, and Political Disinformation: A Review of the Scientific Literature," Hewlett Foundation, March 2018, https://hewlett.org/wp-content/uploads/2018/03/Social-Media-Political-Polarization-and-Political-Disinformation-Literature-Review.pdf.

96 For guidance on overcoming these limitations and building a more democratic digital public sphere, see Joshua Cohen and Archon Fung, "Democracy and the Digital Public Sphere," in *Digital Technology and Democratic Theory*, ed. Lucy Bernholz, Hélène Landemore, and Robert Reich (Chicago: University of Chicago Press, 2021).

97 For more on potential barriers to full participation and how they might be alleviated, see Céline Braconnier, Jean-Yves Dormagen, and Vincent Pons, "Voter Registration Costs and Disenfranchisement: Experimental Evidence from France," *The American Political Science Review* 111, no. 3 (2017): 584–604.

98 For more on the difficulties inherent in implementing a full democracy, see Robert Dahl, "Procedural Democracy," in *Philosophy, Politics and Society*, ed. Peter Laslett and Jim Fishkin (New Haven: Yale University Press, 1979), 97–133.

99 LaTosha Brown in discussion with the authors, December 2019 and February 2021.

100 Theda Skocpol and Morris P. Fiorina, *Civic Engagement in American Democracy* (Washington, DC: Brookings Institution Press, 1999); Theda Skocpol, *Diminished Democracy: From Membership to Management in American Civic Life* (Norman, OK: University of Oklahoma Press, 2003).

101 For France, see the Citizen's Convention on Climate, https://www.conventioncitoyennepourleclimat.fr/en/; For Vancouver, Canada see Edana Beauvais and Mark E. Warren, "What Can Deliberative Mini-Publics Contribute to Democratic Systems?" *European Journal of Political Research* 58, no. 3 (2019): 893–914; and for Ireland, see "Lessons from Ireland's Recent Referendums: How Deliberation Helps Inform Voters," *British Politics and Policy at LSE*, September 9, 2018.

102 Carl Miller, "Taiwan Is Making Democracy Work Again. It's Time We Paid Attention," *Wired UK*, November 26, 2019, https://www.wired

.co.uk/article/taiwan-democracy-social-media; Anne Applebaum and Peter Pomerantsev, "How to Put Out Democracy's Dumpster Fire." *The Atlantic*, March 8, 2021, https://www.theatlantic.com/magazine /archive/2021/04/the-internet-doesnt-have-to-be-awful/618079/.

103 For details of every case, see vTaiwan's website: https://info.vtaiwan.tw /#three.

104 Hélène Landemore, *Open Democracy: Reinventing Popular Rule for the Twenty-First Century* (Princeton, NJ: Princeton University Press, 2020).

CONCLUSION: IT'S UP TO US

1 John Rawls, *A Theory of Justice* (Cambridge, MA: Harvard University Press, 1971).

2 For contemporary accounts and theories of justice that also provide an overview of past work, see Iris Marion Young, *Justice and the Politics of Difference* (Princeton, NJ: Princeton University Press, 1990); Michael J. Sandel, *Justice: What's the Right Thing to Do?* (New York: Farrar, Straus and Giroux, 2009); Amartya Kumar Sen, *The Idea of Justice* (Cambridge, MA: Harvard University Press, 2009); Mathias Risse, *On Global Justice* (Princeton, NJ: Princeton University Press, 2012).

3 Karl Polanyi, *The Great Transformation: The Political and Economic Origins of Our Time*, 2nd Beacon Paperback ed. (Boston, MA: Beacon Press, 2001).

4 Michèle Lamont, "Addressing Recognition Gaps: Destigmatization and the Reduction of Inequality," *American Sociological Review* 83, no. 3 (2018): 419-44.

5 Michèle Lamont, *The Dignity of Working Men: Morality and the Boundaries of Race, Class, and Immigration*, Revised edition (New York: Harvard University Press, 2002); Mark Carney, *Value(s): Building a Better World for All* (Penguin Random House of Canada, 2021).

6 Lakshmi Ramarajan, "Past, Present and Future Research on Multiple Identities: Toward an Intrapersonal Network Approach," *Academy of Management Annals* 8, no. 1 (2014): 589–659.

7 Fabrizio Ferraro, Jeffrey Pfeffer, and Robert I. Sutton, "Economics Language and Assumptions: How Theories Can Become Self-Fulfilling," *Academy of Management Review* 30, no. 1 (2005): 8–24; Michèle Lamont, "From 'Having' to 'Being': Self-Worth and the Current Crisis of American Society," *The British Journal of Sociology* 70, no. 3: 660–707 and *American Sociological Review* 83, no. 3 (2018): 419–44.

8 Elizabeth Anderson, *Value in Ethics and Economics* (Cambridge, MA: Harvard University Press, 1993).

APPENDIX

1   Max Weber, *Economy and Society*, eds. Guenther Roth and Claus Wittich (Berkeley: University of California Press, 1978).

2   Robert A. Dahl, "The Concept of Power," *Behavioral Science* 2, no. 3 (1957): 201–15.

3   Peter Bachrach and Morton S. Baratz, "Two Faces of Power," *American Political Science Review* 56, no. 4 (1962): 47–952.

4   Peter M. Blau, *Exchange and Power in Social Life* (New York: Wiley, 1964).

5   Steven Lukes, *Power: A Radical View* (Houndmills: Macmillan, 1974).

6   Gerald Salancik and Jeffrey Pfeffer, "Who Gets Power — And How They Hold on to It," in *The Management of Organizations: Strategies, Tactics, and Analyses*, eds. M. Tushman, C. O'Reilly, and D. Nadler (New York: Harper & Row, 1989), 268–284.

7   Bertrand Russell, *Power: A New Social Analysis* (London: Allen and Unwin, 1938); Dennis Wrong, *Power: Its Forms, Bases, and Uses* (New York: Harper & Row, 1979).

8   See, for example, John R. P. French and Bertram Raven, "The Bases of Social Power," in *Studies in Social Power*, ed. D. Cartwright (Ann Arbor: University of Michigan, 1959), 150–167.

9   Manuel Castells, "A Sociology of Power: My Intellectual Journey," *Annual Review of Sociology* 42 (2016): 1–19.

10   Richard M. Emerson, "Power-Dependence Relations," *American Sociological Review* 27, no. 1 (1962): 32.

11   Edna B. Foa and Uriel G. Foa, "Resource Theory: Inter-personal Behavior as Social Exchange," in *Social Exchange: Advances in Theory and Research*, eds. K. J. Gergen, M. S. Greenberg, and R. H. Willis (New York: Plenum Press, 1980): 78–79.

12   Peter Morris, *Power: A Philosophical Analysis*, 2nd ed. (Manchester, UK: Manchester University Press, 2002).

13   See, for example, Jeffrey Pfeffer and Gerald Salancik who applied Emerson's exchange theory of power-dependence relations to organizations in their book, *The External Control of Organizations: A Resource Dependence Perspective* (New York: Harper & Row, 1978).

14   See, for example, Robert Keohane and Joseph Nye, *Power and Interdependence* (Boston, MA: Little, Brown & Co., 1977); Joseph Nye, *The Future of Power* (New York: PublicAffairs, 2011).

15   Wrong, *Power*, xxii.

16   Michel Foucault, *The History of Sexuality: The Will to Knowledge* (London: Penguin, 1998), 63.

17   See Talcott Parsons, "On the Concept of Political Power," in *Sociological Theory and Modern Society*, ed. T. Parsons (New York: The Free Press, 1967).

18 Mary Parker Follett, *Dynamic Administration: The Collected Papers of Mary Parker Follett*, eds. H. C. Metcalf and L. Ur-wick (New York–London: Harper & Brothers, 1942).

19 Hannah Arendt, *On Violence* (New York: Harcourt, Inc., 1970).

20 Hanna Fenichel Pitkin, *Wittgenstein and Justice: On the Significance of Ludwig Wittgenstein for Social and Political Thought* (Berkeley: University of California Press, 1972): 276–77.

21 Pamela Pansardi, "Power to and Power over: Two Distinct Concepts of Power?" *Journal of Political Power* 5, no. 1 (2012): 73–89.

22 For reviews of research on power in psychology, management, political science, sociology, and philosophy see Adam D. Galinsky, Derek D. Rucker, and Joe C. Magee, "Power: Past Findings, Present Considerations, and Future Directions," in *APA Handbook of Personality and Social Psychology: Interpersonal Relationships*, eds. Mario Mikulincer and Philip R. Shaver, vol. 3 (Washington, DC: American Psychological Association, 2015): 421–60; Peter Fleming and André Spicer, "Power in Management and Organization Science," *Academy of Management Annals* 8, no. 1 (2014): 237–98; William Ocasio, Jo-Ellen Pozner, and Daniel Milner, "Varieties of Political Capital and Power in Organizations: A Review and Integrative Framework," *Academy of Management Annals* 14, no. 1 (2020): 303–38; Marshall Ganz, "Speaking of Power" (Gettysburg Project, 2014); Archon Fung, "Four levels of Power: A Conception to Enable Liberation," *The Journal of Political Philosophy* 28, no. 2 (2020): 131–157; Roderick Kramer and Margaret Neale, *Power and Influence in Organizations*, 1st ed. (Thousand Oaks, CA: SAGE, 1998); Amy Allen, "Rethinking Power," *Hypatia* 13, no. 1 (2020): 21–40; Stewart Clegg, David Courpasson, and Nelson Phillips, *Power and Organizations* (London: SAGE, 2006); Gerhard Göhler, "'Power to' and 'Power over,'" in *Sage Handbook of Power*, eds. S. R. Clegg and M. Haugaard (London: SAGE, 2009) 27–40; Rachel E. Sturm and John Antonakis, "Interpersonal Power: A Review, Critique, and Research Agenda," *Journal of Management* 41, no. 1 (January 1, 2015): 136–63.

Index

JULIE BATTILANA is a professor of organizational behavior and social innovation at the Harvard Business School and the Harvard Kennedy School, where she is also the founder and faculty chair of the Social Innovation and Change Initiative. Over the past fifteen years, Battilana has studied the politics of change in organizations and in society while teaching on power and leadership. She has advised change-makers around the world in the public, private, and social sectors. She is also the cofounder of the Democratizing Work initiative, a global alliance of researchers and practitioners collaborating toward a more just, green, and fair economic system. Originally from France, she received a joint PhD from INSEAD and from École Normale Supérieure de Paris-Saclay. She lives in Belmont, Massachusetts.

TIZIANA CASCIARO is a professor of organizational behavior at the Rotman School of Management at the University of Toronto. Her research on interpersonal and organizational networks and power dynamics has received distinguished scientific achievement awards from the Academy of Management and has been covered by *The New York Times*, *The Washington Post*, CNN, *The Economist*, *Financial Times*, MSNBC, ABC, CBC, *Fortune*, and *TIME* magazine. She advises organizations and professionals across industries and has been recognized by Thinkers50 as a management thinker most likely to shape the future of how organizations are managed and led. Originally from Italy, she received a Laurea from Bocconi University and a PhD from Carnegie Mellon University. She lives in Toronto.